Modula-2
Programming

Modula-2 Programming

John W. L. Ogilvie
Modula Corporation

McGraw-Hill Book Company

New York St. Louis San Francisco Auckland
Bogotá Hamburg Johannesburg London
Madrid Mexico Montreal New Delhi
Panama Paris São Paulo Singapore
Sydney Tokyo Toronto

Library of Congress Cataloging in Publication Data

Ogilvie, John W. L.
  Modula-2 programming.

  Includes index.
  1. Modula-2 (Computer program language) I. Title.
QA76.73.M63036 1985   001.64'24   84-29742
ISBN 0-07-047770-1

1234567890   DOC/DOC   898765

ISBN 0-07-047770-1

*The editors for this book were Tyler G. Hicks and Nancy Young,
the designer was Naomi Auerbach, and the production supervisor was Sally Fliess.
It was set in Century Schoolbook by Bi-Comp, Incorporated.*

Printed and bound by R. R. Donnelley & Sons Company.

To Mrs. K and Mrs. P
From their student who was
Almost, at times, the Fool

Contents

Preface   xi

Chapter 1   An Overview of Modula-2. . . . .   **1**

How Long Will It Take to Learn Modula-2?   1
The Origins of Modula-2   2
Modula-2 Briefly Described   3

Chapter 2   A First Example **5**

A Simple Program   5
A Capitalization Convention 8

Chapter 3   Modula-2 Compared Briefly with Other Languages. **10**

Modula-2 and Pascal   10
Modula-2 and Ada   15
Modula-2 and C   16
Modula-2 and BASIC   18
Modula-2 and FORTRAN   18

Chapter 4   Modula-2's Basic Data Types **20**

The INTEGER Type   20
The CARDINAL Type   22
The REAL Type   23
The BOOLEAN Type   24
The CHAR Type   26
The BITSET Type 27
Operator Precedence and Associativity   28
Exercises   30

Chapter 5   Declarations **32**

Comments   32
Constant Declarations   33
Variable Declarations   34

Type Declarations   36
Strong Typing and Type Compatibility   39
Exercises   42

Chapter 6   Conditional and Loop Statements. . . .   43

The IF Statement   43
The CASE Statement   44
Loop Statements in Modula-2   46
FOR Loops   48
WHILE and REPEAT. .UNTIL Loops   50
LOOP Loops   51
Exercises   53

Chapter 7   Procedures and Functions   55

Why Use Subprograms?   55
Procedures Versus Functions   59
Subprogram Parameters   59
Functions   63
Naming Procedures and Functions   64
Visibility Rules   65
Recursion   69
Exercises   71

Chapter 8   Modules   73

The Three Kinds of Modula-2 Modules   73
Why Use Modules?   77
Compilation of Library Modules   79

Chapter 9   Controlling Visibility with Modules . . .   81

Listing Procedures Globally without Nesting   81
A Look at Nesting   87
Using Library Modules   88
The Visibility of Exported Items   89
Import Trees   92
Local Modules   94

Chapter 10   Enumeration, Subrange, and Set Types .   98

Enumeration Types   98
Subrange Types   100
Set Types   102
Exercises   103

Chapter 11   Array Data Types.   105

Declaring and Using Arrays   105
Open Array Parameters   107
An Example: String Handling   109
Initializing Arrays   113
Exercises   114

Chapter 12   Records and Pointers 115

Declaring and Using Records   115
The WITH Statement   117
Declaring and Using Pointers   118
Pointers as Value Parameters   124
Exercise   125

Chapter 13   Variant Records 126

Declaring and Using Variant Records   126
An Example: LISP Functions in Modula-2   128
Exercise   136

Chapter 14   Opaque Types 137

Declaring and Using Opaque Types   137

Chapter 15   Software Engineering with Modula-2 . . 141

What Are Desirable Program Qualities?   141
Understandability   142
Correctness   145
Modifiability   146
Efficiency   147
Durability   148
Portability   149
Availability   149

Chapter 16   An Example: A Pattern Matcher. 151

The Algorithms   151
Dividing the Program into Modules   155

Chapter 17   Procedure Types 180

Values Which "Do" Versus Values Which "Say"   180
Using Independent Procedure Variables   182
Procedures as Parameters   185

Chapter 18   Processes 188

Coroutines and Concurrency   188
Coroutines Versus Subprograms   189
Creating Coroutines   190
An Example of the Use of Coroutines   195
Module Priorities   199
Exercise   200

Chapter 19   Modula-2's Low-Level Features 201

Storage Information and Allocation   202
The Type WORD   204

Sidestepping Type Compatibility   209
An Example: Dynamic String Handling   212

Chapter 20   Debugging Modula-2 Programs   216

Causes of Programming Errors   216
Debugging Techniques   219

Chapter 21   A Modula-2 Programming Style   221

Comments   221
Identifiers   223
Format   223
Object Code Style   224

Chapter 22   A Discussion of Modula-2's
Shortcomings   226

Disclaimer   226
Problems Hardly Worth Mentioning   226
Some Truly Annoying Problems   227
Are These Really Shortcomings?   229

Appendix 1   Modula-2's Standard Subprograms . . .   232
Appendix 2   Reserved Words and Standard
Identifiers   235
Appendix 3   Formal Syntax Diagrams   238
Appendix 4   Other Sources of Information
on Modula-2   255
Appendix 5   Revisions and Amendments to
Modula-2   258

Glossary   262
Answers to the Exercises   288
Bibliography   298
Index   299

Preface

This book is intended to serve two somewhat different groups of programmers because Modula-2 may be viewed as two languages. On the one hand, Modula-2 is a clearly improved version of Pascal. Because Modula-2 programs are even easier to read, write, debug, and modify than Pascal programs, Modula-2 is an excellent language for beginners. But Modula-2 also provides powerful low-level features for systems programming which can be used to their full capacity only by experienced programmers.

This book is meant to be both an introduction to Modula-2 and a reference for that language. It is not a guide to the use of Modula-2 on a particular system or implementation. It is assumed that the reader is familiar with the mechanics of using text editors and compilers and has at least a nodding acquaintance with the use of pointers in simple data structures such as linked lists and trees. It is further assumed that once the basic facts associated with a given data type (acceptable values, legal operators, syntax, etc.) are clear, the reader will be able to decide which type is appropriate in a particular set of circumstances. All the programs shown in this book have been successfully compiled and executed.

To assist readers who have little previous programming experience, the material in this book is presented in an easiest-to-hardest sequence, and an extensive glossary is included. A number of exercises have also been provided. The answers for all the exercises are given at the end of the book so that the reader's will power is tested as well as his or her knowledge of Modula-2.

For experienced readers who wish to use the book mainly for reference, I have tried to make the index quite comprehensive. Modula-2's syntax is given in Appendix 3 in the form of "railroad" syntax diagrams for which a separate index has been provided. To the best of my knowledge, this book contains all the hard information on Modula-2 which was available at the time of writing. To supplement the text, Appendix 4 contains a list of other sources of information on Modula-2. Chapter 22 contains a discussion of some of Modula-2's shortcomings. Appendix 5 contains a summary of the changes to Modula-2 which have been approved by Niklaus Wirth as of March 1984.

For both the inexperienced and the experienced reader, I have included a chapter containing what I feel are some useful software engineering techniques and another chapter which lists some of the common and uncommon causes of bugs in Modula-2 programs. A third chapter of friendly advice describes the style used in the program listings in this book.

My current programming philosophy might best be summed up as "Make it readable, make it run, then make it run fast if you need to." A program will be read many times, both while it is being written and afterward when it must be debugged, modified to handle additional inputs, or ported to another machine. A program cannot be made to run fast, or even to run at all, unless it can be understood. And unless one is absolutely certain that the source code for a program will never be looked at again once the program is running, it is worthwhile to write code that will be as clear a year from now as it is today. You are all hereby forewarned of my biases.

I made much use of the Lilith, the Canon LBP-10 Laser Printer, the Lilith software manual, and the Lilith software provided by the Modula Research Institute and the University of Utah Computer Science Department while writing this book. I would like to thank the numerous people associated with those two institutions who helped answer my questions. This group includes, but is not limited to, Rod Schiffman. Lyle Bingham, Gregory Daich, Mike Maloney, Dan Klass, and Chuck Hansen, as well as Drs. Richard Ohran, Richard Fujimoto, P. A. Subrahmanyam, Tom Henderson, and Dave Hanscom. Greg and Mike were especially helpful and patient. Bruce Horton, Peter Jones, Kevin Likes, Genie Ogilvie, and Dr. Bill Salmon all read portions of the manuscript and made many useful suggestions. Vicky Jackson, Joyce Higgenbotham, Jay Lepreau, Fred Wilhelmson, Jimmy Miklavcic, Kevin Deford, Grant Weiler, and many others did not read any of the manuscript, but they were always so helpful that they deserve thanks as well.

I owe a particular debt of gratitude to Dr. Elliott Organick, who gave me such excellent opportunities in the beginning and who has given me more chances to explore than I would have thought possible. Mike Powell from Digital Equipment Corporation's Western Research Lab was also very helpful. Tyler Hicks, Edward Matthews, Nancy Young, Olive Collen, and many other people at McGraw-Hill were courteous, efficient, and very patient. Finally, a truly impressive amount of legitimate criticism was provided by John Craig, who is not only knowledgable and literate but a good friend as well. The responsibility for any mistakes lies solely with myself. I welcome comments and reasonable suggestions from readers; I can be reached via Tyler Hicks, 26th Floor, Professional and Reference Division, McGraw-Hill Book Company, 1221 Avenue of the Americas, New York, New York, 10020.

Salt Lake City   *John W. L. Ogilvie*

An Overview
of Modula-2

How Long Will It Take to Learn Modula-2?

A programmer who knows Pascal can expect to be writing Modula-2 programs which do not require low-level or multiprogramming capabilities in just a few hours. Much of this time will probably be spent finding out what is and is not available in the library of modules on the system being used. Modula-2's syntax includes many improvements over Pascal's which will make debugging simpler once the programmer is aware of them. Modula-2 and Pascal are compared briefly in Chapter 3.

Programmers who already know Ada[1] should be able to master all the features of Modula-2 with very little effort, including those dealing with low-level and multiprogramming. Modula-2 may be viewed as a somewhat disguised but powerful subset of Ada (see Ogilvie, 1984). Some of the main differences between the two languages are discussed in Chapter 3.

Programmers who know BASIC, FORTRAN, or C will need to get used to Modula-2's strong typing, import mechanisms, and generally different syntax. Modula-2 also provides a more powerful group of data structuring capabilities than these readers are probably used to. Some of the differences between Modula-2 and these languages are mentioned in Chapter 3.

Those readers who are unfamiliar with strong typing; conditional and loop statements; the decomposition of programs into procedures, functions, and modules; and other basic aspects of programming in

---

[1] Ada is a Registered Trademark of the U.S. Dept. of Defense.

Modula-2 will need more time to master the ideas involved. They should seriously consider working through an introductory text on structured programming while they read this book. However, this learning process will be easier than it would be in most other high-level languages because of the way Modula-2 is designed. Modula-2's syntax encourages code that is easy to read, and the strong typing also makes it possible for the compiler to find many of the errors in programs written by people who are unfamiliar with the language.

The Origins of Modula-2

Modula-2 was designed by Professor Niklaus Wirth, and it draws on the insights he gained by designing two earlier programming languages, Pascal and Modula. Like Pascal, Modula-2 is a good language for writing programs in which the structure of the algorithms and data structures used is clearly expressed by the program. Pascal has gained wide acceptance since its implementation in 1970 for several reasons. It is much easier to clearly describe algorithms and a wide range of data structures in Pascal than in earlier languages such as FORTRAN and COBOL. Pascal's syntax encourages programs which are both easy to read and powerful. Finally, Pascal's strong type checking makes it possible to detect many errors at compilation time, which in turn makes it easier for programmers to be certain that the compiler agrees with them on the meaning of their code.

Modula-2 has not only inherited all these excellent characteristics from Pascal, but it also contains improvements in syntax, power, efficiency, and the degree to which software engineering techniques may be easily applied while programming. Modula-2 also incorporates the multiprogramming capabilities of Wirth's earlier language, Modula, as well as that language's important module concept. Modula is not used very widely today, so this book follows Wirth's lead and uses "Modula" and "Modula-2" interchangeably.

The first implementation of Modula-2 was in 1979 on a PDP-11 at ETH in Zürich. The ETH compiler was released for outside use in March 1981 after a year of use and testing. Since then, Modula-2 has become available on the Apple II, Apple III, Sage II, Sage IV, IBM PC, TI 9900, 8080/Z80-based systems, and DEC VAX computers, among others. Modula-2 is small enough to be used on single-user machines and to be learned relatively easily. Nonetheless, it is a very powerful language. Among the less-than-completely-obscure high-level languages which are available today, only Ada and perhaps Smalltalk-80 are more powerful.

Modula-2 Briefly Described

Modula-2 is a general-purpose, strongly typed, high-level programming language which provides a number of low-level features and supports coroutines. One of its most distinctive features is the way it allows programmers to break programs into a number of logically distinct, separately compiled modules. Three kinds of modules make up most programs. "Program modules" correspond roughly to programs in other languages. However, program modules virtually always use various data types, procedures, functions, variables, and/or constants which are compiled as parts of other modules. The library modules which export the types, procedures, and so forth used by program modules (and by other library modules) always come in pairs consisting of a "definition module" and an "implementation module."

The definition module in a library module pair contains all the semantic information associated with the exports from the pair and describes the visibility of the exports. The semantic information includes things such as how many parameters an exported procedure has and what type (INTEGER, BOOLEAN, REAL, etc.) of values it expects. Only the objects which are explicitly exported by the definition module can be imported for use in other modules. The corresponding implementation module contains the bodies of exported procedures and functions and other code which supports the exports.

Strong checks are performed to prevent inconsistent use of any objects imported from library modules, just as they are performed on objects declared locally in the module being compiled. For instance, a procedure which was declared to have one parameter cannot be passed two values at once, whether the procedure was declared in the module being compiled or was imported from a pair of library modules. This ability to separately compile modules without losing any syntactic or semantic checking simplifies the construction of large programs by teams of programmers. Modularity also assists portability by localizing machine-dependent objects in a few modules, and it helps provide a growing library of software tools for the programmer.

The facilities for separate compilation which were just briefly described are probably Modula-2's most important features, but Modula-2's low-level facilities also set it apart from many other high-level languages. For instance, one may do things such as reinterpret the bit pattern representing a CARDINAL number as a BOOLEAN value. Several other facilities are also provided to allow one to avoid the consequences of strong typing. One may also easily determine the current address of a variable, perform address arithmetic, or determine storage requirements. Some implementations provide programmers

with the ability to override the compiler's allocation decisions by specifying absolute storage addresses for variables.

Two of Modula-2's other features which deserve mention here are
the capability to work with coroutines and the procedure types which
make it possible to pass procedures and functions as parameters to
other procedures and functions.

It is important to note that all these features are not only available,
but they are also easy to use because Modula-2 source code is much
easier to read than code in many other languages. There are a number
of reasons for this legibility. All modules, procedures, functions, and
compound statements are clearly bracketed, so one can tell at a glance
where they begin and end. There is no goto command in Modula-2, so
programs are easier to understand because there is less jumping
around. Import lists and modularity can be used to make it easy to
locate the code which defines the objects used in a program. Reserved
words are easy to see because they are completely capitalized. Reasonably long identifiers are allowed, so cryptic ones can be avoided. The
fact that a wide range of predefined and user-defined data types is
supported makes it possible to tailor the Modula-2 declaration of a data
structure more closely to the programmer's mental model. Other reasons for Modula-2's legibility will become apparent as the reader gains
experience with the language.

2

A First Example

A Simple Program

This chapter is meant to give some sort of feel for Modula-2 to those readers who are unfamiliar with the language. Listing 2-1 contains the code for a Modula-2 program which reads in a list of integers and prints out the arithmetic average of the list's nonnegative elements. The user specifies the length of the list before entering it. Program module FirstExample uses a number of basic programming constructs such as variable declarations, IF statements, assignment statements, and a FOR loop. FirstExample also contains examples of other features which are more advanced and/or less commonly used in most current programming languages: procedures which are imported from other modules, type conversion, and a call to the standard Modula-2 procedure INC.

The I/O functions used in Listing 2-1, such as READCharacter and WRITEString, are imported from library modules. FirstExample will not run without a definition/implementation module pair called InOut which exports the procedures named in the import list at the top of Listing 2-1. Similarly, FirstExample expects to be able to locate a pair of RealInOut library modules so that it can import WRITEReal. Unfortunately, the Modula-2 library had not been standardized to any real extent at the time of writing; therefore this book follows Wirth (1983) with a few modifications for legibility.

Turning from subprograms to data types, the reader will see that the variable LISTLength has been declared to be of type CARDINAL. The reason for this is that CARDINAL variables cannot assume negative values, although they can equal zero. LISTLength is declared as a CARDINAL because it makes little sense to speak of a list with a negative number of elements. If an error in the program causes it to try

LISTING 2-1 *A first example.*

```
MODULE FirstExample;
  FROM InOut     IMPORT READCardinal, READCharacter, READInteger,
                        WRITEString, WRITELine;
  FROM RealInOut IMPORT WRITEReal;

  VAR  LISTLength: CARDINAL;
       AVERAGE   : REAL;
       AGAIN     : CHAR;

  PROCEDURE IntroAndGetListLength;
  (* Introduce program to user and read in LISTLength, the      *)
  (* length of the list which is used by AverageOfNonnegatives.*)
  BEGIN
    WRITELine;
    WRITEString("This program accepts N integers and outputs");
    WRITELine;
    WRITEString("the floating-point arithmetic average of those");
    WRITELine;
    WRITEString("which are nonnegative. Enter N> ");
    READCardinal(LISTLength);
    WRITELine;
  END IntroAndGetListLength;

  PROCEDURE AverageOfNonnegatives(): REAL;
    VAR Index, NonnegativeCount  : CARDINAL;
        NextInteger, RunningTotal: INTEGER;
  (* Reads in a list of LISTLength integers and returns the     *)
  (* average of the nonnegative elements of the list. Returns  *)
  (* zero if all the elements of the list were negative.        *)
  BEGIN
    NonnegativeCount := 0;
    RunningTotal := 0;
    FOR Index := 1 TO LISTLength DO
      WRITELine;
      WRITEString("Enter next integer> ");
      READInteger(NextInteger);
      IF NextInteger >= 0 THEN
        INC(NonnegativeCount);
        RunningTotal := RunningTotal + NextInteger;
      END; (* IF *)
    END; (* FOR *)
    IF NonnegativeCount > 0 THEN
      RETURN (FLOAT(RunningTotal)/FLOAT(NonnegativeCount));
    ELSE
      RETURN 0.0;
```

```
    END; (* IF *)
    END AverageOfNonnegatives;

BEGIN   (* main body of FirstExample *)
    LOOP
        IntroAndGetListLength;
        AVERAGE := AverageOfNonnegatives();
        WRITELine;
        WRITEString("The average of the nonnegative terms is ");
        WRITEReal(AVERAGE, 6);   (* Write the current value of    *)
        WRITELine;               (* AVERAGE, using six characters.*)
        WRITEString("Want to go again? ");
        READCharacter(AGAIN);
        IF ((AGAIN <> "y") AND (AGAIN <> "Y")) THEN
            WRITEString(" No.");
            WRITELine;
            EXIT;
        ELSE
            WRITEString(" Yes.");
        END; (* IF *)
    END; (* LOOP *)
END FirstExample.
```

to assign a negative value to LISTLength, the programmer will be informed. If LISTLength was declared as an INTEGER, this error might go undetected.

It has been mentioned that Modula-2 is a strongly typed language. This means, for instance, that it is illegal to combine CARDINAL and REAL variables in a single expression. The average of the nonnegative elements in the list read by FirstExample cannot be computed by simply dividing RunningTotal by NonnegativeCount because RunningTotal is an INTEGER, NonnegativeCount is a CARDINAL, and the result of the division is supposed to be a REAL value. To avoid the type incompatibilities, the type conversion function FLOAT has been used to convert the INTEGER RunningTotal and the CARDINAL NonnegativeCount into REALs. Except in the simplest cases, such as the assignment of a CARDINAL variable's value to an INTEGER variable, all such changes from values of one data type to corresponding values of another type must be explicitly requested by the programmer. This is because the correspondence which is to be used is not always clear. Modula-2 provides several predefined type conversion functions such as FLOAT.

In addition to the type conversion functions, a number of other standard or predefined subprograms are provided with every implementation of Modula-2. One of them is the procedure INC, which is called inside function AverageOfNonnegatives to increment the value of NonNegativeCount. The call to INC could be replaced by the statement

NonNegativeCount := NonNegativeCount + 1;

However, on most systems INC would execute faster. Other standard subprograms exist to decrement variables, compute absolute values, make conversions between types, stop programs in mid-execution, and perform several other useful tasks. The standard subprograms are described in Appendix 1.

Listing 2-1 also points out how easy it is to tell where loops, CASE statements, IF statements, procedures, modules, and similar constructs begin and end in a Modula-2 program. The end of a compound statement such as a loop or an IF statement is generally marked with the reserved word END; the FOR loop and IF statements shown in function AverageOfNonnegatives are good examples. The extent of procedures, functions, and modules is also clearly marked, as shown in Listing 2-1.

A Capitalization Convention

A distinction is made in all Modula-2 programs between lower- and uppercase letters. For instance, "AVERAGE" and "Average" are two different variables. Modula-2 reserved words and standard procedure names are always capitalized. In addition to the reserved words, the first words in the names of global variables and most of the imported or exported procedures and functions in the examples in this book have been capitalized, e.g., LISTLength and WRITEString. This helps one differentiate quickly between locally declared objects and ones which are declared globally or imported.

However, the main reason this book uses a convention whereby the first word in an import's name is capitalized is to underline the differences between the libraries which are available on different systems. For example, even though numerous systems may have a subprogram called WriteString which is exported from a pair of library modules called InOut and which writes a string to the screen, there may be any number of differences between the various versions of WriteString. For instance, the WriteString on one system might recognize /t as a request to write eight blank spaces to the screen, while another version of WriteString would simply print the two characters /t.

The practice of capitalizing the first words in the names of global variables and imports was chosen because no existing library I have seen follows that convention. Although I have followed Wirth (1983) fairly closely, I have tried (where possible) not to assume that the reader is working on a particular system with a particular library. Since there are a number of differences between existing libraries, I felt that using a more generic notation would be preferable to using the names defined on a specific system. Therefore, the use of WRITEString in the listings in this book is meant to remind the reader that some modifications may be necessary to get the examples to run correctly on her or his system.

It follows that readers will need to consult their own system documentation to determine the equivalents of the imports used in the examples. This will be quite easy in most cases. For instance, it is more likely than not that your system's equivalent of the import list

```
FROM InOut IMPORT READCardinal, READCharacter, READInteger,
    WRITEString;
```

will be

```
FROM InOut IMPORT ReadCard, Read, ReadInt, WriteString;
```

Since most libraries available at the time of writing seem to bear some resemblance to the definitions given in Wirth (1983), this book uses the same module names as that source whenever possible.

3

Modula-2 Compared Briefly with Other Languages

In this chapter, Modula-2 is compared very briefly with Pascal, Ada, C, BASIC, and FORTRAN. Readers are encouraged to skip those sections which deal with unfamiliar languages. Ideally, this chapter would consist of several book-length primers: Modula-2 for Pascal Programmers, Modula-2 for C Programmers, etc. Unfortunately, the amount of space available does not permit this approach. Listings 3-1 through 3-6 show different versions of the same program written in Modula-2, Pascal, Ada, C, BASIC, and FORTRAN. There are many ways to write any program in a given language; not everyone would agree that the versions shown are the best each language can offer. These programs are only meant to give the reader a rough sense of the differences between the six languages and to illustrate Modula-2's generally greater legibility.

Modula-2 and Pascal

There is at least one book available which explains in depth the differences between Modula-2 and Pascal (see Gleaves, 1984). A very concise but incomplete comparison of Modula-2 and Pascal is given in Muller (1984). Modula-2's syntax is much like Pascal's except that various awkward constructs have been removed or improved. For instance, BEGIN is used in Modula-2 only to separate declarations from statements; the ends of IF statements, CASE statements, and loops are indicated by the key word END. An optional ELSE clause is available in CASE statements. Constants, types, variables, and subprograms may be declared in any order.

LISTING 3-1   *The same program in several languages, Modula-2 version.*

```
MODULE FindMax;
  (* This Modula-2 program accepts a string of integers,  *)
  (* ending in zero, and prints the one which is greatest.*)

  FROM InOut IMPORT READInteger, WRITEInteger, WRITELine, WRITEString;

  VAR    NEXTNumber  : INTEGER;
         PREVIOUSHigh: INTEGER;

  PROCEDURE Max(x, y: INTEGER): INTEGER;
  BEGIN
    IF x >= y THEN
      RETURN x;
    ELSE
      RETURN y;
    END; (* IF *)
  END Max;

BEGIN (* Main body of FindMax *)
  WRITEString("Enter a string of integers, terminated with a zero");
  WRITELine;
  PREVIOUSHigh := 0;
  NEXTNumber := -1;
  WHILE NEXTNumber <> 0 DO
    READInteger(NEXTNumber);
    WRITELine;
    PREVIOUSHigh := Max(NEXTNumber,PREVIOUSHigh);
  END; (* WHILE *)
  WRITEString("The largest number in the stream is ");
  WRITEInteger(PREVIOUSHigh,6);
  WRITELine;
END FindMax.
```

LISTING 3-2   *The same program in several languages, Pascal version.*

```
program findmax(input,output);
{ This Pascal program accepts a string of integers,   }
{ ending in zero, and prints the one which is greatest.}

var NextNumber, PreviousHigh: integer;

function max(x, y: integer): integer;
```

LISTING 3-2 Continued

```
begin
  if x >= y then
    max := x
  else
    max := y;
end;

begin
  writeln('Enter a string of integers, terminated with a zero');
  PreviousHigh := 0;
  NextNumber := -1;
  while NextNumber <> 0 do
  begin
    read(NextNumber);
    PreviousHigh := max(NextNumber,PreviousHigh);
  end;
  write('The largest number in the stream is ');
  write(PreviousHigh);
  writeln;
end.
```

LISTING 3-3 *The same program in several languages, Ada version.*

```
with Text_IO, Int_IO;
use  Text_IO, Int_IO;
procedure Find_Max is
-- This Ada program accepts a string of integers,
-- ending in zero, and prints the one which is greatest.

  next_number  : integer := -1;
  previous_high: integer := 0;

  function max(x, y: in integer) return integer is
  begin
    if x >= y then
      return x;
    else
      return y;
    end if;
  end max;

begin
  put_line("Enter a string of integers, terminated with a zero");
  while next_number /= 0
  loop
    get(next_number);
```

```
    previous_high := max(next_number,previous_high);
  end loop;
  put("The largest number in the stream is ");
  put(natural'image(previous_high));
end Find_Max;
```

LISTING 3-4 *The same program in several languages, C version.*

```c
main()
/* This C program accepts a string of integers,      */
/* ending in zero, and prints the one which is greatest. */

{
int previous, next;

printf("Enter a string of integers, terminated with a zero \n");
previous = 0;
for( next = -1; next != 0; scanf("%d", &next))
  {
    previous = max(next, previous);
  };
printf("The largest number in the stream is %d \n", previous);
}

max(x,y)
int x,y;
{
if (x >= y)
  return(x);
else
  return(y);
}
```

LISTING 3-5 *The same program in several languages,*
BASIC *version.*

```basic
10    REM THIS BASIC PROGRAM ACCEPTS A STRING OF INTEGERS
20    REM ENDING IN ZERO, AND PRINTS THE ONE WHICH IS GREATEST
30    REM
40    DEF FNM(X,Y)
50      IF X >= Y THEN FNM = X
60      ELSE FNM = Y
70    FNEND
80    REM
100   PRINT "Enter a string of integers, terminated with a zero"
```

LISTING 3-5   Continued

```
110  N = -1
120  P = 0
130  WHILE N <> 0
140    P = FNM(N,P)
150    INPUT N
160  WEND
170  PRINT : PRINT "The largest number in the stream is "; P
180  STOP
190  END
```

LISTING 3-6 *The same program in several languages,*
FORTRAN *version.*

```
      PROGRAM FINDMAX
C
C     THIS FORTRAN PROGRAM ACCEPTS A STRING OF INTEGERS,
C     ENDING IN ZERO, AND PRINTS THE ONE WHICH IS GREATEST
C
      INTEGER NEXT, PREV
C
      PRINT*,'Enter a string of integers, terminated with a zero'
      PREV = 0
      NEXT = -1
10    IF (NEXT.NE.0) THEN
        PREV = MAX(NEXT,PREV)
        READ*, NEXT
        GO TO 10
      WRITE(*,100) PREV
100   FORMAT(/' The largest number in the stream is ',I6//)
      STOP
      END
```

Other improvements include support for separately compiled modules with full type checking across module boundaries; low-level programming facilities; open array formal parameters of types such as ARRAY OF CHAR; support for coroutines; and the consistent use of "short-circuit" evaluation for logical expressions, thereby allowing statements such as

```
WHILE ((Pointer <> NIL) AND (Pointer ↑ .Value <= 0)) DO
   Pointer := Pointer ↑ .Next;
END; (* WHILE still looking for first positive *)
       (* value and not at end of linked list   *)
```

Additional improvements over Pascal include the repetition of procedure and module names at their respective ends; the presence of a more general LOOP statement; and variant records whose syntax matches that of the CASE statement. Also, it is not necessary to declare at compilation time all the files which might be used by a Modula-2 program; this accounts for the lack of a list of files after the program module name, e.g.,

Program PascalExample(Input, Output);

In summary, Modula-2 is easier to read than Pascal, and it is more powerful.

Modula-2 and Ada

Modula-2 is essentially a disguised version of a powerful subset of Ada (see Ogilvie, 1984). Both languages support the division of programs into relatively small modules or packages which are related in clearly specified ways. The library modules (packages) each consist of a definition (specification) part which defines the objects and procedures available for use by other compilation units and a body which contains the current implementation of the module's objects and procedures. Modula-2 program modules correspond to main procedures in Ada.

Strong type checking on all objects, including imported ones, is done at compilation time in both languages. Both languages support ways to restrict the information available to an importing module or package. The designers of each language held the view that the intended use of a type or procedure is distinct from the object's current implementation.

Both languages also support some form of concurrency. Modula processes are not as general as Ada tasks, however; they are only quasi-concurrent coroutines. That is, a single processor may divide its efforts among several Modula processes, giving the user the impression of concurrency. Modula-2 assumes a machine with a single central processing unit. Communication between Ada tasks is also easier to program than that between Modula-2 processes.

Both languages provide low-level facilities in the form of type transfer functions, an address type, and standard ways to tell how much memory is used by a variable or type. Modula also has the type WORD, representing an individually accessible memory unit. Modula-2 has no parallel to most of Ada's representation specifications, although both languages allow one to specify absolute storage addresses for variables.

Modula lacks the generic packages, goto statement, exception facilities, and in general the greater power of Ada. Modula-2 functions, for instance, can often only return basic data types and pointers, whereas Ada functions may also return records or arrays. Ada code is a little easier to understand because underscores are allowed in identifiers, and key phrases such as end loop and end if are used where Modula only allows END to be used. Ada procedure calls may use parameter assignment by name or by position, whereas Modula-2 only allows the latter. Ada's designation of parameter modes, using in, in out, and out, is clearer than Modula's use of VAR.

On the other hand, Ada has no direct equivalent to Modula-2's procedure type or type WORD or set types. Modula's standard procedures INC(x) and DEC(x) are defined for all enumeration types; the procedure finds out what x's type is. The comparable Ada code requires the programmer to explicitly state x's type. Ada has nothing comparable to Modula's WITH statement. Modula-2's method of commenting allows large blocks of code to be commented out much more easily than in Ada and allows comments to be placed within a line and to be nested.

Ada is a much larger language than Modula-2. Since Modula-2 is quite powerful, it should be seriously considered as an alternative in many situations in which the more powerful constructs of Ada are not needed. This is especially true since the development environment in Modula-2 is much better at present than in Ada.

Modula-2 and C

Modula-2 and C are quite similar from the point of view of their overall power. Both are good systems programming languages which can be used to bring high-level control structures to bear on low-level programming problems. Both languages make it possible to manipulate addresses and memory contents without observing the restrictions imposed by strong typing. Modula-2 has no predefined bitwise logical operators or shift operators, no register storage class, and no support for macros. But Modula-2 has four major advantages over C: support for separately compiled modules with complete semantic checking across module boundaries, support for concurrency, code which is usually easier to read, and the availability of strong typing if the Modula-2 programmer wishes to take advantage of it.

C has no syntactic equivalent to the Modula-2 module or Ada package to assist in "programming in the large." At least one attempt has been made to graft something similar on to C, but the result was not completely satisfactory (see Boyd, 1983). C also has no syntactic support for coroutines. C code makes common use of operators whose actions are not clear from their names in expressions such as num++

and &(w -> z). Many C programmers also use very terse identifiers, such as auto, id, fn and nom, whose names to not tell the reader very much about their purposes. This is not a problem with the language, but unfortunately it is in accord with the style often used by C programmers. C allows code which is very concise and extremely cryptic. However, it does allow underscores in identifiers where Modula-2 does not.

Various errors and ambiguities which would be reported by a Modula-2 compiler are ignored by C compilers. For instance, consider the problems raised by the acceptance of "if (x = 2) foo;" as legal when the programmer meant to write "if (x == 2) foo;." The first statement assigns x the value 2 and calls procedure foo, while the second calls foo only if the current value of x equals 2. As another example, note that a call which passes only three values to a procedure which was declared to have five will be accepted by a C compiler. The lint program may be used to catch some of the errors missed by C compilers, but Modula-2 compilers provide even stronger semantic checking. Moreover, Modula-2 programmers have the choice of either utilizing strong typing or else avoiding the restrictions imposed by it, while C programmers must make do for the most part without the same kind of strong semantic checks.

The argument may be made that C programs are very efficient in the sense that they run very quickly. A counterexample is provided by an optimizing Modula-2 compiler which runs under 4.2 BSD UNIX on the VAX 11/780 and which produces code whose execution speed is as good as that produced by "the best C and Pascal compilers" (see Powell, "Modula-2: Good News and Bad News"). There is nothing inherent in any language which guarantees the efficiency of object code; it is all a question of the quality of the compiler being used and the speed of the underlying operating system and hardware.

In any case, there are several types of efficiency which should concern programmers. The one which is often considered first is that of speed: how fast will a given program execute? Another, just as important, is the amount of extra work done by a program. A program whose machine instructions execute very quickly but which does too much unnecessary computation may be worse than one whose object code seems to be locally slower but which is better designed and so avoids extra labor.

For large programs, especially those written by more than one person, the efficiency with which code is produced may be the most important factor. Software engineering techniques that help divide the programming effort, test a design at progressively less abstract levels, and ensure that all the pieces produced will fit together properly are necessary to avoid wasted effort by the programmers. Modula-2 was designed with basic software engineering principles in mind. C apparently was not since it lacks separate compilation with strong type checking across module boundaries and the overall relative clarity of Modula-2 code.

Modula-2 and BASIC

BASIC's main advantages over Modula-2 are its size, string-handling capabilities, and current popularity. BASIC is small enough to learn relatively rapidly, and many home computers are equipped to handle BASIC. BASIC is especially good for interactive I/O and for string manipulation. However, if one compares loop statements or legal variable names or most of the other features the two languages have in common, then Modula-2 code is seen to be not only more powerful but also easier to understand. BASIC's heavy reliance on goto statements, short identifier names, and numbered statements makes clarity much harder to achieve in programs more than a hundred or so lines long.

Modula-2 also has many important features which BASIC does not offer. These include support for separately compiled modules, set and procedure types, and support for low-level and multiprogramming. BASIC has many disadvantages when it comes to writing large programs which interact at all with their environments and has relatively little of Modula-2's clarity and data-structuring power.

Modula-2 and FORTRAN

FORTRAN is a better language than Modula-2 for certain numeric calculations because Modula-2 implementations are only required to support one precision for each of the numeric types INTEGER, CARDINAL, and REAL (however, see Appendix 5) and because a large library of specialized FORTRAN applications already exists. FORTRAN also has a predefined exponentiation operator, a key phrase END IF, a PAUSE facility, and a few other features which are missing in Modula-2.

On the other hand, FORTRAN source code is harder to understand than Modula-2 code, mainly because of the heavy reliance on the goto statement but also because of the restriction on identifier length, the tendency toward large monolithic programs, the lack of extensive data-structuring facilities, the weak semantic checks on CALLed subprograms, the common lack of run-time range checking on array indices, and various other elements. The need to fit statements into fixed fields, as if punched cards were still being used, is also an unnecessary annoyance.

Except for numerical applications, Modula-2 is much more powerful since FORTRAN provides no set types, no support for concurrency, very little support for programming low-level procedures in anything except assembly code, and no recursive subprograms.

4

Modula-2's Basic
Data Types

Modula-2 has six basic types of data: INTEGER, CARDINAL, REAL, BOOLEAN, CHAR, and BITSET. Later chapters discuss ways to use arrays, records, pointers, and other types to build more complex structures from these basic types. The six basic types are described below, along with the operators which can be used on them. The chapter closes with a brief look at operator precedence and associativity.

The INTEGER Type

In mathematics, the integers are all the numbers . . . $-3, -2, -1, 0, 1,$ $2, 3, \ldots$ . . On a computer, however, there will be limits to the size of an INTEGER value. The allowable range of INTEGERs on any implementation of Modula-2 is finite: MinInt, . . . , $-2, -1, 0, 1, 2, \ldots$, MaxInt. On computers with 16-bit words, for instance, MaxInt is often equal to 32,767. If some computation tries to produce a value outside the range allowed, the user will be given an error message such as "INTEGER overflow," and the program will probably stop running. Some implementations may support a LONGINT type which uses more bits to represent a larger range of values than INTEGER. However, Modula-2 compilers are not required to support any type except INTEGER, and the number of bits which must be used for INTEGER or LONGINT values is not specified in the language's definition.

Note that large INTEGER values are written without commas or spaces; one writes 20000, for instance, not 20,000 or 20 000. The operators which may be used on values of the type INTEGER are listed in Table 4-1. Operators may not be written next to each other. For instance, 3 * − 2 is illegal; this should be written instead as 3 * (− 2). Operator precedence is discussed at the end of this chapter.

The operator DIV takes two INTEGER values and returns an INTEGER. In algebra, 13 ÷ 5 = 2.6. However, using DIV is equivalent to doing long division and ignoring the remainder. Thus, 13 DIV 5 = 2 because 5 goes into 13 twice. The sign of x DIV y is the same as the sign of x divided by y in the usual algebraic way. That is, (13 DIV 5) = (−13 DIV −5) = 2, and (−13 DIV 5) = (13 DIV −5) = −2. The value (x MOD y) is the same as the remainder after doing a long division of y into x. For instance, 5 goes into 13 twice, with a remainder of 3, so 13 MOD 5 = 3. Note that x MOD y is only defined for positive values of x and y.

ABS and ODD are both functions which return a value; they may appear anywhere an INTEGER value is needed. For instance, one may write

Length := ABS(b-a);

DEC and INC, by contrast, do not return values but rather execute

TABLE 4-1   INTEGER Operators

Binary operators:

:=	assignment; x := 3 is read aloud as "x gets three"
−	subtraction; also indicates negative integers, e.g. −2
+	addition; can be used to indicate positive integers, e.g., one could write 2 as +2
*	multiplication
DIV	integer division
MOD	remainder upon integer division; defined only for positive operands

Relational operators:

=	equals
#	does not equal; may be used instead of <>
<>	does not equal; may be used instead of #
<	is less than
<=	is less than or equal to
>	is greater than
>=	is greater than or equal to

Standard Subprograms:

ABS(x)	returns the absolute value of x; ABS(−3) = ABS(+3) = 3
ODD(x)	returns TRUE if x is odd and returns FALSE otherwise
DEC(x)	subtracts one from the current value of x if MinInt < x; after executing x := 12; DEC(x); x has the value 11
INC(x)	adds one to the current value of x if x < MaxInt after executing x := 12; INC(x); x has the value 13
TRUNC(x)	returns the value obtained by truncating the REAL x; returns an INTEGER on some systems and a CARDINAL on others; TRUNC(2.76) = 2

actions; they are procedures. The statement

x := DEC(x); (* ILLEGAL *)

is not correct. Instead, one could write

x := −2;
DEC(x);

After executing this correct code, x has the value −3. All four standard subprograms are predefined, so they are visible to every Modula-2 program; they do not need to be imported from a library module or declared locally in order to be used.

Modula-2 INTEGER values may also be written in base 8 or base 16. Octal values are followed by a capital B; hexadecimal values end with an H. The letters A through F are used to represent the six greatest hex digits. Thus, 1DH, 35B, and 29 represent twenty-nine in base 16, base 8, and base 10, respectively.

The CARDINAL Type

In mathematics, the cardinal numbers are zero and the positive integers, i.e., 0, 1, 2, 3, ... The range of CARDINAL values on any computer is finite: 0, 1, 2, . . . , MaxCard. In general, MaxCard will be greater than MaxInt since it will be equal to (MaxInt − MinInt + 1). That is, the range of legitimate CARDINAL values may be viewed on many systems as the interval of INTEGER values shifted to the right so that the left-most value is now zero. Although some implementations may support a type LONGCARD, this is not required. Moreover, the number of bits used to represent CARDINAL and LONGCARD values is implementation-dependent.

The operators applicable to variables of type CARDINAL are nearly the same as those given for the type INTEGER in Table 4-1. Since CARDINAL variables cannot hold negative values, there is no need for ABS(x). The operator IN may be also used with CARDINAL values; this operator is discussed later in connection with the basic type BITSET.

To illustrate the use of CARDINAL values, suppose one is writing a program to produce statistics from test scores and an error in the program causes an average to be computed with subtraction instead of addition. If CARDINAL variables are used to hold the averages, the user will be notified of a "CARDINAL overflow" when the program tries to assign a negative value as an average. However, if the averages were INTEGERs, the program would go merrily on its erroneous way, and the error might never be detected if the output was incorrect but within reason.

The REAL Type

Mathematical real numbers are all those found on the usual number line. The square root of 2, -12.0, 5.38, pi, and $-7/3$ are all real. The sets of integers, cardinals, and rationals (fractions) are all subsets of the real numbers. That is, every integer, cardinal, and rational is a real number, although the real line contains many values which are in none of these subsets. Unlike integers and cardinals, real values cannot be enumerated as the elements of some set. It is possible to list all the rational numbers, such as $-7/3$, in that way, but all the irrationals such as pi and the square root of 2 would be missing. In a way which requires some careful mathematics to make precise, there are more real numbers than fractions, and the reals are closer together than the rationals are.

The result is that one can get a computer to use 3.14 or 3.1416 or even 3.1415926 as the value of pi, but these are all approximations of the actual value of pi. In order to work with the true values of such numbers, symbols such as π must be used. Real numerical calculations performed on a computer will almost always give an answer that is different from the exact answer because only a finite number of digits are used. The main advantage of using the computer is the speed with which the calculations can be performed.

To get from the mathematical real numbers to the type REAL on a computer, two things must be done. First, as with the integers, one must throw out numbers which are too far toward either end of the number line. If REALs can only use eight digits plus two for an exponent, the largest REAL is MaxReal = $+9999999.9E+99$. This limit is not part of the language Modula-2; the values of MaxReal, MinReal, MaxInt, MinInt, and MaxCard all depend on the implementation one uses. The number of bits used to represent REAL values is implementation-dependent. Some implementations may provide higher-precision floating-point arithmetic by way of 32-, 48-, or 64-bit REAL or LONGREAL types, but compilers are not required to support such features.

Secondly, many of the numbers which are between MinReal and MaxReal also get thrown out because they require too much precision. For example, there is certainly no lack of real numbers between $+9999999.8E+99$ and $+9999999.9E+99$, $+9999999.85E+99$ for in-

TABLE 4-2 REAL Operators

Binary operators:
   :=   assignment
   −   subtraction; also indicates negative reals
   +   addition; can be used to indicate positive reals
   *   multiplication
   /   division

Relational operators:
   =   equals
   #   does not equal
   <>   does not equal
   <   is less than
   <=   is less than or equal to
   >   is greater than
   >=   is greater than or equal to

Standard Subprograms:
   ABS(x)   returns the absolute value of x; ABS(−3.0) = ABS(+3.0) = 3.0
   FLOAT(x)   returns the REAL value which corresponds to x; on different systems, x
              may be a CARDINAL, an INTEGER, or both; FLOAT(2) = 2.0

Note that INC(x), DEC(x), ODD(x) might not accept REALs on your system.

stance, but one cannot represent any of these intervening numbers if only ten digits (including two for an exponent) are used.

Real numbers include the integers and the cardinals, but in Modula-2 one writes, for example, −12 to mean an INTEGER, and −12.0 to mean a REAL number. One could also write −1.2 E1 or −0.12 E2; an E2 following a REAL number means "multiplied by 10 to the 2," i.e., by 100. As illustrated in Listing 2-1, INTEGERs and REALs may not be mixed in expressions without using type conversion functions such as FLOAT (or some other method) to change all the values into a single type. The operations which may be applied to variables of type REAL are summarized in Table 4-2.

The BOOLEAN Type

BOOLEAN variables, named after the English mathematician George Boole, may have either of two values: FALSE or TRUE. Boolean expressions are formed by using the logical operators AND, OR, and NOT; AND is also denoted by &, and NOT will be synonymous with ~ in the second version of Modula-2 (see Appendix 5).

If One and Two are two BOOLEAN variables,

   One AND Two will be TRUE when both One and Two are TRUE; this expression is FALSE otherwise

One OR Two will be TRUE when either One or Two or both are TRUE

NOT One will be TRUE when One is FALSE, and FALSE when One is TRUE

The expressions are evaluated from left to right. The order of the operands may make a difference if one of them is not well defined. For instance,

(4 = 2 + 2) OR (6 / 0 = 3)

is TRUE even though division by zero is not defined because Modula-2 uses "short-circuit" evaluation of logical expressions. The second operand, (6 / 0 = 3), is never evaluated; there is no point in checking it since the fact that (4 = 2 + 2) is TRUE makes the entire OR expression TRUE. Similarly,

(4 = 2 + 3) AND (6 / 0 = 3)

is FALSE even though the second operand is not well defined. On the other hand, if one writes (6 / 0 = 3) AND (4 = 2 + 3), an error message will be generated as a result of the attempt to divide by zero. Short-circuit logical evaluation is used in function CATENATEDStrings in Listing 11-3 and procedure ADDNameToList in Listing 12-2. Because Modula-2 uses short-circuit evaluation of logical expressions, the expression One AND Two may be thought of as a call to a function whose body is the statement

```
IF One THEN
    RETURN(Two);
ELSE
    RETURN(FALSE);
END;
```

Similarly, One OR Two may be viewed as a call to a function whose body is

```
IF One THEN
    RETURN(TRUE);
ELSE
    RETURN(Two);
END;
```

Certain rules of logic exist for reducing boolean expressions. One of the simplest is de Morgan's law, which states: ((NOT One) AND (NOT

Two)) is equivalent to NOT(One OR Two) and ((NOT One) OR (NOT Two)) is equivalent to NOT(One AND Two).

Arithmetic expressions formed with the relational operators =, <>, <, and so forth are some of the most common uses of BOOLEAN values. Note that expressions such as

0 <= x < 5

are illegal. Instead, one must write

(0 <= x) AND (x < 5)

Also, although one could write

IF One = TRUE THEN . . .

this is poor style. A better choice is to write

IF One THEN . . .

Similarly, instead of

IF Two = FALSE THEN . . .

use

IF NOT Two THEN . . .

The CHAR Type

One of the most widely used sets of characters is ASCII (American Standard Code for Information Interchange), pronounced ask-ee. The ASCII elements are tabulated in Table 4-3.

Each character has a CARDINAL number associated with it, known as its "ordinal number." To find the ordinal number of a character, add its row and column numbers, which are taken from Table 4-3. The standard procedure ORD(char) returns the ordinal number of the character char. For instance, ORD(ack) = 6. Depending on the machine's implementation of ORD(), one might get ORD(ht) = 9, or ORD(ht) = 11. The apparent discrepancy is caused by the fact that 11 is the base 8 representation of 9. The row and column numbers in Table 4-3 are given in octal form, i.e., in base 8. ORD() might return an octal value on one machine and return the equivalent decimal value on another. Readers unfamiliar with octal numbers may consult the glossary.

TABLE 4-3   The ASCII Character Set

	0	20	40	60	100	120	140	160
0	nul	dle		0	@	P	`	p
1	soh	dc1	!	1	A	Q	a	q
2	stx	dc2	"	2	B	R	b	r
3	etx	dc3	#	3	C	S	c	s
4	eot	dc4	$	4	D	T	d	t
5	enq	nak	%	5	E	U	e	u
6	ack	syn	&	6	F	V	f	v
7	bel	etb	'	7	G	W	g	w
10	bs	can	(	8	H	X	h	x
11	ht	em	)	9	I	Y	i	y
12	lf	sub	*	:	J	Z	j	z
13	vt	esc	+	;	K	[	k	{
14	ff	fs	,	<	L	\	l		
15	cr	gs	-	=	M	]	m	}
16	so	rs	.	>	N	↑	n	~
17	si	us	/	?	O	—	o	del

The entries in the first two columns and the last entry, del, are called "control characters." These characters are usually not printable. They are used to indicate carriage returns, backspaces, the ends of files, and so forth. The meanings assigned to these characters may differ from machine to machine.

Modula-2 refers to characters by their ordinal numbers followed by C, not by the abbreviations listed in Table 4-3. The escape character, for instance, is denoted 33C, not esc. However, one could declare CONST Escape = 33C; and then refer to the ASCII esc character as Escape.

It is easy to confuse octal values and characters since character values may be written as a sequence of digits ending in a C and octal numbers are sequences of digits ending in B: 100C denotes the character @ and 100B is the base 8 number which is equal to 64 in base 10. Just plain 100, with no B or C following, is the base 10 number one hundred. Incidentally, sequences of digits ending in H denote hexadecimal numbers; see the section on type INTEGER earlier in this chapter.

The BITSET Type

Variables of this type take on values which are sets of integers between 0 and N-1. The value of N is system-dependent but is usually either the word length or else a small multiple of it. The name BITSET is used for these variables because they are represented inside the computer as a set of bits. This representation makes the set operators very efficient; they are usually much faster than operators on numbers, for example.

CARDINALSET or SUBRANGESET might have been better names since a BITSET variable could, for instance, take on the value {0, 1, 2}, the value {5, 11}, or the value {3, 7, 8, 9, 10, 11}. This last set could also be written {3, 7..11}. The set with no elements, known as the "empty set," is written { }. There are six operators which take two variables of type BITSET. These are shown in Table 4-4 with some examples of their use.

All the set expressions formed using the set braces { and } are called "set constants." Only constant elements like 0, 1, and 2 may appear between the braces at the time of writing, but this is being changed; see Appendix 5. Even if a variable CardinalVariable is of type CARDINAL, one may not write statements such as

BitsetVariable := {CardinalVariable};

using the original version of Modula-2. To include the current value of a CARDINAL variable in a BITSET, one must use the standard procedure INCL:

INCL(BitsetVariable, CardinalVariable);

The Element in calls on EXCL or INCL may be a constant such as 5 or a variable. Different compilers may expect a variable Element to be of INTEGER type or of CARDINAL type or may accept both.

Operator Precedence and Associativity

Operator precedence and associativity are briefly explained below. The reader should be aware that there will be less trouble understanding programs or porting them to another machine if no assumptions about precedence or associativity are made. Instead, programmers should use as many parentheses and separate statements as necessary to make the order of evaluation clear.

Recall from algebra that in evaluating $3 + 4 * 5$, the multiplication is done first, then the addition; the expression evaluates to 23, not to 35. In algebra, multiplication has been assigned a higher precedence than addition. This means that multiplications are always done before additions in the absence of parentheses which indicate some other

TABLE 4-4   **Set operators and examples of their use**

Binary and Relational Operators:
:=   assignment; BitsetVariable := {1, 3}; is legal. Elements can also be added to sets or removed from sets by using INCL and EXCL.
=   test for equality; takes two sets, the result is either TRUE or FALSE. {1, 3} = {1..3} is FALSE and {1, 3, 4, 5} = {1, 3..5} is TRUE.
inequality; takes two sets, the result is either TRUE or FALSE.
+   set union; takes two sets, the result is another set which contains all values which were in either set. {1, 2} + {2, 3} = {1..3} and {1, 2} + { } = {1, 2}.
−   set difference or complementation; takes two sets, the result is another set which is obtained by removing all elements of the second set from the first set. {1, 3, 4} − {2, 4} = {1, 3}.
*   set intersection; takes two sets, the result is another set which contains those values that were in both of the sets. Thus, {1, 2, 3} * {2, 4} = {2} and {1, 2} * {3, 4} = { }.
/   symmetric set difference; takes two sets, the result is another set which contains those elements that were in one of the sets but not in both. {1, 2, 3, 4} / {1, 3, 7} = {2, 4, 7}. If A and B are two sets, then A / B = (A + B) − (A * B).
<=   test for "improper" inclusion; takes two sets, the result is a BOOLEAN. A <= B is TRUE if and only if every element of A is also an element of B. S <= S is TRUE for every set S. {1, 2} <= {1..3} is TRUE, but {1, 2} <= {1, 3} is FALSE.
>=   test for "improper" containment; takes two sets, the result is a BOOLEAN. A >= B is TRUE if and only if every element of B is also an element of A. S >= S is TRUE for every set S.
IN   test for membership; takes a possible element E and a set S and gives the result TRUE if E is an element of S; E IN S is FALSE otherwise. 2 IN {1..4} is TRUE and 7 IN {1, 3, 5} is FALSE.

Standard Procedures:
INCL(Set, Element)   adds the current value of Element to Set if that value is not out of range for the set. Thus, after executing

Set := { };
Card := 3;
INCL(Set, Card);

one has Set = {3}.

EXCL(Set, Element)   removes the current value of Element from Set if that value is in Set. Thus, after executing

Set := {5, 7};
Card := 3;
EXCL(Set, Card);

one has Set = {5, 7}. If one executes

Set := {5, 7};
Card := 5;
EXCL(Set, Card);

then one has Set = {7}.

order. All the operators discussed in this chapter have been divided into four precedence groups, as shown in Summary 4-1.

SUMMARY 4-1	Grouping of Modula-2's operators by precedence
1. Negation; highest precedence	NOT; unary −, as in −4
2. Multiplication, division, intersection	*, /, DIV, MOD, AND
3. Addition, subtraction and union	+, −, OR
4. Relational operators; lowest precedence	=, #, <>, <, <=, >, >=, IN
No precedence is specified for unary +.	

As indicated in Summary 4-1, the precedence of unary +, as in +3 − 5 or +2 * 6, is left unclear, but since the presence or absence of a unary plus makes no difference to the way an expression is evaluated, any precedence will do.

Whenever there is any doubt that the precedence rules will cause an expression to be evaluated as desired, parentheses should be used. For instance, if the relative precedence of + and * is momentarily forgotten, one can write 3 + (4 * 5) to ensure that the multiplication is done first or (3 + 4) * 5 if the addition should be done first.

When operators with the same precedence are used several times in an expression without parentheses, associativity determines the value of the expression. For example, 16 / 2 / 4 could be evaluated as 8 / 4 = 2 if the divisions are done left to right or as 32 if they are done right to left. The division operator is said to be left- or right-associative, respectively. Left associativity is used in Modula-2. However, one usually has enough to remember without worrying about either precedence or associativity. You can always make your intentions clear by inserting parentheses properly, e.g., (16 / 2) / 4 or 16 / (2 / 4), whichever is desired.

Exercises

1. Find three things wrong with this BOOLEAN expression:

2.0 = (13,002 div 5)

2. Find two things wrong with this BITSET assignment:

BSet := (−2, −1, 0, 1, 2)

3. Evaluate

3 IN ({1, 2, 3} * ({2, 3, 4} − {3, 4, 5}))

4. What basic data type might be preferable when representing
   (*a*) The number of children in a household?
   (*b*) A checking account balance?
   (*c*) The truth of "Sam Clemens is a valid user of this machine"?

5. Try to write an expression for "H cubed divided by K cubed" for REAL H and K without using parentheses. Rewrite the statement using parentheses. Will H * H * H / K * K * K give the right answer?

5

Declarations

Every constant, variable, data type, procedure, or function used in a module M must be introduced before it can be used so that the compiler can check for inconsistencies. This introduction may be accomplished in three ways: the object in question may be "predeclared," it may be imported from a library module, or it may be declared within module M.

The predeclared (also known as "standard" or "predefined") identifiers include the names of Modula-2's standard procedures and functions, the names of certain types (including those introduced in Chapter 4), and the predefined constant values NIL, TRUE, and FALSE. Appendix 2 contains a complete list of standard identifiers and reserved words.

Every nonstandard constant, variable, data type, procedure, or function used in a module must either be imported or else it must be declared within that module. The import mechanisms are discussed in Chapter 9; procedures and functions are presented in Chapter 7. This chapter presents most of the details of constant, variable, and type declarations as they are used within a given module. First, however, comments are briefly discussed since they are often associated with declarations.

Comments

Comments are often used to help document programs. Documentation for a program should explain what the program does, how it is done, what the program's limitations are, and perhaps what the reasoning behind a certain choice of algorithm is. The documentation might also contain other information which is useful to the program's author or people who would like to run or modify the program. All this information can be included in the Modula-2 version of a program, next to the items concerned, by putting it inside comments. Comments may contain any string of characters, including other comments, fragments of Modula-2 code, or English text. The presence or absence of commentary in a program has virtually no direct effect on the way the program compiles or runs. But clear, carefully placed, and concise commentary may greatly improve the program's clarity.

Most of the listings presented so far have contained comments. The start of a comment is marked by a left parenthesis followed immediately by an asterisk: (*. Any text between this delimiter and the next end-of-comment marker *) will have no effect on the execution of the surrounding program. The first asterisk which is directly followed by a right parenthesis *) read by a Modula-2 compiler after it reads a (* will be taken as the end of the comment. Comments can be nested. For instance, this is a valid comment:

(* Here comes a nested comment: (* This is a comment. *) *)

The ability to nest comments is particularly useful during debugging since large portions of code may easily be made invisible to the compiler without simply deleting them and thus losing the work invested in typing them in. Of course, one must be careful not to accidentally exclude part of a program which was meant to be processed by the compiler:

(* The rest of the code (* In a program containing no more comment delimiters than these three *) will be ignored by the compiler

Notice that it is necessary to keep track of the level of nesting when one checks for comments which have been left open by mistake.

The reader may note in passing that many implementations of Modula-2 also allow the programmer to use comments to specify certain compilation options, such as turning off the normal run-time checks on array indices and subrange types. Implementations of Modula-2 are not required to support these options, and their use is not recommended except in extraordinary cases.

Constant Declarations

Numbers, character strings, BITSETs, and other values which are used but never changed by a program and which have a special significance may be named appropriately and listed as constants at the top of the program. For example, suppose one is writing a program which produces form letters seeking donations to the Pi Truncation Society. The program will be easier to understand if it includes some constant declarations such as these:

```
CONST  PI              = 3.14159;
       LETTERHead      = "Truncate Pi For Tomorrow's Children";
       MINIMUMDonation = "$5.00";
```

String constants like LETTERHead are discussed at more length in Chapter 11 since they are considered to be arrays of characters. Other than string constants, Modula-2 allows no constant records and no constant arrays.

If a constant value is given a symbolic name by using a declaration such as

```
CONST NUMBEROfElements = 1000;
```

and that symbolic name is used throughout a program in place of the actual value:

```
IF Element < NUMBEROfElements THEN . . .
```

one can change the value used by the program simply by changing the declaration. For instance, if more conservative forces gain control of the Pi Truncation Society, all references to the value of pi can be changed by simply changing the constant declaration:

```
CONST PI = 3.14;
```

If symbolic names are not used, one is forced to search the entire program for instances of the constant value and change each instance separately. If any instances are missed, the program may fail to run correctly. Descriptive symbolic names can also help clarify the significance of a constant. System-dependent values such as the screen width or word size should also be given descriptive names and declared as constants at the beginning of any program which uses them explicitly. This makes the program easier to port because new values for system constants only need to be inserted in a program at a few easy-to-find places, namely, the constant declarations.

Variable Declarations

The data type of each variable used in a module must be declared before the variable's first use unless the variable is imported from a library module. This includes loop indices. As an illustration, suppose that a programmer wants to write a program which adds up the squares of all the integers between two limits which will be provided by the program's user. A variable will be needed to hold the limits since they may differ from one execution of the program to the next. Other variables will be needed to hold the sum of the squares computed thus far and to keep track of progress toward the upper limit. The types of all these variables must be explicitly declared.

When writing a variable declaration, try to decide whether the declaration would still tell something about the variable's intended purpose if it was surrounded by several hundred (or thousand) lines of code and the program had been ignored for six months. Like comments, good variable names can be very useful to someone who is trying to understand a program. The clarity gained by typing descriptive variable names such as the following is well worth the time spent:

```
VAR SquaresLowerLimit, SquaresUpperLimit: INTEGER;
    (* Limits on summation of squares. *)
    TotalOfSquares, SquaresSumIndex        : INTEGER;
```

As far as the computer is concerned, one could use shorter declarations:

```
VAR LL,UL,tot,ind:INTEGER
```

However, this use of cryptic identifiers and the lack of commentary forces the programmer to remember more, thereby making logic errors more likely. It also creates more work for other people who would like to understand the code, modify it, or perhaps help the programmer debug it. Of course, each system places an upper bound on the length of variable names and other identifiers, but this bound is usually fairly large. Programmers are encouraged to use descriptive identifiers instead of cryptic abbreviations.

Variable declarations never assign values. No automatic initializations are performed, so it is essential that each variable is explicitly assigned a value before a computation tries to make use of its value. Unfortunately, Modula-2 compilers do not always inform the programmer when an attempt is made to access the value of a variable which has not been initialized.

Syntactically, a variable declaration consists of a variable name, possibly preceded or followed by the names of other variables of the same type, with a comma following each name except the last. The last variable name is followed by a colon and the data type of the variable(s); a final semicolon marks the end of the declaration. The list of variable declarations must be preceded by the reserved word VAR, just as constant declarations are preceded by CONST.

Legal variable names consist of a letter, possibly followed by other letters and digits. The only exception is that reserved words cannot be used. Thus, these two declarations are legal:

```
VAR integer: INTEGER;
VAR Integer: INTEGER;
```

but this declaration is not legal:

```
VAR INTEGER: INTEGER; (* ILLEGAL *)
```

Remember that Modula-2 is case sensitive, so "integer" and "Integer" are distinct identifiers.

Unlike Pascal, Modula-2 allows constant, variable, and type declarations in any order. One does not need to declare all constants, then all variables, then all types, and so forth. This is very useful since it allows one to group related declarations together. For instance, one could declare a set type, then declare variables of that type, and then give the procedures and functions which operate on such variables. These declarations could be followed by a declaration of types needed to build a linked list and the variables and subprograms associated with these types.

Readers may note in passing that it is possible in some implementations of Modula-2 to override the allocation scheme used by a Modula-2 compiler by giving an absolute address in a variable's declaration:

```
VAR DeviceStatus[11111B]: BITSET;
```

This feature allows programmers to control memory locations which are reserved for some specific purpose, such as the device registers on computers which use memory-mapped I/O. This facility must be used very carefully if one is to avoid overwriting critical sections of memory; see Chapter 19 for more details.

Type Declarations

Every variable, including the formal parameters in procedures and functions, must be declared to have exactly one type. Constants and functions also have types. Chapter 7 presents the syntax for declaring which data type is returned by a function. The type of a constant is implicit in the constant's declaration:

```
CONST   EMPTYSet = {};       (* Can only be a BITSET    *)
        ROOTTwo = 1.414214;  (* Must be a REAL constant *)
```

In a well-written program, the type of a variable describes the smallest possible set of legitimate values for the variable. Typing should be used to express intentions about the way a variable should be used. This is one of the reasons Modula-2 allows programmers to define their own types, as well as providing a number of predefined types. For instance, one would normally declare a variable called CurrentNumberOfChildren to be of type CARDINAL because values of that type are never negative and the programmer would like to be informed when a program thinks that someone has −3 children.

By making a variable's range of legitimate values clear to the compiler, a programmer can enlist the compiler's aid during debugging. If a program mistakenly passes CurrentNumberOfChildren to a procedure which expects CurrentGrossIncome and these two variables are of different types, the procedure will not blithely figure someone's taxes on an income of $4 instead of $20,000. Without strong typing, it might well be left to the programmer to notice that the final output is wrong and to figure out why.

In addition to delimiting the range of acceptable values for a variable, types may be used to help organize data. Array types, record types, and pointers, for instance, are commonly used to build data structures which are better suited to particular problems than basic types such as INTEGER and CHAR. From this point of view, Modula-2 types fall into two classes. The basic types INTEGER, CARDINAL, BITSET, CHAR, BOOLEAN, and REAL; types which are subranges of these six; and enumeration types are all known as "unstructured types." Arrays, records, sets (except BITSET), and other types whose values may have several distinct components are known as "structured types." Pointer types and procedure types, presented in later chapters, are considered to be unstructured.

The distinction between structured and unstructured types is important for two reasons. First, Modula-2 functions may usually only return pointers and other unstructured types. A function may not return an array, for instance, although it can return a pointer to an array. Some implementations allow functions to return structured types, but compilers are not required to support this facility, so programs which depend on it may be hard to port. Second, the rules concerning type compatibility are different for structured and unstructured types. Two structured types which are not declared to be equal will be incompatible, even if they have precisely the same structure. This is not the case for unstructured types. Type compatibility is examined in more detail later in this chapter.

Syntactically, a type declaration consists of a type name followed by =, followed by a type. The type may be one of the basic types, such as BITSET or BOOLEAN, or it may be an enumeration, a subrange, an array, a record, a set, a pointer, or a procedure type. Each of the structured types have their own syntax, of course, as do enumerations, subranges, and procedure types (see Appendix 3). Several examples of type declarations are shown in Listing 5-1.

LISTING 5-1 *Some sample type declarations.*

```
TYPE  PointerType   = POINTER TO ArrayType;
      RecordType    = RECORD
                        FieldOne: BITSET;
                        FieldTwo: BOOLEAN;
                        END; (* RECORD *)
      Subrange      = [-2..5];
      Enumeration   = (line, square, triangle, other);
      ArrayType     = ARRAY[1..5],[0..10] OF INTEGER;
      SetType       = SET OF Enumeration;
      ProcedureType = PROCEDURE(REAL, VAR CHAR);
```

Note that Modula-2, unlike Pascal, allows constant, variable, and type declarations to be given in any order. However, except for certain declarations involving pointer types, compilers may require that type declarations only involve previously declared types. Thus, to enhance portability, Enumeration should be declared before one declares SetType to be a SET OF Enumeration.

One is allowed to use certain declarations which refer to later declarations, such as the ones for RecordPointer and the two mutually recursive procedures in Listing 5-2.

LISTING 5-2 *In Modula-2, certain declarations are allowed to refer to objects which are defined later in the same block.*

```
TYPE  RecordPointer = POINTER TO RecordType;
      RecordType    = RECORD
                        Value: INTEGER;
                        NEXT : RecordPointer;
                        END; (* RECORD *)
```

```
PROCEDURE MutuallyRecursiveOne(x: CARDINAL);
BEGIN
  IF x > 0 THEN
    WRITECardinal(x,6);
    MutuallyRecursiveTwo(x-1);
  END; (* IF *)
END MutuallyRecursiveOne;

PROCEDURE MutuallyRecursiveTwo(x: CARDINAL);
BEGIN
  IF x > 0 THEN
    WRITECardinal(x,6);
    MutuallyRecursiveOne(x-1);
  END; (* IF *)
END MutuallyRecursiveTwo;
```

Strong Typing and Type Compatibility

Modula-2 is called a strongly typed language because most statements which try to mix types are illegal. For instance, we saw in Chapter 2 that it is illegal to simply divide an INTEGER by a CARDINAL and expect a REAL result. Hoare (1983) lists several reasons why strong typing is preferable to the use of automatic type transfers and coercions. Apart from the important role typing plays in the design and documentation of programs during their development, there is the problem that the rules governing the various conversions may greatly complicate the language. Some complication is inevitable, whether or not type conversions are done at the programmer's explicit request. But compilers which perform coercions without informing anyone force every programmer to learn essentially every rule concerning type conversions. If conversions are made only at the behest of the programmer, then programmers can safely ignore any complexities associated with conversions they have not explicitly requested.

Hoare also points out that quite often the errors introduced by conversions are small, so it is more difficult to detect and correct them. Automatic type conversions also introduce machine dependencies at unwanted places and may be much less efficient than one would have hoped. However, in my own opinion the most frustrating part of working in a language which uses automatic type conversions is the feeling that one does not have complete control over a program any more. Trying to eliminate errors caused by typing mistakes or oversights in logic is frustrating enough; one should not also need to take into account the quirks of an overzealous compiler which is "only trying to help."

In any case, programmers need to understand the rules which govern type compatibility in Modula-2 in order to use the language. If two variables in a module are of different types and there is not a single, obvious correspondence between the allowed values for the two types, it is not legal to use the two variables in the same expression without using FLOAT or some other conversion or coercion. The correspondence between the values of two types must be made clear to the compiler before it will allow expressions which mix variables of the two types. For instance, consider the code in Listing 5-3.

LISTING 5-3   *Examples for the discussion of type compatibility.*

```
VAR   IntegerX, IntegerY  : INTEGER;
      RealVariable        : REAL;
      CardinalVariable    : CARDINAL;
      CharacterVariable   : CHAR;
      IntegerCompatible   : [-10..10]; (* Subrange of INTEGER  *)
      CardinalCompatible  : [10..100]; (* Subrange of CARDINAL *)

      (* These statements involve no type incompatibilities: *)
      IntegerX := IntegerY;
      IntegerCompatible := IntegerY;
      CardinalVariable := CardinalCompatible;
      IntegerY := CardinalVariable;
      CardinalVariable := IntegerX;
```

Note first that CARDINAL and INTEGER variables are "assignment compatible," that is, INTEGER values may be assigned to CARDINAL variables and vice versa. Of course, the assignment of a negative INTEGER value to a CARDINAL variable will result in an error. INTEGER, CARDINAL, and subranges of INTEGER and CARDINAL are all assignment compatible.

Assignment compatibility imposes weaker restrictions than full type compatibility. Any types which are fully compatible are also assignment compatible, but the reverse is not true. One cannot, for instance, add or multiply an INTEGER variable and a CARDINAL variable. The statements

```
Integer Y := IntegerX + CardinalVariable;
Integer X := RealVariable;
CardinalVariable := CharacterVariable;
```

are all illegal because they contain type incompatibilities.

The rules governing full type compatibility (as opposed to assignment compatibility) are shown in Summary 5-1. Types BasicOne and BasicTwo in Listing 5-4 are fully compatible because they are both renamings of CARDINAL. Types StructuredOne and StructuredTwo in that example are not compatible, even though they have the same structure. Type BasicThree is compatible with both the other basic types shown, but type StructuredThree is compatible only with StructuredOne, even though it has the same structure as type StructuredTwo.

SUMMARY 5-1   The rules which govern type compatibility

1. The types TypeOne and TypeTwo are compatible if they were declared as

TYPE TypeOne = TypeTwo;

or if

TYPE TypeTwo = TypeOne;

2. TypeOne and TypeTwo are compatible if TypeOne is a subrange of TypeTwo or vice versa.

3. TypeOne and TypeTwo are compatible if TypeOne and TypeTwo are both subranges of the same type.

4. TypeOne and TypeTwo are compatible if TypeOne and TypeTwo are both renamings of a third type, i.e., if they were declared as

TYPE TypeOne = TypeThree;
TYPE TypeTwo = TypeThree;

5. The only way for two structured types to be compatible is for them to have been declared as equal. This could be done by declaring

TYPE StructuredTwo = StructuredOne;

or by declaring StructuredOne and StructuredTwo both equal to some third structured type.

6. Nonnegative INTEGER values may be assigned to CARDINAL variables; CARDINAL values which do not exceed MaxInt may be assigned to INTEGER variables.

7. There are two exceptions to the compatibility rules just given. These exceptions will be discussed later in connection with formal "open array" parameters of types such as ARRAY OF CHAR and in the discussion on type WORD.

LISTING 5-4 *More declarations used in the discussion of compatibility.*

```
TYPE  BasicOne     = CARDINAL;
      BasicTwo     = CARDINAL;
      BasicThree   = BasicOne;

      StructuredOne    = ARRAY[1..100] OF CHAR;
      StructuredTwo    = ARRAY[1..100] OF CHAR;
      StructuredThree  = StructuredOne;
      StructuredFour   = ARRAY[1..50] OF CHAR;
```

Exercises

1. Which of the following are legal variable names?
   (*a*) realestate
   (*b*) real estate
   (*c*) profits83
   (*d*) 1983
   (*e*) real-estate
   (*f*) real
   (*g*) REAL
   (*h*) Real_Estate

2. Given the declarations
   ```
   x, y   :INTEGER;
   r, s   :REAL;
   card   :CARDINAL;
   char   :CHAR;
   george:BOOLEAN;
   ```
   which of the following statements are legal? Assume that TRUNC converts REAL values into corresponding INTEGER values by removing everything to the right of the decimal point, e.g., TRUNC(12.34) = 12.
   (*a*) x := y*r;
   (*b*) x := CARDINAL(s);
   (*c*) x := TRUNC(r)*TRUNC(s);
   (*d*) real := FLOAT(x*y);
   (*e*) george := card;
   (*f*) x := TRUNC(r*s); (* Is this always the same as (*c*)? *)
   (*g*) card := CARDINAL(TRUNC(FLOAT(card)));

6

Conditional and Loop Statements

The IF Statement

Listing 6-1 shows a simple function which might be called at the beginning of every programming session. As part of an actual log-in sequence it has numerous drawbacks; it is meant mainly as an illustration of Modula-2 IF statements. The function MayLogin assumes the visibility of the imported procedures WRITEString and READInteger, as well as the global variables INVOICESNeedProcessing, SUPER-UserLoggedOn, SYSTEMLoad, and JASONSPriority. Notice how Modula-2's syntax, descriptive identifier names, and comments combine to produce code which is easy to understand.

LISTING 6-1 *An example of nested Modula-2* **IF** *statements.*

```
PROCEDURE MayLogin(): BOOLEAN;
  CONST SusanPassNumber = 123;
        SandyPassNumber = 25;
        JasonPassNumber = 900;
  VAR   PassNumber  : INTEGER;
        UserIsValid : BOOLEAN;
BEGIN (* MayLogin *)
  UserIsValid := TRUE;
  WRITEString("Enter your passnumber: ");
  READInteger(PassNumber);
  IF ((PassNumber=SusanPassNumber) AND (NOT INVOICESNeedProcessing)) THEN
    (* Only allow Susan to log on if she is caught up with her work. *)
    WRITEString("Hello, Susan.");
```

LISTING 6-1 Continued

```
ELSIF (PassNumber = SandyPassNumber) THEN
  WRITEString("Hello, Sandy.");
  SUPERUserLoggedOn := TRUE;
ELSIF (PassNumber = JasonPassNumber) THEN
  IF (SYSTEMLoad <= JASONSPriority) THEN
    (* Jason has low priority as a user. *)
    WRITEString("Hello, Jason.");
  ELSE
    WRITEString("Sorry, Jason. The system is too busy.");
    UserIsValid := FALSE;
  END; (* IF system not too busy *)
ELSE
  WRITEString("Sorry, you are not a valid user.");
  UserIsValid := FALSE;
END; (* IF PassNumber = SusanPassNumber *)
RETURN UserIsValid;
END MayLogin;
```

The expressions which follow IF and ELSIF must give BOOLEAN values. These expressions are evaluated in the order of their occurrence until one is found to be TRUE. The associated sequence of statements is then executed, and control passes to the next statement after the IF statement. The number of ELSIF portions allowed depends on the Modula-2 implementation being used; the syntax imposes no limit. If none of the expressions are TRUE and an ELSE clause is present, its sequence of statements will be executed; otherwise, control passes to the next statement after the IF statement. Pascal programmers should notice how the lack of begin . . . end bracketing makes nested IF statements easy to read.

The CASE Statement

Listing 6-2 shows an example of a Modula-2 CASE statement. Every CASE statement starts with the key word CASE followed by some expression, i.e., some combination of identifiers and operators which can be evaluated at run time to give a single value. This controlling expression must evaluate to an INTEGER, CARDINAL, CHAR, BIT-SET, BOOLEAN, enumeration, or subrange value. The variable ThisUser.Kind in Listing 6-2, for instance, is of the programmer-defined enumeration type KindOfUser.

After the controlling expression comes the reserved word OF, followed by a nonempty list of cases. Each of the cases starts with a label which distinguishes it from all other cases. This label is usually a constant expression which has a single value, but one may also use a

LISTING 6-2 *Examples of the* **CASE** *statement in Modula-2.*

```
TYPE KindOfUser = (BadUser, Student, Staff, Faculty, Operator);
TYPE UserDescription = RECORD
                    Name: ARRAY[1..NameLength] OF CHAR;
                    Kind: KindOfUser;
                    END; (* UserDescription RECORD *)
VAR  ThisUser: UserDescription;


(* This CASE statement uses the definitions above *)
CASE ThisUser.Kind OF
  BadUser       : GoNab(ThisUser);       |
  Student       : PrintStudentNews;      |
  Staff, Faculty: PrintAllNews;          |
  Operator      : PrintSystemStatistics;
                  PrintHelpRequests;
END; (* CASE ThisUser.Priority *)


(* This should not be programmed as a CASE statement: *)
CASE IntegerVariable OF
  1    : WRITEString(" That is a one ");     |
  10   : WRITEString(" That is a ten ");     |
  100  : WRITEString(" That is a hundred "); |
  1000 : WRITEString(" That is a thousand ");
ELSE
  WRITEString(" I do not know what that is ");
END; (* CASE which should be rewritten as an IF statement *)


(* IF statement which is logically equivalent to the CASE *)
(* statement above, but which is often more efficient:    *)
IF IntegerVariable = 1 THEN
  WRITEString(" That is a one ");
ELSIF IntegerVariable = 10 THEN
  WRITEString(" That is a ten ");
ELSIF IntegerVariable = 100 THEN
  WRITEString(" That is a hundred ");
ELSIF IntegerVariable = 1000 THEN
  WRITEString(" That is a thousand ");
ELSE
  WRITEString(" I do not know what that is ");
END; (* Reformulation of CASE statement above as an IF statement *)
```

range of values such as 1..10, a list such as 2, 3, 5, 7, or a mixture such as 1, 11..22. The same value should not appear in more than one label, and the labels must be of a type which is compatible with the controlling expression.

The labels used in a CASE statement should also be essentially adjacent in value because of the way CASE statements are usually handled by a compiler. A CASE statement which uses 1 and 100 as labels, for instance, and skips the values in between should be reformulated as an IF statement; Listing 6-2 contains an example. A label such as 1..100 is fine. Continuing with the syntax, the reader will note that a colon separates each label from the list of statements which are to be executed if the value of the controlling expression falls within the range defined by the label. A vertical bar, |, separates all but the last of the cases from their successors. Notice that it is possible to associate several statements with a given label. In the second version of Modula-2, a bar may be placed after the last case as well (see Appendix 5).

Now suppose that the controlling expression's value falls outside the set defined by the labels; this should generally occur only when something unusual has happened. If there is an ELSE portion in the CASE statement, control will be passed to the statement which follows the key word ELSE. For instance, if IntegerVariable = 5 when the second CASE statement in Listing 6-2 is reached, "I do not know what that is" will be printed. If there is no ELSE portion, the computer should *not* be relied upon to pass control to the statement which follows the CASE statement. It is more likely that some sort of run-time error will occur, and the program will crash. For this reason, it is sometimes a good idea to include an ELSE portion which contains something like

WRITEString("ELSE in CASE IntegerVariable unexpected");

even in CASE statements which should never need them, so that the programmer will be informed whenever the ELSE portion is unexpectedly executed.

Loop Statements in Modula-2

Modula-2 recognizes four kinds of loop statements: the FOR loop, the WHILE loop, the REPEAT..UNTIL loop, and the just plain LOOP loop. Listing 6-3 shows an example of each; the four loops shown are equivalent in the sense that Total will contain the same value after leaving each loop. Different styles of commentary are used to mark the ends of the loops shown, but in each case it is clear what kind of statement (FOR loop, WHILE loop, etc.) has been finished. In addition, it may be useful to follow the style of the LOOP and WHILE loops in Listing 6-3 and indicate which particular loop was just completed when the body of a loop extends over several lines.

The body of a loop can only be executed a finite number of times on any computer. The loop shown in Listing 6-4 is an example of an

LISTING 6-3 *Modula-2's four kinds of loop statements.*

```
Total := 0;
FOR Index := 3 TO 33 BY 3 DO
  Total := Total + Index;
END; (* FOR *)

Total := 0;
Index := 3;
WHILE Index <= 33 DO
  Total := Total + Index;
  Index := Index + 3;
END; (* WHILE Index <= 33 *)

Total := 0;
Index := 3;
REPEAT
  Total := Total + Index;
  Index := Index + 3;
UNTIL Index > 33;

Total := 0;
Index := 3;
LOOP (* Sum multiples of 3 *)
  Total := Total + Index;
  Index := Index + 3;
  IF Index > 33 THEN
    EXIT;
  END; (* IF *)
END; (* LOOP summing multiples of 3 *)
```

LISTING 6-4 *An infinite loop.*

```
Index := 0;
WHILE Index <= 0 DO
  Index := Index - 1;
END; (* WHILE Index <= 0 *)
WRITEString(" Out of infinite loop. ");
```

"infinite" loop. If the body of the loop is entered, control will never pass to the call to WRITEString; Index <= 0 will always be true. The assignment statement in the body of the loop will be executed and re-executed repeatedly until a range error, a hardware failure, or something similar brings the program to a halt. The conditions which control the number of iterations made through a loop should always be carefully considered in order to avoid unwanted infinite loops.

Also, computations which can be done outside a loop should not be part of the loop's body. Leaving them inside the loop probably causes them to be executed many more times than is necessary. Thus, although the first loop in Listing 6-5 is correct, the second version is more efficient. Some compilers will make similar optimizations, but one cannot rely on their doing so. More examples are given in the exercises at the end of this chapter.

LISTING 6-5 *Avoiding unecessary computation in loops.*

```
WHILE Index < UpperBound - LowerBound DO
   Total := Total + Factor*Height + Index;
   Index := Index + 2*Step;
   George := FALSE;
END; (* WHILE *)


UpperIndex := UpperBound - LowerBound;
FactorHeight := Factor*Height;
IndexStep := 2*Step;
George := FALSE;
WHILE Index < UpperIndex DO
   Total := Total + FactorHeight + Index;
   Index := Index + IndexStep;
END; (* WHILE *)
```

FOR Loops

In a FOR statement such as

```
FOR Index := Lower TO Upper BY Step DO
   StatementSequence;
END; (* FOR *)
```

StatementSequence is executed repeatedly, with Index assuming the successive values Lower, Lower + Step, Lower + 2 * Step, . . . , Lower + K * Step, where t the largest cardinal for which Lower + K * Step <= Upper is K. If the BY Step clause is left out, the increment Step is assumed to be 1. For instance, executing

```
FOR Index := 7 TO 12 DO
   WRITECardinal(Index, 6);
END; (* FOR *)
```

will produce

```
7    8    9    10    11    12
```

FOR loops may be made to execute with a decreasing sequence of values for the control variable by using a negative increment, e.g., executing

```
WRITEString("Seconds to blastoff:");
FOR TimeLeft := 10 TO 0 BY −1 DO
   WRITECardinal(TimeLeft,2);
END; (* FOR *)
```

will produce

Seconds to blastoff: 10 9 8 7 6 5 4 3 2 1 0

A FOR loop such as

```
FOR Index := 10 TO 1 DO
   StatementSequence;
END; (* FOR *)
```

is skipped over during program execution; Index cannot get from 10 to 1 using the default step size +1. Note also that the value of the control variable after the loop is finished depends on the implementation of Modula-2 being used.

The index or control variable of a FOR loop may not be a component of a structured variable such as an array or record. The control variable must be of a nonstructured type, such as CARDINAL or an enumeration type; it cannot be of type REAL. The index cannot be an imported variable, nor can it be a parameter if the loop is inside a procedure or function. Finally, note that statements in the body of the FOR loop should not attempt to change the value of the loop's control variable:

```
FOR Index := 1 TO 10 DO
   Index := 2*Index;      (* NOT A GOOD IDEA *)
   WRITEInteger(Index, 6);
END; (* Bad FOR loop *)
```

Incidentally, programmers who commonly use FOR loops such as

```
FOR Index := LowBound TO HighBound DO
  ArrayOne[Index] := ArrayTwo[Index];
END; (* FOR *)
```

to copy the contents of one array into another one should note that assignments involving entire arrays are allowed. Thus, although the loop shown is correct, the assignment may be done more easily with the statement

```
ArrayOne := ArrayTwo;
```

WHILE and REPEAT..UNTIL Loops

The number of times the body of a FOR loop will be executed is fixed at the point at which the loop is first entered; statements in the body of a FOR loop should not attempt to change the number of iterations which will be made through that body. However, the number of times the body of a WHILE or a REPEAT..UNTIL loop is executed depends on the value of some BOOLEAN expression. The value of this controlling expression must be changed somewhere in the body of the loop or the loop will never be exited, and one must contend with an infinite loop such as the one shown in Listing 6-4.

There are two basic differences between WHILE loops and RE-PEAT..UNTIL loops. The first is that the controlling BOOLEAN expression is evaluated before each execution of the body of a WHILE loop, but after each execution of the body of a REPEAT..UNTIL loop. The second difference is that a WHILE loop finishes execution when the controlling expression becomes FALSE, but a REPEAT..UNTIL loop finishes when the controlling expression becomes TRUE. If the flow of control ever reaches the top of the loop, the body of a WHILE loop will be executed zero or more times, while the body of a RE-PEAT..UNTIL loop will always be executed one or more times.

If the controlling expression in a WHILE loop evaluates to TRUE, the statements in the body of the loop will be executed in sequence. The expression is then evaluated again. If it is TRUE, the body is executed again. These alternating evaluations of the expression and executions of the loop's body are repeated until the BOOLEAN expression is found to be FALSE. Control then passes to the statement which follows the loop. The simplest infinite WHILE loop is of the form

```
WHILE TRUE DO
  SomeStatements;
END; (* WHILE *)
```

The body of a REPEAT..UNTIL loop, on the other hand, will always be executed once before the controlling expression is evaluated. Thus, the BOOLEAN expression controlling a REPEAT..UNTIL loop may involve variables which are given their initial values the first time through the loop. If the expression is FALSE, the body is executed again. The expression is then evaluated again. If it is FALSE, the body is executed one more time. These alternating evaluations of the expression and executions of the loop's body are repeated until the BOOLEAN expression is found to be TRUE. The simplest infinite RE-PEAT..UNTIL loop looks like

```
REPEAT
    SomeStatements;
UNTIL FALSE;
```

LOOP Loops

LOOP loops allow programmers to specify several possible points of exit from a loop so that the body of the loop is executed, for instance, 3½ times. By contrast, the body of a WHILE or a REPEAT..UNTIL loop will always be executed zero, one, two, or some other cardinal number of times. Once the body of a LOOP loop is entered, the statements in it will be executed repeatedly until the statement EXIT; is encountered. EXIT statements may only be used in connection with LOOP loops. If several LOOP loops are nested, only the one immediately surrounding the EXIT statement will be terminated. FOR, WHILE, and REPEAT..UNTIL loops can all be expressed as LOOP loops which contain a single EXIT statement. LOOP statements are the most convenient way to program loops with more than one exit, such as the one shown in Listing 6-6. The reader is invited to attempt an equivalent formulation using, say, nothing but WHILE loops.

LISTING 6-6   *A LOOP loop with two exits.*

```
PROCEDURE LookForCharacter;
    VAR Found                 : BOOLEAN;
        TryAgain, NextCharacter,
        DesiredCharacter      : CHAR;
BEGIN
    Found := FALSE;
    WRITEString(" What character are we looking for? ");
    READCharacter(DesiredCharacter);
    LOOP
```

LISTING 6-6   Continued

```
WRITEString(" What file shall we look in? ");
OPENInput(""); (* Try to open INPUTFile to read from it *)
WHILE (NOT DONE) DO
  WRITEString(" Could not open input file. ");
  WRITEString(" Want to try again? ");
  READCharacter(TryAgain); (* This assumes that input is read *)
  (* from the keyboard until INPUTFile is opened.            *)
  IF ((TryAgain = "y") OR (TryAgain = "Y")) THEN
    OPENInput("");
  ELSE
    WRITEString(" No. ");
    EXIT; (* leave surrounding LOOP loop *)
  END; (* IF user is not tired of looking *)
END; (* WHILE still have no input file to scan *)
READCharacter(NextCharacter); (* This value will be read from *)
                              (* opened INPUTFile             *)
WHILE ((NextCharacter <> ENDOfFile) AND (NOT Found)) DO
  IF NextCharacter = DesiredCharacter THEN
    WRITEString(" Found it! ");
    CLOSEInput;
    EXIT; (* leave surrounding LOOP loop *)
  END; (* IF DesiredCharacter found *)
  READCharacter(NextCharacter);
END; (* WHILE more of current file and DesiredCharacter not found *)
END; (* LOOP through some number of files looking for the *)
     (* DesiredCharacter; EXIT when user gets tired of     *)
     (* looking or when the character is found.            *)
END LookForCharacter;
```

LOOP loops are also convenient for writing loops which one intends to be executed an arbitrarily large number of times before execution is stopped by some force external to the program. These loops are not to be confused with infinite loops, such as the one in Listing 6-4, which are the result of a programming error. The arbitrarily long loop is useful, for instance, when one wishes to write a "watchdog" process for some application. Such a loop is shown in Listing 6-7 as part of a simple MonitorVatTemperature procedure which monitors the temperature of a vat and raises an alarm if necessary. Incidentally, MonitorVatTemperature could be made into a Modula-2 PROCESS in such a way as to allow more or less continuous monitoring of the vat without preventing other computations from moving forward.

LISTING 6-7   *A LOOP loop with no explicit exits.*

```
PROCEDURE MonitorVatTemperature;
  VAR VatTemp: TEMPERATURE;
BEGIN
  LOOP
    VatTemp := GETVatTemperature();
    IF VatTemp > MAXSafeVatTemperature THEN
      RAISEAlarm(VATTooHot);
    END; (* IF vat too hot *)
  END; (* watchdog LOOP *)
END MonitorVatTemperature;
```

Exercises

1. Try to rewrite each of the following IF statements as a CASE statement:

```
IF IDNumber = EmployeeNumber THEN
  WRITEString("Hello, employee.");
ELSIF IDNumber = ForemanNumber THEN
  WRITEString("Hello, foreman");
ELSIF IDNumber = BossNumber THEN
  WRITEString("Hello, boss");
ELSIF IDNumber = PresidentNumber THEN
  WRITEString("Hello, Mr. President.");
ELSE
  WRITEString("Sorry, I can't let you in.");
END; (* IF IDNumber = EmployeeNumber *)

IF PatientCondition = Critical THEN
  CallEMTs;
ELSIF StomachCondition = Empty THEN
  GetSomeFood;
ELSE
  GoToSleep;
END; (* IF PatientCondition = Critical *)
```

2. Give two reasons why a logically equivalent IF statement would be preferable to the following CASE statement:

```
CASE AmountOwed OF
  5    : WRITEString("Have you sent your payment?");|
  50   : WRITEString("Hurry up; You owe us money."); |
  500  : WRITEString("We've impounded your car."); |
  5000 : WRITEString("We're taking possession of your house.");
END; (* CASE AmountOwed *)
```

3. Rewrite the following code using comments, format, and suggestive identifier names to help clarify it. Assume that its purpose is to find the sum of the cubes of the integers between two given limits:

```
a,b,c,d:INTEGER;
    .
    .
d:=0;
FOR a:=b TO c DO
d:=d+a*a*a;END;
```

4. Try to find the value of Total after the following code is run:

```
Total := 0;
Index := 3;
WHILE Index <= 35 DO
    Total := Total + Index;
END; (* WHILE Index <= 35 *)
```

5. State the results of trying to execute each of the following pieces of code:

```
Total := 0;
Index := 1;
LOOP (* loop (a) *)
    Index := Index + 2;
    Total := Total + Index;
    IF Index = 6 THEN EXIT; END;
END; (* loop (a) *)
Total := 0;
Index := 1;
LOOP (* loop (b) *)
    Index := Index + 2;
    Total := Total + Index;
    IF Index > 5 THEN EXIT; END;
    Index := 0;
END; (* loop (b) *)
```

6. Use each of the four kinds of loops to find the sum of all the odd numbers between LowerLimit and UpperLimit; include UpperLimit if it is odd. Assume LowerLimit is odd. What does your answer give as the sum if LowerLimit = UpperLimit or if LowerLimit > UpperLimit?

7. How many times is the assignment to George done when the first loop below is executed? Try to rewrite both loops so that the final values of all variables are the same, but less work is done.

```
FOR Index := 2 TO 11 DO
    Total := Total + Index;
    George := FALSE;
END; (* FOR Index := 2 TO 11 *)

WHILE Index < (3*UpperLimit - 2) DO
    Total := Factor1*(1-Factor2) + Factor3*Index;
    NewLimit := OldLimit - UpperLimit;
END; (* WHILE Index < (3*UpperLimit - 2) *)
```

7

Procedures and Functions

Why Use Subprograms?

The term "subprogram" is used in this book to mean both procedures and functions. Some reasons for using subprograms are given in Summary 7-1.

SUMMARY 7-1   Reasons to use procedures and functions

1. Subprograms can make the purpose of code more evident by keeping details which are inappropriate to the current level of abstraction hidden from the reader. Descriptive procedure and function names are important for this reason.

2. Procedures and functions may make programming more efficient by preventing unnecessary repetition of similar pieces of code throughout a particular program.

3. The use of subprograms may make it easier to debug, test, and modify programs by helping to clarify the structure of a program at its various levels of abstraction and by localizing actions.

4. In Modula-2, procedures and functions may make later programming easier by becoming elements of a library which can be used in other modules. This helps prevent the unnecessary repetition of similar pieces of code throughout many different programs.

The first entry in Summary 7-1 refers to the fact that it is usually a good idea to hide details which the computer needs but which can be ignored by the programmer. Thus, a simple procedure call such as

WRITEString("Hello!");

is preferable to something such as

WRITECharacter("H");
WRITECharacter("e");
WRITECharacter("l");
WRITECharacter("l");
WRITECharacter("o");
WRITECharacter("!");

Notice how the longer version still relies on procedures; without them it would be even longer. The example above also illustrates the second and third points in Summary 7-1; a single call on WRITEString is both more concise and easier to understand than the alternative. The fourth point will be ignored for now, but it will be seen in Chapter 9 that new procedures or functions can be added to a system's library quite easily.

As another illustration, consider the program in Listing 7-1. This program accepts the cartesian coordinates of three points and then determines whether the figure obtained by connecting the points is a point, a line, or a triangle. The program uses three imported I/O procedures, but no procedures or functions have been declared locally in the program module Geometer. Listing 7-2 contains the same program, rewritten to make better use of procedures and functions. In Listing 7-2, the newly added procedures and functions serve the first three purposes mentioned in Summary 7-1.

LISTING 7-1 *A monolithic program module.*

```
MODULE Geometer;
  FROM InOut IMPORT WRITEString, WRITELine, READInteger;

  VAR X1, Y1, X2, Y2, X3, Y3: INTEGER;

BEGIN (* main body of Geometer *)
  WRITEString(" This program determines whether three points form a ");
  WRITEString(" point, a line segment, or a triangle.  ");
  WRITELine;
  WRITEString(" Enter the three pairs of (integer) coordinates. ");
  READInteger(X1);
  READInteger(Y1);
  READInteger(X2);
```

```
READInteger(Y2);
READInteger(X3);
READInteger(Y3);
IF ((X1 = X2) AND (Y1 = Y2)) THEN
  IF ((X2 = X3) AND (Y2 = Y3)) THEN
    WRITEString(" Figure formed is a point. ");
  ELSE
    WRITEString(" Figure formed is a line segment. ");
  END; (* IF *)
ELSIF ((X2 = X3) AND (Y2 = Y3)) THEN
  IF ((X1 = X3) AND (Y1 = Y3)) THEN
    WRITEString(" Figure formed is a point. ");
  ELSE
    WRITEString(" Figure formed is a line segment. ");
  END; (* IF *)
ELSIF ((X1 = X3) AND (Y1 = Y3)) THEN
  IF ((X2 = X3) AND (Y2 = Y3)) THEN
    WRITEString(" Figure formed is a point. ");
  ELSE
    WRITEString(" Figure formed is a line segment. ");
  END; (* IF *)
ELSE
  WRITEString(" Figure formed is a triangle. ");
END; (* IF *)
END Geometer.
```

LISTING 7-2 *The program of Listing 7-1, rewritten to use procedures and functions.*

```
MODULE Geometer;
  (* Revised to make better use of procedures and functions. *)
  FROM InOut IMPORT WRITEString, WRITELine, READInteger;

  TYPE FigureType = (Point, LineSegment, Triangle);

  VAR X1, Y1, X2, Y2, X3, Y3: INTEGER;

  PROCEDURE Introduce;
  BEGIN
    WRITEString(" This program determines whether three points form a ");
    WRITEString(" point, a line segment, or a triangle. ");
    WRITELine;
  END Introduce;
```

LISTING 7-2   Continued

```
PROCEDURE GetPoint(VAR x, y: INTEGER);
BEGIN
  WRITELine;
  WRITEString(" Enter integer x coordinate> ");
  READInteger(x);
  WRITELine;
  WRITEString(" Enter integer y coordinate> ");
  READInteger(y);
END GetPoint;

PROCEDURE SamePoint(x1, y1, x2, y2: INTEGER): BOOLEAN;
BEGIN
  RETURN ((x1 = x2) AND (y1 = y2));
END SamePoint;

PROCEDURE FigureIs(x1, y1, x2, y2, x3, y3: INTEGER): FigureType;
BEGIN
  IF SamePoint(x1, y1, x2, y2) THEN
    IF SamePoint(x2, y2, x3, y3) THEN
      RETURN Point;
    ELSE
      RETURN LineSegment;
    END; (* IF *)
  ELSIF SamePoint(x2, y2, x3, y3) THEN
    IF SamePoint(x1, y1, x3, y3) THEN
      RETURN Point;
    ELSE
      RETURN LineSegment;
    END; (* IF *)
  ELSIF SamePoint(x1, y1, x3, y3) THEN
    IF SamePoint(x2, y2, x3, y3) THEN
      RETURN Point;
    ELSE
      RETURN LineSegment;
    END; (* IF *)
  ELSE
    RETURN Triangle;
  END; (* IF *)
END FigureIs;

BEGIN (* main body of Geometer *)
  Introduce;
  GetPoint(X1, Y1);
  GetPoint(X2, Y2);
  GetPoint(X3, Y3);
  CASE FigureIs(X1, Y1, X2, Y2, X3, Y3) OF
```

```
  Point       : WRITEString(" Figure formed is a point. ");        |
  LineSegment: WRITEString(" Figure formed is a line segment. ");|
  Triangle    : WRITEString(" Figure formed is a triangle. ");
  END; (• CASE FigureIs •)
END Geometer.
```

Procedures Versus Functions

Procedure calls stand for a sequence of statements which are to take the values given and perform some actions with them. Functions, on the other hand, return values. In both cases, the source code which is to be executed is found at some other location than the point at which the subprogram is called. Procedure calls may appear anywhere another complete Modula-2 statement could appear; function calls may appear wherever a value of the type returned by the function is expected. This rules out constructions such as

X1 := READInteger(X1);

since READInteger is a procedure, not a function. Similarly

ABS(x);

is illegal; since ABS returns a value, one must do something such as

y := ABS(x);

Except for the fact that procedure calls are (syntactically) statements and function calls are factors, there is no difference between procedures and functions in Modula-2.

Subprogram Parameters

Listing 7-3 shows some procedure and function headings. Along with any declarations of local objects and the statements which are to be executed when the subprogram is called, headings form part of the declarations of all procedures and functions. Each heading must contain the following information: the subprogram's name; the names, types, and modes of its formal parameters; and the type of value returned if the subprogram is a function. The terms "mode" and "parameter" require further explanation.

The variables which appear in a procedure or function's heading are known as "formal parameters." The variables, constants, or expres-

LISTING 7-3   *Some procedure and function headings.*

```
PROCEDURE GetPoint(VAR x, y: INTEGER);
(* This procedure has two variable parameters. *)

PROCEDURE OneOfEach(VAR x: CARDINAL; y: CARDINAL);
(* This procedure has one variable parameter, x, and *)
(* one value parameter, y.                           *)

PROCEDURE Introduce;
(* This procedure has no parameters. *)

PROCEDURE READInteger(VAR x: INTEGER);
(* This procedure has one variable parameter. *)

PROCEDURE SamePoint(x1, y1, x2, y2: INTEGER): BOOLEAN;
(* This function has four value parameters and returns *)
(* a BOOLEAN value.                                    *)

PROCEDURE Obscure(VAR x: CARDINAL; y: CARDINAL): CARDINAL;
(* This is the heading of a function which may cause   *)
(* "side-effects" because it uses a variable parameter; *)
(* see the section on "Functions" in this chapter.     *)
```

sions which are used to carry values between a subprogram and the environment from which it is called are known as "actual parameters." A subprogram always has the same formal parameters, but a different group of actual parameters may be supplied each time the subprogram is called to perform its particular job.

For instance, in Listing 7-2 the actual parameters X1, Y1 are matched to formal parameters x, y when the first call to GetPoint is made. Later calls supply X2, Y2 and X3, Y3 as actual parameters. While it is legal to use the same name for a formal parameter and some corresponding actual parameter, this may make a program harder to understand.

Two modes of formal parameters are available in Modula-2: value parameters and variable parameters. The actual parameter which is matched to a variable parameter must be a variable. The reason for this is that variable parameters are used to get information out of a subprogram back to the calling environment, so the actual parameter must be something that can be assigned a value within the subprogram. The following call is illegal because no variable was supplied to hold the INTEGER value which is to be read:

READInteger(34);

Value parameters, on the other hand, are used only to pass values into the subprogram, so their corresponding actual parameters may be constants, variables, or any expression which can be evaluated to yield a value. Function SamePoint in Listing 7-2, for instance, accepts four values and then takes some actions which are based on the values received; this function uses value parameters.

Some readers may know the terms "call-by-value" and "call-by-reference." Value parameters correspond to call-by-value parameters, and variable parameters correspond to call-by-reference parameters.

Variable parameters are preceded in the subprogram heading by the reserved word VAR. Every formal parameter between the VAR and the next formal type name is considered to be a variable parameter. Thus, both of GetPoint's parameters are variable, even though VAR is used only once. Any formal parameters not marked as VAR parameters are automatically value parameters.

Another way to understand the differences between value and variable parameters is to notice that formal value parameters are essentially local variables. They are initialized with the values of the corresponding actual parameters each time the subprogram is called. Their values may be used inside the subprogram, but assignments to them have no effect on any variable in the calling environment.

The names of formal variable parameters, on the other hand, are pseudonyms for the variables which are passed as actual parameters at the point of call. As an example, consider the program in Listing 7-4.

The output in Listing 7-4 illustrates the fact that the act of making an assignment to a value parameter does nothing to the value stored in the corresponding actual parameter. Indeed, the actual parameter might not even be a variable. ValueParameter could have been called with the constant Ten or an expression such as 2 + Ten * I as the actual parameter, instead of the variable I. An assignment to a formal variable parameter, however, results in an identical change in the corresponding actual parameter, as shown. Recall that the actual parameter matched to a formal variable parameter cannot be a constant or an expression but must be a variable.

The allowable data types for formal parameters include all the legal Modula-2 types. The actual parameters which correspond to a formal

LISTING 7-4 *Illustration of the difference between value and variable parameters.*

```
MODULE Example;
  FROM InOut IMPORT WRITEString, WRITELine, WRITEInteger;

  CONST Ten = 10;
  VAR I: INTEGER;

  PROCEDURE VariableParameter(VAR x: INTEGER);
  BEGIN
    WRITELine;
    WRITEString("Value for x passed into VariableParameter: ");
    WRITEInteger(x, 6);
    x := 12345;
    WRITELine;
    WRITEString("Last value of x in VariableParameter: ");
    WRITEInteger(x, 6);
  END VariableParameter;

  PROCEDURE ValueParameter(x: INTEGER);
  BEGIN
    WRITELine;
    WRITEString("Value for x passed into ValueParameter: ");
    WRITEInteger(x, 6);
    x := 12345;
    WRITELine;
    WRITEString("Last value of x in ValueParameter: ");
    WRITEInteger(x, 6);
  END ValueParameter;

BEGIN (* main body of Example *)
  I := 0;
  VariableParameter(I);
  WRITELine;
  WRITEString("Value of I after passing it to VariableParameter: ");
  WRITEInteger(I, 6);
  I := 0;
  ValueParameter(I);
  WRITELine;
  WRITEString("Value of I after passing it to ValueParameter: ");
  WRITEInteger(I, 6);
END Example.
```

Output when Example is executed:

Value for x passed into VariableParameter: 0

```
Last value of x in VariableParameter:   12345
Value of I after passing it to VariableParameter:   12345
Value for x passed into ValueParameter:       0
Last value of x in ValueParameter:   12345
Value of I after passing it to ValueParameter:        0
```

parameter must be of a type which is compatible with the formal parameter's type. One cannot do something such as

```
VAR Ch: CHAR;
READInteger(Ch);
```

Readers may note in passing that the order in which actual parameters are evaluated when a subprogram is called is system-dependent. If an actual parameter involves indices, they are evaluated at the time the call is made.

Functions

As noted earlier, functions are identical to procedures except that functions return a value to the calling environment. Notice that both functions and procedures begin with the reserved word PROCEDURE. Unlike Pascal, values are not returned by making an assignment to the function name. Instead, a RETURN statement is used, as shown in Listing 7-5. RETURN statements may also be used to leave procedures when unusual conditions make it unwise to continue with the procedure's execution. In this case, no expression follows the reserved word RETURN since procedures cannot return values.

LISTING 7-5 *A simple function.*

```
PROCEDURE CubeOf(Number: INTEGER): INTEGER;
(* Accepts one INTEGER value parameter and returns an INTEGER *)
BEGIN
   RETURN (Number*Number*Number);
END CubeOf;
```

The type of value returned must be indicated in the function's heading, after the list of formal parameters. Normally, Modula-2 functions may only return unstructured types and pointers. Thus, a function could not return an array, but it could return a pointer to an array. (Pointers are variables whose values are the storage locations of other variables; although an array cannot be returned by a function, the location of the array can be returned and used to access the array itself.) Some implementations allow functions to return structured types such as arrays, but compilers are not required to support this facility.

Functions can only return a single value directly, but by using VAR parameters, it is possible to pass other data back out to the calling environment. As Listing 7-6 illustrates, this facility must be used with care if one is to avoid writing code which is difficult to understand and debug. Listing 11-2 contains other examples of functions which use variable parameters.

LISTING 7-6   VAR *parameters in functions must be used carefully.*

```
PROCEDURE Obscure(VAR x: CARDINAL; y: CARDINAL): CARDINAL;
BEGIN
  x := x + 1;
  RETURN (x + y);
END Obscure;
          .
          .
          .
x := 4;
y := 2;
x := Obscure(x,y);
y := Obscure(y,x);
(* What are the values of x and y now? *)
```

Naming Procedures and Functions

Procedures are often best thought of as actions and are named appropriately: Introduce and GetPoint, for instance. The purpose of a function, on the other hand, is usually dominated by the value returned, so functions are often given nouns as names, e.g., SQUARERoot or FLOAT. Those which return a BOOLEAN value are often named for conditions which are TRUE or FALSE, e.g., SamePoint or OUT-PUTExists. One can also use a fill-in-the-blank technique so that the function's name and the value it returns form a sentence: FigureIs returns Point, LineSegment, or Triangle. Appropriate, descriptive subprogram names can add much to a program's clarity.

Visibility Rules

Subprograms are often used to control the area of code over which an identifier such as a variable or a type name may be legally referenced. This area is known as the identifier's scope or region of visibility. The extent of an identifier's scope is determined according to the rules given in Summary 7-2. These rules are fairly complex, but an understanding of them is necessary to write any but the simplest of programs.

SUMMARY 7-2   Summary of the rules which govern visibility in subprograms

1. If an identifier is used in a declaration in a subprogram or is listed in the subprogram's heading as a formal parameter, the object declared is visible everywhere inside that subprogram. There is one exception; if another subprogram is nested inside the first and the identifier is also used in a declaration in the nested subprogram, the object that was declared in the original subprogram is not visible inside the nested one. The declaration in the nested subprogram is said to "mask" the declaration in the original one. In other words, the first declaration one comes to as one moves outward through nested subprograms toward the surrounding module is the one that determines which variable (or type or other construct) an identifier refers to.

2. If an object is declared in a subprogram or is listed in the subprogram's heading as a formal parameter, the object is invisible outside the subprogram.

3. The standard identifiers of Modula-2 behave as though they were declared in an imaginary procedure which encloses any given program module. In other words, they are visible everywhere some declaration does not "mask" them; see rule 1. The standard function HIGH, for instance, is visible everywhere there is no other object (not necessarily a function) called HIGH. To avoid confusion, these standard identifiers should not be used for any purposes except the ones described in Appendix 2.

4. The rules of visibility in modules that are summarized in Table 9-2 also apply to subprograms.

For example, consider the module VisibilityExample in Listing 7-7. Figure 7-1 uses a "block diagram" to show how the procedures used in Listing 7-7 are nested, and Table 7-1 summarizes the visibilities of the variables used. The assignment statement in ChangeGlobalVariable refers to the variable called C which is declared at the top of the module. In ChangeLocalVariable, however, the "nearest" declaration

LISTING 7-7 *An example illustrating the scoping rules.*

```
MODULE VisibilityExample;
  FROM SomeOtherModule IMPORT SomeProcedure, SomeVariable,
                              SomeType, SomeConstant;

  VAR   C : CHAR;          (* These variables are "global" to *)
        J : INTEGER;       (* everything else in this module. *)

  PROCEDURE ChangeGlobalVariable;
    TYPE SomeType = BITSET;
  BEGIN
    C := "A";
  END ChangeGlobalVariable;

  PROCEDURE ChangeLocalVariable;
    VAR C: CHAR;
  BEGIN
    C := "A";
  END ChangeLocalVariable;

  PROCEDURE OuterMost(B: INTEGER);
    CONST SomeConstant = 12;
    VAR x, y, z: INTEGER;

    PROCEDURE InnerMost(B: BOOLEAN);
      VAR x: CARDINAL;
          C: CHAR;
    BEGIN
      (* body of InnerMost goes here *)
    END InnerMost;

  BEGIN
    (* body of OuterMost goes here *)
  END OuterMost;

BEGIN
  (* Main body of the module VisibilityExample goes here *)
END VisibilityExample.
```

is the one local to ChangeLocalVariable, so the assignment is made to this local variable.

The value of the local variable C becomes undefined as soon as control leaves ChangeLocalVariable. The only ways to get data out of a

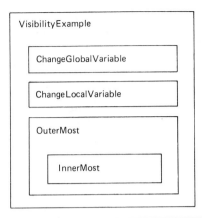

Figure 7-1   A visibility block diagram for Listing 7-7.

TABLE 7-1   Summary of the visibility of items in Listing 7-7

Object	Where declared	Kind of object
	Visibility Example	
Visible:		
C	VisibilityExample	CHAR variable
J	VisibilityExample	INTEGER variable
SomeProcedure	VisibilityExample	Imported procedure
SomeVariable	VisibilityExample	Imported variable
SomeType	VisibilityExample	Imported type
SomeConstant	VisibilityExample	Imported constant
	ChangeGlobalVariable	
Visible:		
SomeType	ChangeGlobalVariable	Type
C	VisibilityExample	CHAR variable
J	VisibilityExample	INTEGER variable
SomeProcedure	VisibilityExample	Imported procedure
SomeVariable	VisibilityExample	Imported variable
SomeConstant	VisibilityExample	Imported constant
Not Visible:		
SomeType imported by Visibility-Example; masked by declaration in ChangeGlobalVariable		

TABLE 7-1   Continued

Object	Where declared	Kind of object
ChangeLocalVariable		
Visible:		
C	ChangeLocalVariable	CHAR variable
J	VisibilityExample	INTEGER variable
SomeProcedure	VisibilityExample	Imported procedure
SomeVariable	VisibilityExample	Imported variable
SomeType	VisibilityExample	Imported type
SomeConstant	VisibilityExample	Imported constant
Not Visible:		
C declared at top of Visibility-Example; masked by declaration in ChangeLocalVariable		
OuterMost		
Visible:		
B	OuterMost	INTEGER parameter
x, y, z	OuterMost	INTEGER variables
SomeConstant	OuterMost	Constant
C	VisibilityExample	CHAR variable
J	VisibilityExample	INTEGER variable
SomeProcedure	VisibilityExample	Imported procedure
SomeVariable	VisibilityExample	Imported variable
SomeType	VisibilityExample	Imported type
Not Visible:		
SomeConstant imported by VisibilityExample; masked by declaration in OuterMost		
InnerMost		
Visible:		
B	InnerMost	BOOLEAN parameter
x	InnerMost	CARDINAL variable
C	InnerMost	CHAR variable
y, z	OuterMost	INTEGER variables
SomeConstant	OuterMost	Constant
J	VisibilityExample	INTEGER variable
SomeProcedure	VisibilityExample	Imported procedure
SomeVariable	VisibilityExample	Imported variable
SomeType	VisibilityExample	Imported type
Not Visible:		
x declared in OuterMost; masked by declaration in InnerMost		
SomeConstant imported by VisibilityExample; masked by declaration in OuterMost		
C declared in Visibility-Example; masked by declaration in InnerMost		

procedure or function are by using VAR parameters, RETURN statements, or assignment to a variable which is global to the procedure. One consequence of the visibility rules is that local variables cease to exist once control passes outside their scope. In fact, the storage space set aside for use by local variables is made available for other use as soon as the procedure is completed. New space is allocated for all value parameters and local variables each time a procedure or function is entered; any previous values are lost. This is not true of coroutines; see Chapter 18 for the details.

The use of local declarations has several advantages over the use of global ones. First, local declarations make debugging easier by restricting the scope of identifiers. If some local variable has an erroneous value, for instance, we know it could only have been given that value within the surrounding procedure or function. The visibility rules also make it possible for the compiler to detect inadvertant uses of local objects by parts of a program which lie outside the object's scope. Finally, the visibility rules make it possible to decrease the storage required by a program since the memory resources used by local variables are released for other uses each time a call to the surrounding subprogram is finished.

Recursion

Since a Modula-2 subprogram can call any other subprogram which is visible, it can call itself. It could also call another subprogram which makes a call that results in yet another call, and so forth, until the chain of calls leads to a call to the original subprogram. A call made by a subprogram on itself is an instance of "direct recursion." The procedure CountDown in Listing 7-8 is directly recursive. The reader should take note that recursion is generally an expensive way to do things and should be used only when necessary. There are more efficient ways to perform the tasks in the examples presented in this section.

LISTING 7-8 *A directly recursive procedure.*

```
PROCEDURE CountDown(From: CARDINAL);
BEGIN
  WRITECardinal(From, 6);
  IF From <> 0 THEN
    CountDown(From-1);
  END; (*IF not done *)
END CountDown;
```

If two subprograms make calls on each other, such as the two procedures in Listing 5-2, we have an instance of "mutual recursion." A certain amount of care must be taken to avoid the problems depicted in Listing 7-9. An "escape hatch" must be provided whenever recursion is used to avoid an attempt to make an infinite number of recursive calls. The escape hatch is simply some part of a subprogram which will be executed after some finite number of calls on the subprogram and which either makes no more subprogram calls or only makes calls that cannot continue the recursion. The need for an escape hatch implies that one should only place (directly) recursive calls inside conditional statements.

Listing 7-9 shows two versions of a function which is supposed to return the Nth number in the Fibonacci series. The Fibonacci series is 1, 1, 2, 3, 5, 8, 13, 21, 34, ... Each number in the series except the first two is the sum of the two which preceded it. The first version of function NthFibonacci in Listing 7-9 fails to provide an escape hatch by ignoring the fact that the first two elements of the series are both 1. Any call to NthFibonacciOne will result in an attempt to execute an infinite direct recursion. The second version of the function recurses infinitely for negative values of N; the escape hatch provided by Nth FibonacciTwo does not always work. The third and fourth versions both provide a complete escape hatch. Calls on either of these last two versions cannot result in an infinite recursion.

LISTING 7-9 *Examples illustrating the need for an escape hatch whenever recursion is possible.*

```
PROCEDURE NthFibonacciOne(N: INTEGER): INTEGER;
(* Provides no escape hatch; any call causes an infinite recursion. *)
BEGIN
   RETURN( NthFibonacciOne(N-1) + NthFibonacciOne(N-2) );
END NthFibonacciOne;

PROCEDURE NthFibonacciTwo(N: INTEGER): INTEGER;
(* Only provides a partial escape hatch; any call *)
(* passing an N <= 0 causes an infinite recursion. *)
BEGIN
   IF ((N = 1) OR (N = 2)) THEN
      RETURN 1;
   ELSE
      RETURN( NthFibonacciTwo(N-1) + NthFibonacciTwo(N-2) );
   END; (* IF *)
END NthFibonacciTwo;
```

```
PROCEDURE NthFibonacciThree(N: INTEGER): INTEGER;
(* Provides a complete escape hatch; any call passing an    *)
(* N <= 0 causes an error message and a returned value of 0. *)
BEGIN
  IF (N <= 0) THEN
    WRITEString(" NthFibonacciThree passed nonpositive value ");
    RETURN 0;
  ELSIF ((N = 1) OR (N = 2)) THEN
    RETURN 1;
  ELSE
    RETURN( NthFibonacciThree(N-1) + NthFibonacciThree(N-2) );
  END; (* IF *)
END NthFibonacciThree;


PROCEDURE NthFibonacciFour(N: CARDINAL): CARDINAL;
(* Provides a complete escape hatch; any call passing an *)
(* N < 0 will be caught, since N is now a CARDINAL.      *)
BEGIN
  IF (N = 0) THEN
    RETURN 0;
  ELSIF ((N = 1) OR (N = 2)) THEN
    RETURN 1;
  ELSE
    RETURN( NthFibonacciFour(N-1) + NthFibonacciFour(N-2) );
  END; (* IF *)
END NthFibonacciFour;
```

Exercises

1. Assume the following declarations and assignments:

CONST b = 2;
VAR   x, y, z: CARDINAL;
        w   : REAL;
PROCEDURE Example(i, y: CARDINAL; VAR j: CARDINAL);
BEGIN
  i := 5;
  j := i + y;
  y := y + 1;
END Example;
.
.
.
x := 4;
y := 0;
z := 3;
(* A call to Example comes here. *)

Trace the execution of the following procedure calls; assume the calls are made

after the third assignment statement, z := 3;. If the call will result in some sort
of error, indicate the reason for the error.
(a) Example(x, y, z);
(b) Example(b, y, z);
(c) Example(x, y, b);
(d) Example(z, y, z);
(e) Example(y, y, b);
(f) Example(x, y, x+z);
(g) Example(x+y, y, z);
(h) Example(x, y, w);

8

Modules

The Three Kinds of Modula-2 Modules

Every Modula-2 compilation unit is one of three types of modules: it may be a program module, a definition module, or an implementation module. This chapter describes the different uses of the three kinds of modules and looks briefly at the actions caused by submitting each to a compiler. The next chapter continues this discussion with a look at ways to control the visibility of objects in Modula-2 by using the import/export mechanisms and local modules. The fact that each module is a separate compilation unit means that any single module may be submitted to the compiler. No smaller units are accepted by compilers. Procedures and functions, for instance, must always be embedded in a module.

All the modules seen up to this point have been program modules. These modules correspond to main programs in most other languages; in particular, they bear a strong resemblance to Pascal programs. They are used to execute algorithms. Program modules always begin with the reserved word MODULE. Program modules may import functions, procedures, types, variables, or constants from library modules.

Library modules supply pieces of programs for use by other library modules and by program modules. Library modules always come in pairs consisting of one implementation module and one definition module. As suggested by Figure 8-1, a definition module answers the question "What can you do?" Definition modules contain information which is used by the compiler to check, to the best of its ability, that the exports are only used as the programmer who wrote the definition module intended them to be used.

The question "How do you do what you do?" is answered by an implementation module. Listing 8-1 shows a simple program module

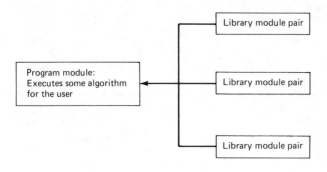

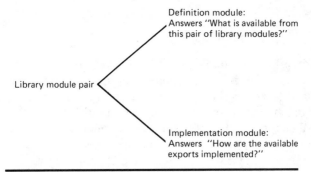

Figure 8-1   Overview of the purpose and interrelationships of the three types of compilation units.

LISTING 8-1   *A simple program module which uses the library modules shown in Listing 8-2.*

```
MODULE TestForRepetition;
    (* Import lists: *)
    FROM PlaneGeometry IMPORT GETIntegerPoint, SAMEIntegerPoint,
                             INPUTReadFromFile;
    FROM InOut        IMPORT WRITELine, WRITEString, DONE, CLOSEInput;

    (* Global variables: *)
    VAR REPETITIONFound: BOOLEAN;
        LASTX, LASTY,
        NEXTX, NEXTY   : INTEGER;
```

```
BEGIN (* body of program module TestForRepetition: *)
  REPETITIONFound := FALSE;
  GETIntegerPoint(LASTX, LASTY);
  GETIntegerPoint(NEXTX, NEXTY);
  WHILE ((NOT REPETITIONFound) AND (DONE (* not at end of file *))) DO
    REPETITIONFound := SAMEIntegerPoint(LASTX, LASTY, NEXTX, NEXTY);
    LASTX := NEXTX;
    LASTY := NEXTY;
    GETIntegerPoint(NEXTX, NEXTY);
  END; (* WHILE no repetition *)
  WRITELine;
  IF REPETITIONFound THEN
    WRITEString(" Found a repetition ");
  ELSE
    WRITEString(" No repetition found ");
  END; (* IF repetition found *)
  IF INPUTReadFromFile THEN
    CLOSEInput;
  END; (* IF need to close file opened by PlaneGeometry *)
END TestForRepetition.
```

which uses the pair of library modules shown in Listing 8-2. A particular definition module and its corresponding implementation module are often referred to by their common name, e.g., "TestForRepetition imports two subprograms and a variable from PlaneGeometry."

LISTING 8-2 *Library modules used by the program module shown in Listing 8-1.*

```
DEFINITION MODULE PlaneGeometry;
  EXPORT QUALIFIED GETIntegerPoint, SAMEIntegerPoint, INPUTReadFromFile;

  VAR INPUTReadFromFile: BOOLEAN; (* TRUE if a file has been opened *)
                                  (* and GETIntegerPoint reads its *)
  (* values from the file; the file should be closed by the       *)
  (* importer of GETIntegerPoint if INPUTReadFromFile = TRUE.      *)

  PROCEDURE GETIntegerPoint(VAR x, y: INTEGER);
  (* Reads a coordinate pair from the keyboard or from a file, as *)
  (* specified by the user.                                       *)
  PROCEDURE SAMEIntegerPoint(x1, y1, x2, y2: INTEGER): BOOLEAN;
  (* Returns ((x1 = x2) AND (y1 = y2)).                           *)
END PlaneGeometry.
```

LISTING 8-2   Continued

```
IMPLEMENTATION MODULE PlaneGeometry;
  FROM InOut IMPORT WRITELine, WRITEString, READInteger, OPENInput, DONE;


  VAR OPENFile: CHAR; (* "Y" or "y" for yes, anything else for no *)


  PROCEDURE GETIntegerPoint(VAR x, y: INTEGER);
  BEGIN
    WRITELine;
    WRITEString(" Enter integer x coordinate> ");
    READInteger(x);
    WRITELine;
    WRITEString(" Enter integer y coordinate> ");
    READInteger(y);
  END GETIntegerPoint;


  PROCEDURE SAMEIntegerPoint(x1, y1, x2, y2: INTEGER): BOOLEAN;
  BEGIN
    RETURN ((x1 = x2) AND (y1 = y2));
  END SAMEIntegerPoint;

BEGIN (* initialization of PlaneGeometry *)
  WRITELine;
  WRITEString(" Is input coming from a file?");
  READCharacter(OPENFile);
  IF ((OPENFile = "Y") OR (OPENFile = "y")) THEN
    WRITEString(" File name>");
    OPENInput("");
  END; (* IF need to open file *)
  IF NOT DONE THEN
    WRITELine;
    WRITEString(" PlaneGeometry: Could not open input file.");
    INPUTReadFromFile := FALSE;
  ELSE
    INPUTReadFromFile := TRUE;
  END; (* IF could not open input file *)
END PlaneGeometry.
```

Each definition module contains an export list such as the one shown
in Listing 8-2 for PlaneGeometry. This list names all the procedures,
functions, variables, types, and constants which may be imported from
the pair of library modules. As noted in Appendix 5, the second public
version of Modula-2 does not use export lists but assumes instead that
everything shown in a definition module is exported. In any case, the
exports become part of a library which is available to every other
module via an import list such as the ones in module TestForRepetition.

If any functions or procedures are exported, the definition module must contain a heading for each, such as

PROCEDURE GetIntegerPoint(VAR x, y: INTEGER);

Headings are included so that the number, mode, and types of the actual parameters used in each call to an exported subprogram can be checked at compilation time, no matter what module the call is made in. A compiler will use the information in the definition module to ensure as completely as it can that exports are only used in ways which agree with the intentions of the author of the definition module. Of course, the compiler cannot distinguish between a call to SINE and one to COSINE, for instance. Therefore, enough comments should be included in the definition module to make the intended use of an export clear to other programmers.

The implementation module which corresponds to a given definition module may only be compiled after its definition module has been compiled. Among other things, the implementation module contains the implementations of all the subprograms listed as exports from its definition module. Implementation modules may also contain subprograms, types, constants, and variables which are not actually part of the library but which are used inside the implementation module to support the exports.

The implementation of PlaneGeometry in Listing 8-2 also contains some initialization code. The body of an imported module will always be executed before the body of any module which imports it. However, the order in which the initializations are executed when several modules are imported is system-dependent. Thus, the bodies of InOut and PlaneGeometry will both be executed before the body of TestForRepetition, but the body of InOut will not necessarily run before that of PlaneGeometry.

Why Use Modules?

Summary 8-1 lists the reasons why one ought to break large programming tasks into several modules. By using modules to group related data structures and subprograms, programmers can impose additional structure on large or even moderately sized programs. For instance, when writing a debugger it would be reasonable to break this task into the coding of a main program module Debug and several pairs of library modules such as WindowHandler, FileHandler, InOut, DataDisplayer, and so forth. Some of these, such as InOut and FileHandler, will already be available, while others will need to be written. Each of the newly proposed modules may need to be broken in turn into modules with tasks which are even more specific. This hierarchical division into modules which perform clearly defined jobs can contribute additional clarity to nearly any program which is more than a few hundred lines long.

SUMMARY 8-1   Reasons for breaking programs into modules

1. To impose additional clarity on large programs by allowing importing modules to concern themselves only with the question of what imports do, not with how things are done

2. To decrease the amount of work involved in programming by adding to a library of types, subprograms, and other objects which may be imported instead of being recoded in each program which needs them

3. To cut down on the amount of code which must be recompiled to reflect a change in a program

4. To allow several programmers to work on separate portions of a large program at the same time

---

Breaking a large program into a number of smaller interrelated modules may significantly decrease the amount of code which must be recompiled each time a change is made to the program. This is true because a given implementation module may be changed and recompiled any number of times without forcing the recompilation of other modules which import from it. There is also another good reason for pulling some type or subprogram out of a program module, placing it in a new pair of library modules, and then importing it for use in its original home. The reason is that the exported object becomes part of the library which is available not only to the original program but to other modules (program, definition, or implementation) as well.

Yet another reason to break large programming tasks into several modules is that different programmers may work freely on different implementation modules once the definition modules are available. This is possible because the implementation modules are hidden from the other modules; potential importers only need to see the definition modules to know what is available. Thus, TestForRepetition does not need to know how SAMEIntegerPoint checks two points to see if they are identical; it only needs to know that that is what SAMEInteger-Point does.

The compiler checks for correct usage of types, the right number of parameters in a procedure or function call, agreement between actual parameters and the modes of corresponding formal parameters, and so forth on imported items just as it would on those declared and used inside a single module. No semantic checks are lost if a large program is divided into several smaller modules, and all the benefits listed in Summary 8-1 may be gained.

Compilation of Library Modules

There are two main points to be noted in connection with the compilation of library modules. First, an implementation module cannot be compiled until its corresponding definition module has been written. On some systems, the definition module must also be compiled before the implementation module is compiled. On others, the definition module need only to have been placed where the compiler can find it. In any case, an implementation module cannot be compiled when a corresponding definition module does not exist. This makes good sense since one must answer the question "What does this pair of library modules export?" before one can begin worrying about how to implement the exports.

The second point to note is that an implementation module can be changed and recompiled any number of times without recompiling either the corresponding definition module or the modules which import from the pair. As long as the information in the definition module is not changed, it is only necessary to recompile the implementation module to produce a program which reflects all the changes made. Recompilation of the definition module is only necessary if the information in the definition module has changed. You should be aware that changes to a definition module will also force the recompilation of any importers whose imports have been modified. Some systems force the recompilation of every module which imports an item from a pair of library modules when the definition half of the pair is changed; others require recompilation only if changes are made to the imports actually used by the importer.

For instance, suppose we decide to modify the body of procedure GETIntegerPoint in Listing 8-2 so that it looks like this:

```
PROCEDURE GETIntegerPoint(VAR x, y: INTEGER);
BEGIN
    WRITEString("Enter coordinates>");
    READInteger(x);
    READInteger(y);
END GETIntegerPoint;
```

The implementation half of PlaneGeometry will need to be recompiled to reflect the change, but the definition portion is unchanged since GETIntegerPoint still takes two variable INTEGER parameters. Therefore it is unnecessary to recompile TestForRepetition. If the system binds modules at run time instead of loading previously linked object code files, the new version of GETIntegerPoint will be used automatically. If a linked version of TestForRepetition is used, the new version of PlaneGeometry will need to be linked in as a replacement for the previous version before the object code version of TestForRepetition will reflect the change.

Suppose we decide instead to add a pair of functions, GETRealPoint and SAMERealPoint, to library module PlaneGeometry in Listing 8-2. The bodies of the two new subprograms will need to be added to implementation module PlaneGeometry. Also, the appropriate headings will have to be added to the definition module, and the export list will need to be expanded. It may or may not be necessary to recompile TestForRepetition since the definitions of GETIntegerPoint, SAMEInteger-Point, and INPUTReadFromFile have not been changed. Strictly speaking, it should not be necessary to recompile TestForRepetition since the definitions of the imports it uses are unchanged, but the recompilation is required on some systems nonetheless. These systems can only tell when a new definition module is being used; they cannot tell whether the changes leave particular exports unchanged or not. It is therefore necessary on such a system to recompile every importer in order to be sure that all exports are used only in ways which are consistent with their current definitions.

9

Controlling Visibility with Modules

In Modula-2, there are three basic ways to organize the declarations of subprograms, data types, and other objects used by a given program: list them more or less arbitrarily, nest some of them inside others according to their dependencies, or break the program module into a smaller program module and a number of new library modules and import some of the objects. These three approaches are represented by the diagrams in Figures 9-1, 9-2, and 9-3, respectively, and Modula-2 examples are sketched out in Listings 9-1, 9-2, and 9-3. In practice, a mixture of all three methods is generally used.

This chapter compares the three approaches by showing how each might be used to make five procedures available to a program module. The ideas presented may also be applied, to a certain extent, to the placement of function, type, variable, and constant declarations. We will also examine the details of Modula-2's import/export mechanisms and take a brief look at "import trees." The chapter closes with a look at the visibility rules for local modules, concluding the visibility discussion which was begun in Chapter 7 in connection with subprograms.

Listing Procedures Globally without Nesting

Perhaps the easiest way to organize the procedures used in a given program is to list all procedure declarations and bodies globally at the topmost level of visibility. The list must be placed in the program module's declaration section, above the main body of the program. This approach results in programs which look like the one in Listing 9-1.

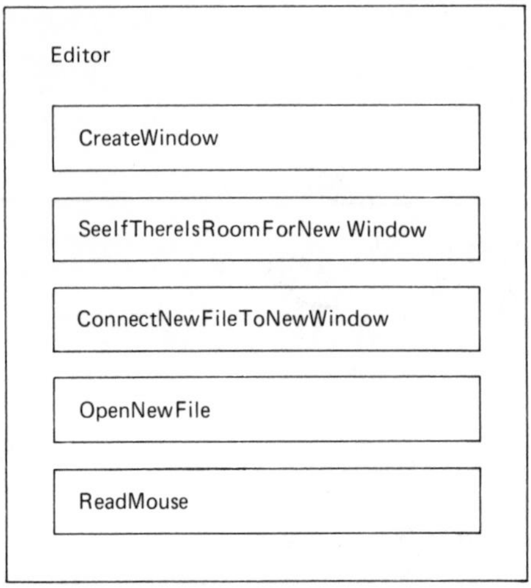

Editor

CreateWindow

SeeIfThereIsRoomForNew Window

ConnectNewFileToNewWindow

OpenNewFile

ReadMouse

Figure 9-1   Scope diagram for Listing 9-1 in which the procedures used are simply listed one after another.

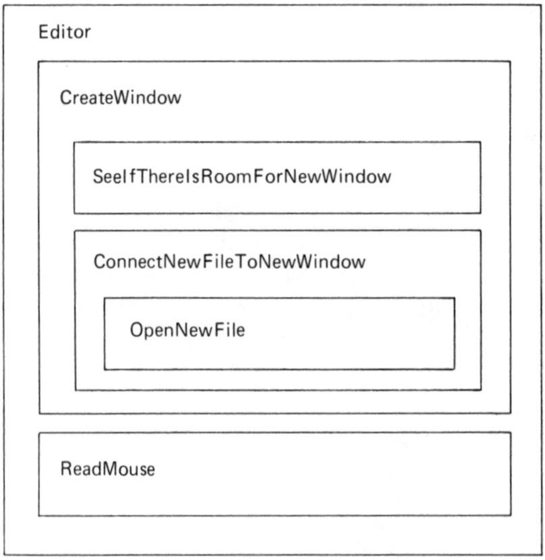

Editor

CreateWindow

SeeIfThereIsRoomForNewWindow

ConnectNewFileToNewWindow

OpenNewFile

ReadMouse

Figure 9-2   Scope diagram for Listing 9-2 in which the procedures are nested according to the uses made of them.

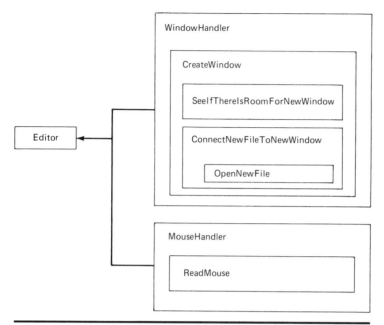

Figure 9-3   Scope diagram for Listing 9-3 in which the procedures are nested or listed in newly created library modules and imported by a smaller program module.

LISTING 9-1   *Listing procedures globally without nesting.*

```
MODULE Editor;
    .
    .
    .
    PROCEDURE CreateWindow;
    BEGIN
        (* body of CreateWindow *)
    END CreateWindow;

    PROCEDURE SeeIfThereIsRoomForNewWindow;
    BEGIN
        (* body of SeeIfThereIsRoomForNewWindow *)
    END SeeIfThereIsRoomForNewWindow;
```

LISTING 9-1 Continued

```
PROCEDURE ConnectNewFileToNewWindow;
BEGIN
  (* body of ConnectNewFileToNewWindow *)
END ConnectNewFileToNewWindow;

PROCEDURE OpenNewFile;
BEGIN
  (* body of OpenNewFile *)
END OpenNewFile;

PROCEDURE ReadMouse;
BEGIN
  (* body of ReadMouse *)
END ReadMouse;
  .
  .
  .
BEGIN
  (* main body of program module Editor *)
END Editor.
```

LISTING 9-2 *Nesting procedures according to usage.*

```
MODULE Editor;
  .
  .
  .
  PROCEDURE CreateWindow;
    PROCEDURE SeeIfThereIsRoomForNewWindow;
    BEGIN
      (* body of SeeIfThereIsRoomForNewWindow *)
    END SeeIfThereIsRoomForNewWindow;

    PROCEDURE ConnectNewFileToNewWindow;
      PROCEDURE OpenNewFile;
      BEGIN
        (* body of OpenNewFile *)
      END OpenNewFile;
    BEGIN
      (* body of ConnectNewFileToNewWindow *)
    END ConnectNewFileToNewWindow;
  BEGIN
    (* body of CreateWindow *)
  END CreateWindow;
```

```
PROCEDURE ReadMouse;
BEGIN
  (* body of ReadMouse *)
END ReadMouse;
  .
  .
  .
BEGIN
  (* main body of program Editor *)
END Editor.
```

LISTING 9-3 *Importing procedures to a program module.*

```
MODULE Editor;
  FROM WindowHandler IMPORT CreateWindow;
  FROM MouseHandler  IMPORT ReadMouse;
  .
  .
  .
BEGIN
  (* main body of program Editor *)
END Editor.

DEFINITION MODULE WindowHandler;
  EXPORT QUALIFIED CreateWindow;
  PROCEDURE CreateWindow;
END WindowHandler.

IMPLEMENTATION MODULE WindowHandler;
  PROCEDURE CreateWindow;
    PROCEDURE SeeIfThereIsRoomForNewWindow;
    BEGIN
      (* body of SeeIfThereIsRoomForNewWindow *)
    END SeeIfThereIsRoomForNewWindow;

    PROCEDURE ConnectNewFileToNewWindow;
      PROCEDURE OpenNewFile;
      BEGIN
        (* body of OpenNewFile *)
      END OpenNewFile;
    BEGIN
      (* body of ConnectNewFileToNewWindow *)
    END ConnectNewFileToNewWindow;
```

LISTING 9-3   Continued

```
BEGIN
    (* body of CreateWindow *)
END CreateWindow;
END WindowHandler.

DEFINITION MODULE MouseHandler;
    EXPORT QUALIFIED ReadMouse;
    PROCEDURE ReadMouse;
END MouseHandler.

IMPLEMENTATION MODULE MouseHandler;
    PROCEDURE ReadMouse;
    BEGIN
        (* body of ReadMouse *)
    END ReadMouse;
END MouseHandler.
```

Figure 9-1 shows the corresponding "scope diagram." The rules governing visibility in subprograms (given in Table 7-2) imply that code in a nested box in Figure 9-1 can see any object declared in a surrounding box if a local declaration does not mask the object by reusing the same identifier. Code in a surrounding box, on the other hand, cannot see objects which are declared inside nested boxes. Thus, any constants, types, variables, or subprograms declared inside CreateWindow are invisible in the main body of program module Editor.

Recall the benefits of using subprograms which were mentioned in Chapter 7: to provide a reader with just those details necessary to understand the program at the current level of abstraction; to prevent unnecessary repetition of similar pieces of code throughout both this and other programs; to help clarify the structure of a program at its various levels; and to make the program easier to modify.

Simply listing the procedures virtually always provides a reader with much more detail than is necessary to understand the program at whatever level of abstraction is currently of interest. The reader may be forced to scan over many details which are of no interest at present. Roughly speaking, the reader who wants to understand how a given procedure works by examining its code is forced to find the code by using a linear search to locate it in the list of procedure declarations.

On the positive side, this global listing of all the procedures makes each of them available at every point in the program. Procedure ConnectNewFileToNewWindow in Listing 9-1, for example, may be called inside procedure CreateWindow or in procedure OpenNewFile. Note that the declaration of a subprogram does not have to precede the first call on the subprogram. Since all the procedures are visible everywhere, this organization helps prevent the unnecessary repetition of similar pieces of code throughout program module Editor. However, none of the procedures are available to other program modules since they have not been exported.

Moreover, simply listing all the procedures used in a program one after another does virtually nothing to help clarify the structure of the program. And the fact that all of a program's procedures lie in the same compilation unit means that even small changes to improve the procedure require us to recompile relatively large amounts of unchanged code. Therefore this method has some serious drawbacks.

A Look at Nesting

Because of the problems caused by simply listing all of a program's procedures at the same level of visibility, procedures are often nested inside each other according to their use by other procedures. For instance, if procedure CreateWindow used procedures SeeIfThereIsRoomForNewWindow and ConnectNewFileToNewWindow and ConnectNewFileToNewWindow used OpenNewFile, one might rearrange the program module of Listing 9-1 to reflect these facts. One such rearrangement is shown in Listing 9-2.

Using nesting alone, such as simply listing all the procedures, forces the programmer to place all the details of a program in the same compilation unit. Small changes to the code may still require large amounts of recompilation time. Readers are still required to scan over unwanted details, but now the procedures at the topmost level of nesting may act as an index, so the problem has been reduced somewhat. However, the visibility rules presented in Table 7-2 must be kept in mind at all times when nesting is used.

In order to place a procedure at its proper nesting depth, one must have a clear idea which other procedures require its services. If the procedure is nested too deeply, it may be necessary to either move it up to a higher level and thereby increase its visibility or duplicate it in several places. If the procedure is placed at too high a level, one begins to lose the main advantage of nesting over the simple listing examined above, namely, the information on how the program is structured at its various levels.

Programs which nest their procedures are harder to modify than those which do not, for two reasons. First, there is the need to maintain a proper level of nesting. Secondly, one does not necessarily have a one-to-one correspondence between storage locations and identifiers because the visibility rules make it possible for the same identifier to be used for different objects. Some renaming may be necessary if procedures are moved.

Using Library Modules

Modula-2 provides a third way to organize the procedures used in a given program module. They may be listed or nested inside library modules according to their logical relationships and imported into the main program module. This approach is shown in Listing 9-3. Import and export in Modula-2 are dominated by two simple rules: the only objects visible inside a module are those which were declared in the module or imported into it; the only objects visible outside a module are those which it exports. These rules have some subtleties which will be investigated later in this chapter, but these guidelines will serve for now.

Breaking a large program down in a fashion similar to that shown in Listing 9-3 requires the use of more modules than nesting or simple listing does. The total amount of code required is a little greater, mainly because the appropriate definition modules must be provided. However, this method has two main advantages over the others: the potentially significant reduction in the amount of code which must be recompiled when a change is made and the fact that the exported procedures are now available to any program module since they belong to the library. Listing and nesting arose in languages which have relatively ad hoc modularization and import/export facilities. Notice that listing and nesting are still used. However, the number of procedures listed or nested in a given module has been significantly reduced.

A reader who wishes to examine the code for a particular procedure is no longer forced to skim over nearly all of the procedures used in order to find the desired one. It is only necessary to look among the procedures which are declared in the same module as the one sought; the rules governing import lists make it easy to determine which module contains the code for any given object. Using library modules also helps prevent unnecessary repetition of similar pieces of code throughout many program modules since any object which might be useful in more than one location can be made available for import by other modules.

There are other benefits as well. The import/export relationships help clarify the structure of a program. And programs may be easier to modify because recompilations can often be restricted to the implementation half of one of the library module pairs.

Program modules should be broken into a number of library modules and a smaller main program module (as shown in Listing 9-3) when a procedure or data structure becomes very complicated or when it appears that some object might be useful in programs other than the one at hand. The possible benefits of modularization, listed in Summary 8-1, should be kept in mind.

Note that none of Modula-2's strong semantic checking is lost when an imported procedure is used in some program module instead of listing or nesting the procedure inside that module. That is, the compiler still makes sure that the type, number, and mode (value or variable) of the parameters in a call to an imported procedure match the procedure's declaration. Imported types and variables must also be used in a fashion which is compatible with their declarations. This semantic checking across module boundaries makes Modula-2's separate compilability more rigorous and more useful than the modularity which is supported by many other languages.

Note also that it is not necessary to list each import explicitly. For instance, module Editor in Listing 9-3 could simply state that it wished to

```
IMPORT MouseHandler;
```

instead of listing each import by name:

```
FROM MouseHandler IMPORT ReadMouse;
```

If this approach is taken, everything exported by MouseHandler is visible in Editor. However, any use of an import must be prefaced by the name of the module which exported it if the import is not listed explicitly in an import list. In Editor, for instance, one must write MouseHandler.ReadMouse instead of simply writing ReadMouse. This makes it easy to find out exactly where the code for a given object resides. If the imports needed are explicitly named in an import list, as shown in Listing 9-3, the module name prefixes will be necessary only to distinguish identically named imports which come from different modules, e.g., DiskHandler.OpenFile and TapeDriveHandler.OpenFile.

The Visibility of Exported Items

We will now take a closer look at Modula-2's import/export mechanisms. The discussion which follows assumes that the reader is using the original public version of Modula-2. In the second version export lists are no longer used; everything defined in a definition module is exported. Appendix 5 summarizes the differences between the two versions of Modula-2.

In both versions, the import/export mechanisms have two aspects: visibility control and semantic checking. The semantic checking aspect has already been mentioned: any Modula-2 compiler performs the same tests on imported objects as it performs on objects which are declared within a module.

The rest of this chapter looks at how the import/export mechanisms can be used to make part or all of an object visible inside or outside a given module. These rules are somewhat complicated, but they are very important if you want to write even simple programs in Modula-2. A compiler which recognizes the second version of Modula-2, in which export lists are not used, was unavailable at the time of writing. I am uncertain how much of the discussion in this section will carry over to that version.

The objects defined in a definition module are visible to varying degrees in other modules. Their visibility depends mainly on whether they are exported but also on where their implementation details reside. Everything declared in a definition module is visible throughout the corresponding implementation module. Any object defined in a definition module is also visible throughout the part of the definition module which follows its declaration.

Depending on the kind of object which is declared in a definition module, the details of the object's implementation may either be given there in the definition module or be elaborated in the corresponding implementation module. Procedure and function bodies, for instance, must always be placed in the implementation module. The implementation of constants, i.e., their values, must be given in the definition module if they are exported. Certain types (mainly pointers) may either be completely declared in the definition module or they may be made into "opaque exports," as shown in Chapter 14.

The possibilities and some examples are given in Summary 9-1. The rules may be summarized as follows: If an object is exported from a definition module, all the information given in the definition module is visible to any module which imports the object; otherwise, nothing is visible outside the pair of library modules. In any case, objects declared in a definition module are visible throughout the corresponding implementation module.

A few points need to be made in connection with exported functions and procedures. In addition to the formal parameters and items declared locally in an imported subprogram, all the objects declared in the subprogram's environment are known and accessible in the subprogram after it is imported. Even if N modules import SomeSubprogram, there will still be only one instance of SomeSubprogram. What

**SUMMARY 9-1   The possible relationships between
the location of an object's
implementation details, its presence
on an export list, and its visibility**

1. Implementation details are given in the definition module, and the object is exported. In this case, both the object and its details are visible to any importing modules. One such definition module is the following:

```
DEFINITION MODULE ExportsEverything;
    EXPORT QUALIFIED THIRTYTwo, NAMEType, FILEOpened;
    CONST   THIRTYTwo = 32;
    TYPE    NAMEType  = ARRAY[1..20]OF CHAR;
    VAR     FILEOpened : BOOLEAN;
END ExportsEverything.
```

If some module Importer imports type NAMEType and declares a local variable

VAR MyName: NAMEType;

statements such as

MyName[6] := "W";

are possible; the fact that NAMEType is an ARRAY[1..20]OF CHAR was exported along with everything else.

2. Implementation details are given in the definition module, but the object is not exported. When this happens, neither the object nor its details are visible to any importing modules. This cannot be done in the second version of Modula-2 (see Appendix 5). In the original version of Modula-2, however, one could do something such as

```
DEFINITION MODULE HidesSomeDetails;
    EXPORT QUALIFIED ARRAYOfWhat;

    TYPE MysteryType = BITSET;
        ARRAYOfWhat = ARRAY[1..10]OF MysteryType;
END HidesSomeDetails.
```

Type MysteryType cannot be imported since it is not exported. Suppose module Importer imports type ARRAYOfWhat and declares a local variable

VAR MyArray: ARRAYOfWhat;

Then a statement such as

MyArray[2] := {};

is not legal because it uses the unexported fact that MyArray is an array of BITSET.

3. A type is exported, but the definition module contains nothing except the type's name. All details reside in the implementation module. This is an "opaque" export, discussed in detail in Chapter 14. The type is visible to importing modules, but none of its details are visible. For instance, given

```
DEFINITION MODULE ExportOpaqueType;
    EXPORT QUALIFIED OPAQUEType;

    TYPE OPAQUEType;
END ExportOpaqueType.
```

```
IMPLEMENTATION MODULE ExportOpaqueType;
   TYPE LongName    = Array[1..50]OF CHAR;
        OPAQUEType = POINTER TO LongName;
END ExportOpaqueType.
```

an importer can declare OPAQUEType variables, apply tests for equality and inequality, and make some assignments. However, if the importer has declared

VAR MyOpaque: OPAQUEType;

a statement such as

MyOpaque ↑ .[35] := "Q";

is illegal because it uses information which is hidden in the implementation module. Only the information exported from the definition module is visible outside any pair of library modules.

4. Implementation details are given in the implementation module, and the object is not exported. In this case, neither the object nor its details are visible to any importing modules. The type LongName in implementation module ExportOpaqueType, above, falls in this category.

the N modules really import is effectively a pointer to SomeSubprogram, which still resides in the environment of the library module pair in which it was declared. Listing 9-4 contains three modules which illustrate the way in which one automatically imports the environment of a subprogram along with the code, formal parameters, and local objects associated with the subprogram.

The first call to WriteGlobal in ImportEnvironment will cause a 0 to be written. Notice that Global is initialized to zero in the body of implementation module Exporter; this initialization code will always be executed before any of the statements in modules which import from Exporter. The call to IncrementGlobal will assign Global the value 1, even though Global was not explicitly imported into ImportEnvironment, so 1 will be printed when the second call to WriteGlobal is made. Similarly, the third call to WriteGlobal will cause a 2 to be written.

Import Trees

Import trees are diagrams that summarize the import/export relationships between modules. For instance, suppose we are writing a text editor in Modula-2. Breaking the problem into the construction of a main program module and a number of implementation/definition module pairs may result in the organization shown in Figure 9-4. In that figure, implementation/definition module pairs are referred to by their common name.

LISTING 9-4 *An illustration of the way in which one imports the environment of a subprogram along with the subprogram.*

```
DEFINITION MODULE Exporter;
  EXPORT QUALIFIED IncrementGlobal, WriteGlobal;

  PROCEDURE IncrementGlobal;
  PROCEDURE WriteGlobal;
END Exporter.

IMPLEMENTATION MODULE Exporter;
  FROM InOut IMPORT WRITECardinal;
  VAR  Global: CARDINAL;

  PROCEDURE IncrementGlobal;
  BEGIN
    INC(Global);
  END IncrementGlobal;

  PROCEDURE WriteGlobal;
  BEGIN
    WRITECardinal(Global,6);
  END WriteGlobal;
BEGIN (* main body of Exporter *)
  Global := 0;
END Exporter.

MODULE ImportEnvironment;
  FROM Exporter IMPORT IncrementGlobal, WriteGlobal;
BEGIN (* main body of ImportEnvironment *)
  WriteGlobal;
  IncrementGlobal;
  WriteGlobal;
  IncrementGlobal;
  WriteGlobal;
END ImportEnvironment.

Output when ImportEnvironment is executed:
  0    1    2
```

The ultimate root of every import tree is a program module; the rest of the tree contains pairs of library modules. Import trees are sometimes referred to as "compilation-dependency trees" because the definition modules lower in the tree must be available before the modules above them can be compiled.

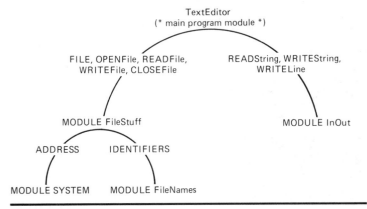

Figure 9-4   An import tree.

Recall that the order in which the bodies of the implementation modules are executed is indeterminate. The bodies of modules File-Stuff and InOut in Figure 9-4, for example, will be executed before the execution of TextEditor begins, but there is no guarantee that the code in InOut will be executed first, or vice versa. However, it is clear from the tree in Figure 9-4 that the initializations of FileNames and SYS-TEM must be completed before the initialization code in implementation module FileStuff can begin execution.

The actual import tree for a given program module may be much larger than the subtree the programmer is aware of since the modules it imports usually import other modules the programmer did not write. For example, most program modules indirectly import a number of items that define the terminal, the screen, and the disk drive(s) being used on a particular system.

For some applications, an import tree like the one in Figure 9-4 will not show sufficient detail. In particular, it may be necessary to distinguish between definition and implementation modules. Wiener and Sincovec (1984) present a more detailed design aid which they call a "modular design chart." In these charts, every import to every module in a compilation-dependency tree is graphically depicted.

Local Modules

We have seen how to control the visibility of objects which are declared outside a given module by using Modula-2's import/export mechanisms. The visibility of objects declared within a given module may be controlled in two ways. One may use the visibility rules presented in

Table 7-2. By nesting procedures and functions, one can control to a certain extent both their visibility and the visibility of the variables, types, and constants declared in the module. The second way to control visibility in a particular module is to declare other modules locally within that module. This facility has some of the same problems as nesting, namely, the potential for confusion if the rules governing visibility are not kept in mind and the renaming which may be necessary if an object is moved. Listing 9-5 and Figure 9-5 illustrate the visibility rules that are listed in Summary 9-2.

LISTING 9-5 *An illustration of the visibility rules for local modules.*

```
MODULE OuterMost;
  VAR OuterOne, OuterTwo: INTEGER;

  MODULE FirstMidLevel;
    IMPORT OuterOne;
    EXPORT FirstMidThree, InnerOne;
    VAR  FirstMidOne,
         FirstMidTwo,
         FirstMidThree: INTEGER;
         FirstMidFour : CARDINAL;

    MODULE InnerMost;
      IMPORT FirstMidOne;
      EXPORT InnerOne, InnerTwo;
      VAR InnerOne, InnerTwo, InnerThree: INTEGER;
    BEGIN
      (* body of InnerMost *)
    END InnerMost;
  END FirstMidLevel;

  MODULE SecondMidLevel;
    EXPORT QUALIFIED SecondMidOne, SecondMidTwo;
    VAR  SecondMidOne, SecondMidTwo: INTEGER;
  BEGIN
    (* body of SecondMidLevel *)
  END SecondMidLevel;

BEGIN
  (* body of OuterMost *)
END OuterMost.
```

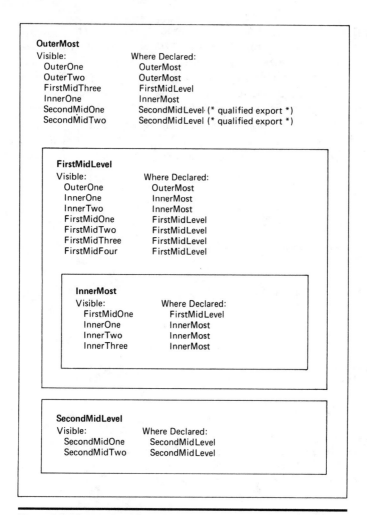

Figure 9-5   Scope diagram for the program in Listing 9-5.

Local modules are always nested in a surrounding program or implementation module. Notice that the word QUALIFIED, which always appears in the export list of a definition module, is optional in the export lists of local modules. If an export is listed as qualified, as SecondMidOne and SecondMidTwo are in Listing 9-5, references to it outside the module containing its declaration must use the dot notation. SecondMidOne alone is illegal in the body of OuterMost; SecondMidLevel.SecondMidOne must be used instead. The scope of visibility

---

**SUMMARY 9-2   Summary of the rules which govern
visibility in modules**

---

1. There are three ways to make an item visible inside any local module: declare the item in that local module, import the item from the environment in which the local module is nested, or export the item from another local module which is nested in the given local module. In the latter case, the local module containing the declaration of the item may be deeply nested in other local modules, which are nested in turn inside the given local module. If this occurs, the item will need to be passed outward from local module to local module via export lists until it reaches the one in which it is needed.

2. Items declared in a program module are invisible outside that module.

3. Items declared in a definition module are visible in the corresponding implementation module. These items are visible in another module only if they are exported from the definition module and imported by the other module. The importer may be another definition module, an implementation module, or a program module. The only facts which are exported along with an export's name are those which appear in the definition module (see Chapter 14).

4. Items declared in an implementation module are invisible in all other modules unless they are listed as exports from the corresponding definition module.

5. Items may be made visible in a program, definition, or implementation module by declaring them in that module or by importing them. In program and implementation modules but not in definition modules, items can also be made visible by exporting them from a local module which is nested in the program or implementation module.

6. The rules of visibility in subprograms summarized in Table 7-2 apply.

---

of an identifier exported from a local module extends only over the block which contains that local module. Thus, it was necessary in Listing 9-5 to name InnerOne in two export lists in order to make that variable visible in the body of module OuterMost.

10

Enumeration, Subrange, and Set Types

Enumeration Types

The days of the week, the gears on a car, and the ranks of military officers could all be modeled in a Modula-2 program by using an enumeration type. The list of possible values for a variable such as Today, CurrentGear, or MyRank is relatively stable over time, and in the case of MyRank, the values have a fixed order from least to greatest. All the values have names, and it would be inconvenient to represent them using INTEGERs or CARDINALs. All these characteristics suggest the use of an enumeration data type to represent these real world objects. Listing 10-1 contains some declarations of enumeration types and variables.

The variable CurrentGear in Listing 10-1 can take any of the five values enumerated for its type, ImpalaGears. For instance,

CurrentGear := Reverse;

is a legal assignment statement. The operations applicable to enumeration variables are :=, =, #, <, <=, >, >=, and operations defined by subprograms. In particular, one may call the standard subprograms ORD, VAL, INC, DEC, INCL, and EXCL.

All the identifiers which comprise the values of an enumeration type are exported when the type is exported (unless the enumeration type is exported opaquely; see Chapter 14). The values given must be identifiers, i.e., they must consist of a letter followed by zero or more letters or digits. Therefore +, −, *, and / are all illegal enumeration values for ArithmeticOperators because they are not identifiers. The values

LISTING 10-1 *Some statements involving enumeration types and variables.*

```
TYPE ImpalaGears    = (Park, Reverse, Neutral, Drive, Low1, Low2);
     ProcessStatus  = (Running, Ready, Blocked, Suspended, Terminated);
     VowelCharacter     = (A,E,I,O,U,a,e,i,o,u);
     SomeHolidays       = (July4, Thanksgiving, Christmas);
     TwoBitCardinal     = (0,1,2,3);              (* illegal *)
     WrittenTwoBitCardinal = (Zero, One, Two, Three);(* legal *)
     ArithmeticOperators  = (+, -, *, /, DIV, MOD); (* illegal *)
     ArithmeticOperators  = (plus, minus, times, divide, Div, Mod);
                          (* Legal version of ArithmeticOperators *)

VAR  CurrentGear              : ImpalaGears;
     FileTransferProgramState: ProcessStatus;
     LastVowelFound           : VowelCharacter;
          .
          .
          .

PROCEDURE ProcessCouldProceed(Status: ProcessStatus): BOOLEAN;
BEGIN
   IF ((Status = Blocked) OR (Status = Terminated)) THEN
      RETURN FALSE;
   ELSE
      RETURN TRUE;
   END; (* IF *)
END ProcessCouldProceed;
(* The following two statements will each cause *)
(* the same value to be assigned to BooleanOne. *)
BooleanOne := (ORD(LastVowelFound) >= ORD(U));
BooleanOne := (LastVowelFound >= U);
```

given for type TwoBitCardinal are illegal because an identifier may
not begin with a number, although it may contain one, e.g., July4 is
legal. Reserved words such as FOR, WHILE, and INTEGER may not
be used as values in enumeration type declarations, so the values DIV
and MOD in the first declaration of ArithmeticOperators are illegal. In
short, the values enumerated must be unreserved identifiers.

It is wise to avoid using enumeration values which are only a single
character long whenever possible because they are easy to confuse
with CHAR values. Although the statements

CharVariable := "A";

and

CharVariable := A;

both look valid, the second statement is illegal. One cannot assign an enumeration value to a CHAR variable. In the first statement A is used as an ASCII character, whereas the A in the second assignment is an identifier which denotes a VowelCharacter value.

Notice that one of the basic data types can be viewed as an enumeration type:

TYPE BOOLEAN = (FALSE,TRUE);

One reason why INTEGER, REAL, CARDINAL, and BITSET cannot be defined as enumeration types is that their values are not identifiers. Another reason is that the number of values allowed for an enumeration type is often limited to the number of bits in a memory word on the machine being used or to a small multiple of that value.

The values of an enumeration type are ordered by their listing in the declaration. For instance, the declarations in Listing 10-1 imply that Park < Reverse and Terminated > Running. The ordinal number of an enumeration value is a CARDINAL which indicates how far from the left the value is in the declaration; the count starts with zero. An enumeration value's position in the type declaration may be obtained by using the standard Modula-2 function ORD(x). If the declarations of Listing 10-1 are used, ORD(Park) = 0, and ORD(Blocked) = 2.

It is best if the values of an enumeration type do not change often because any change forces a recompilation of the surrounding module. For instance, although the declaration of type ValidUser below is legal, there are better ways to represent the valid users of a computer than to declare

TYPE ValidUser = (Susan, Maury, Jason, Me);

What if a new user is added every other day or so? A lot of time could be spent recompiling the module which contains the declaration of an enumeration type such as ValidUser.

Subrange Types

Suppose now that one wishes to define a type whose allowable values are in some group of CHAR values, such as the alphabetic characters. One could define types CapitalCharacters and SmallCaseCharacters as shown in Listing 10-2. These types illustrate the differences between subrange and enumeration types. The allowable values for an

LISTING 10-2   *Some declarations of subrange types.*

```
TYPE CapitalCharacters    = ["A".."Z"];    (* Subrange of CHAR *)
TYPE SmallCaseCharacters  = ["a".."z"];    (* Subrange of CHAR *)
TYPE DigitCharacters      = ["0".."9"];    (* Subrange of CHAR *)
TYPE SeatingCapacity      = [0..9];        (* Subrange of CARDINAL *)
TYPE CapturedCheckers     = [-12..12];     (* Subrange of INTEGER *)
TYPE ForwardGears         = [Drive..Low2]; (* Subrange of ImpalaGears *)
```

enumeration type are specified as a complete list of identifiers. One cannot expect the compiler to interpret

TYPE EnumeratedColors = (Red..Green);

as

TYPE EnumeratedColors = (Red, Orange, Yellow, Green);

The values must be individually enumerated.

The values of a subrange type, on the other hand, are selected from the values already defined for some other type which is known as the "base type" for the subrange. The operations applicable to variables of a subrange type are exactly those defined for the base type. However, the range of allowable values has been restricted. For instance, an operation which tries to assign a SeatingCapacity variable the value 10 will result in an error message.

One can define new subrange types using any of the following as a base type: CHAR, CARDINAL, INTEGER, BOOLEAN, or previously defined enumeration types. The first and last values for definitions of CHAR subranges must be listed in quotes as shown in Listing 10-2 since they are character values, not identifiers. In the case of the numeric subrange types, the subrange elements are of type CARDINAL if the lower limit specified in the type declaration is not negative. Otherwise the values are of type INTEGER. This has been changed in the second public version of Modula-2; see Appendix 5 for details.

Variables and values of any type which is a subrange of a given base type are fully compatible with variables and values of the base type. Subranges also inherit the order associated with their base type. For example, if one uses the ASCII character set and its associated ordering, it is not possible to define a Modula-2 subrange type which includes only the upper- and lowercase alphabetic characters. This is because the characters [, \,], and several others appear between Z and a in the ASCII table which defines type CHAR. All these nonalphabetic characters would be included in the subrange ["A".."z"].

Suppose that SomeVariable's values should fall only within clearly specified limits. There are two alternatives to using a subrange type to enforce the limitations. One may simply ignore operations which assign values outside the desired range, or one may choose to test SomeVariable after every possible change in its value. Neither of these is very efficient, and the first is likely to produce incorrect programs. By declaring SomeVariable to be of an appropriate subrange type, programmers can have the system do the checking for them. The price one pays is that any attempt to assign SomeVariable a value outside the declared range will generally cause the program to terminate. On the other hand, if explicitly programmed tests are used to check SomeVariable's value instead of declaring SomeVariable to be of a subrange type, an error message can be sent to the user and the program can continue execution.

Set Types

Set types could be used conveniently by a program which needs to keep track of the assignments of some people who serve on various committees if the number of people involved is small enough. One is only allowed to declare a SET OF a previously defined subrange or enumeration type, and if this underlying type is too large, then a SET OF that type will not be allowed. For instance, type SET OF CHAR is not allowed on many systems. This deficiency may be remedied somewhat by using library modules such as those in Listings 16-8 and 16-9.

Any set whose elements are listed in between curly braces { and } and which is not preceded by a type name is assumed to be a BITSET. Programmer-defined sets must be preceded by the set type's name when the curly brace notation is used, as shown in Listing 10-3. The operations defined for BITSET variables in Table 4-4 are also applicable to variables of any other set type; recall that these include assignment; test for (in)equality, union, difference, intersection, and symmetric difference; tests for inclusion; and test for membership.

Standard procedures INCL and EXCL can only add or remove one element at a time to or from a set, but they can accept variables as parameters. This is especially useful because the original version of Modula-2 does not allow sets whose elements are variables; all elements must be constants. For instance, the assignment

FoodCommittee := Committee{Somebody, Anybody};

LISTING 10-3 *Some statements involving set types.*

```
TYPE People     = (Tom, Lee, Elliott, Vicky, Joyce, Barbara);
TYPE Committee  = SET OF People;
VAR  FoodCommittee, RecreationCommittee, Everybody: Committee;
     Somebody, Anybody                            : People;
     .
     .
     .

FoodCommittee := Committee{};
RecreationCommittee := Committee{};
Everybody := Committee{Tom, Lee, Elliott, Vicky, Joyce, Barbara};
INCL(FoodCommittee, Tom);
INCL(FoodCommittee, Lee);
INCL(FoodCommittee, Vicky);
RecreationCommittee := Committee{Lee, Vicky, Joyce, Elliott};
```

is illegal since the set braces contain variables. This assignment could be done legally with the calls

```
INCL(FoodCommittee, Somebody);
INCL(FoodCommittee, Anybody);
```

The restriction that set elements be constants is lifted in the second version of Modula-2 (see Appendix 5).

Exercises

1. You are given the following declarations:
```
TYPE CoinTossOutcomes = (Edge, Tail, Head);
TYPE CoinTosses       = SET OF CoinTossOutcomes;
VAR  ThisToss         : CoinTossOutcomes;
     ResultsUpToNow    : CoinTosses;
```
Write an IF or a CASE statement, using curly brace set notation, which will add the value of ThisToss to the set ResultsUpToNow of CoinTossOutcomes. Then do the same assignment using INCL(Set, Element).

2. Find as many syntactic and semantic errors as you can in the following enumeration type declaration:
```
TYPE Verbs is [RUN!, JUMP!, DO, SEE, HALT]
```
Rewrite the declaration so it is legal. What is ORD(SEE) in the revised version?

3. If an enumeration or subrange type SomeType contains three values, how many values will the type SET OF SomeType contain? What if Sometype has n values?

4. Would it make sense to think of type CARDINAL as a subrange of INTE-GER?

11

Array Data Types

Declaring and Using Arrays

It is often desirable to group variables of the types already seen together into larger data structures. Modula-2 provides array and record
types to make this possible. If all the variables being grouped are of the
same type, an array may be used to organize them. For instance, one
could declare

VAR ManyIntegers: ARRAY[1..100] OF INTEGER;

If the variables being grouped are of different types, records must be
used. Record types are discussed in Chapters 12 and 13.

One may think of an array as a row of identical boxes, each with a
different label. In the case of ManyIntegers, the boxes are INTEGER
variables, and the labels on the boxes are the numbers from 1 to 100.
The labels are referred to as "indices" into the array. The indices need
not be numbers; any subrange or enumeration type may be used. An
individual array element is referred to by using its index, e.g.,

ManyIntegers[23] := −5;
ManyIntegers[k] := IntegerVariable;

ManyIntegers is a "one-dimensional" array because each of its elements can be specified with a single index, e.g., ManyIntegers[23]. A
table of data values, on the other hand, might be better represented
using a two-dimensional array:

VAR DataValues: ARRAY[1..10],["a".."f"] OF REAL;

DataValues has 10 * 6 = 60 elements, each of which is a REAL variable. Listing 11-1 shows some other declarations and statements which involve arrays.

LISTING 11-1 *Some statements involving arrays.*

```
TYPE Name          = ARRAY[1..20] OF CHAR;
     People        = (Tom, Lee, Elliott, Vicky, Joyce, Barbara);
     IllegalArray  = ARRAY[1..5, 0..10] OF INTEGER; (* Illegal *)
     LegalArrayType = ARRAY[1..5],[0..10] OF INTEGER;(* Compare *)
     (* this with IllegalArray above. Square brackets must be  *)
     (* included for each subrange; see Appendix 3.            *)


VAR  CurrentUser,
     LastUser   : Name;
     HoursWorked: ARRAY People OF REAL;
     DataValues : ARRAY[1..10],["a".."f"] OF REAL;
     .
     .
     .
IF HoursWorked[Tom] < 20.0 THEN
  Fire(Tom);
END; (* IF *)
FOR Worker := Tom TO Barbara DO
  INC(TotalHours, HoursWorked[worker]);
END; (* FOR *)
FOR i := 1 TO 10 DO
  FOR ch := "a" TO "f" DO
    DataValues[i,ch] := 0.0;
  END; (* FOR *)
END; (* FOR *)
LastUser := CurrentUser; (* entire arrays may be assigned at once *)
```

Declarations of multidimensional arrays such as

TYPE MDA = ARRAY [1..10], [−1..1], People of INTEGER;

are understood to be abbreviations for longer, nested declarations such as

TYPE MDA = ARRAY [1..10] OF
           ARRAY [−1..1] OF
           ARRAY People OF INTEGER;

As shown in the last statement of Listing 11-1, the assignment operator may be applied to entire arrays. For instance although

```
FOR i := 1 TO 20 DO
   LastUser[i] := CurrentUser[i];
END; (* FOR *)
```

is legal, one need only write

```
LastUser := CurrentUser;
```

to assign the values stored in CurrentUser to the variables which constitute the array LastUser. The operators =, <, <=, >, and >= are not defined for arrays, although they may be defined for the elements of an array.

Programmers should be aware that single character literals such as A and # are not compatible with CHAR arrays of length 1 in the original version of Modula-2. For instance, one cannot pass WRITE-String a single CHAR because it expects an ARRAY OF CHAR. This has been fixed in the second version. To avoid the error message caused by a call such as

```
WRITEString("A");
```

one may first assign to an array such as

```
VAR OneChar: ARRAY[1..1]OF CHAR; (* CHAR array of length 1 *)
```

the value which is to be passed. Then the illegal call can be replaced by

```
OneChar[1] := "A";
WRITEString(OneChar);
```

Open Array Parameters

In Modula-2, it is possible to declare a formal "open array" parameter that will match actual parameters of any length as long as the formal and actual element types are assignment compatible. For instance, recall that the procedure WRITEString has the heading

```
PROCEDURE WRITEString(Message: ARRAY OF CHAR);
```

This means that WRITEString expects actual parameters which are strings, i.e., arrays of CHAR values. This is very useful because the length of the actual string passed may vary widely from call to call. Thus,

WRITEString("Short string");
WRITEString("A longer string");
WRITEString("A string of a different length");

are all legal calls. Of course, array variables can also be passed to formal open array parameters in subprogram calls.

The size of the actual array which is matched to a formal open array parameter in a subprogram call may be found with the standard function HIGH. For instance, immediately after the call

WRITEString("Hello!");

we have

Message[0] = "H"
Message[4] = "o", and
HIGH(Message) = 5

Suppose that ActualArray is declared by

VAR ActualArray: ARRAY[Low..High] OF Elements

and OpenArray is a formal parameter which is an ARRAY OF Elements. If ActualArray is matched to OpenArray in a subprogram call, the indices of OpenArray will run from 0 to HIGH(OpenArray) = High − Low. So OpenArray[k] is matched to ActualArray[Low + k].

Open arrays may only be used as formal parameter types, so a declaration such as

TYPE String = ARRAY OF CHAR;

is illegal. The elements of an open array may not be open arrays, so headings such as

PROCEDURE Illegal(M: ARRAY OF ARRAY OF CHAR);

will not be accepted by a Modula-2 compiler. However, Wiener (1983) describes a library module that makes two-dimensional open arrays possible. This library module could be generalized to provide n-dimensional open arrays.

One of the most common uses of open arrays involves the next topic, string manipulation.

An Example: String Handling

Unfortunately, Modula-2's support for string manipulation leaves something to be desired. There is no all-purpose STRING type; one is usually forced into using fixed-length arrays of CHAR instead. As noted earlier, one may not declare

TYPE STRING = ARRAY OF CHAR;

because open arrays may be used only as formal parameters. The string operators for inclusion, concatenation, and so forth are not pre-defined. It is possible to perform some assignments, but the need for the arrays involved to be of the same lengths and of compatible types makes it quite awkward to do so.

Fortunately, the lack of string-handling facilities is not necessarily a permanent condition. We saw in Chapter 9 how easy it is to add new subprograms to the user library. Listings 11-2 and 11-3 show the code for a pair of library modules which export some string-handling sub-programs; more examples are given in the exercises. The exports make use of the standard function HIGH to determine the sizes of the actual arrays matched to their formal open arrays.

LISTING 11-2 *Descriptions of some library subprograms to handle strings.*

```
DEFINITION MODULE StringStuff;
   (* Exports string-manipulation procedures. Assumes that the *)
   (* meaningful portion of a string of characters which is    *)
   (* stored in an array ends in 0C, the ASCII null character, *)
   (* if it does not completely fill the array.                *)

   EXPORT QUALIFIED COPIEDString, STRINGSAreEqual, CATENATEDStrings;

   PROCEDURE COPIEDString( Old: ARRAY OF CHAR;
                           VAR New: ARRAY OF CHAR ): BOOLEAN;
   (* Copies as much as possible of Old to New. If the length of *)
   (* Old's meaningful portion is less than or equal to the space*)
   (* available in New, returns TRUE; otherwise, returns FALSE.  *)

   PROCEDURE STRINGSAreEqual(One, Two: ARRAY OF CHAR): BOOLEAN;
   (* Returns TRUE if the meaningful portions of One and Two match.*)
```

LISTING 11-2   Continued

```
PROCEDURE CATENATEDStrings( One, Two: ARRAY OF CHAR;
                           VAR OneTwo: ARRAY OF CHAR ): BOOLEAN;
(* Copies as much as possible of One and then of Two to OneTwo. *)
(* If the sum of the lengths of One's and Two's meaningful       *)
(* portions is less than or equal to the space available in      *)
(* OneTwo, returns TRUE; otherwise, returns FALSE.               *)


END StringStuff.
```

LISTING 11-3 *Implementations of some library subprograms to handle strings.*

```
IMPLEMENTATION MODULE StringStuff;
  CONST NULLChar = 0C;

  PROCEDURE COPIEDString( Old: ARRAY OF CHAR;
                          VAR New: ARRAY OF CHAR ): BOOLEAN;
  VAR Index: CARDINAL;
  BEGIN (* COPIEDString *)
    IF Old[0] <> NULLChar THEN
      Index := 0;
      WHILE ((Index <= HIGH(New)) AND (Index <= HIGH(Old))
                          AND (Old[Index] <> NULLChar)) DO
        (* Notice that the short-circuit evaluation of BOOLEAN *)
        (* expressions guarantees that no attempt will be made *)
        (* to reference Old[Index] if Index is out of range,   *)
        (* i.e., if Index > HIGH(Old).                         *)
        New[Index] := Old[Index];
        Index := Index + 1;
      END; (* WHILE *)
      IF (Index <= HIGH(New)) THEN
        (* New was large enough to hold Old's meaningful portion *)
        New[Index] := NULLChar;
        RETURN TRUE;
      ELSE
        IF (Index <= HIGH(Old)) THEN
          RETURN (Old[Index] = NULLChar)
        ELSE (* Old, New are of same length and now both are full of *)
             (* the same characters, all of which are meaningful.    *)
          RETURN TRUE;
        END; (* IF *)
      END; (* IF *)
    ELSE (* Old has empty meaningful portion. *)
      New[0] := NULLChar;
```

```
    RETURN TRUE;
  END; (* IF Old[0] <> NULLChar *)
END COPIEDString;

PROCEDURE STRINGSAreEqual(One, Two: ARRAY OF CHAR): BOOLEAN;
VAR   Equal: BOOLEAN;
      Index: CARDINAL;
BEGIN
  Equal := TRUE;
  Index := 0;
  LOOP
    IF One[Index] <> Two[Index] THEN
      (* Strings cannot be equal. *)
      Equal := FALSE;
      EXIT;
    END; (* IF *)
    IF ((One[Index] = NULLChar) OR (Two[Index] = NULLChar)) THEN
      (* Have reached the end of the meaningful characters *)
      (* in one or both of the strings.                    *)
      EXIT;
    END; (* IF *)
    INC(Index);
    IF Index > HIGH(One) THEN
      (* Have reached end of string One. *)
      IF Index <= HIGH(Two) THEN
        Equal := (Two[Index] = NULLChar);
      END; (* IF *)
      EXIT;
    ELSIF Index > HIGH(Two) THEN
      (* Have reached end of string Two. *)
      IF Index <= HIGH(One) THEN
        Equal := (One[Index] = NULLChar);
      END; (* IF *)
      EXIT;
    END; (* IF Index > HIGH(One) *)
  END; (* LOOP *)
  RETURN Equal;
END STRINGSAreEqual;

PROCEDURE CATENATEDStrings( One, Two: ARRAY OF CHAR;
                           VAR OneTwo: ARRAY OF CHAR ): BOOLEAN;
VAR Index, NullInOneAt: CARDINAL;
    Done : BOOLEAN;
BEGIN
  Done := TRUE;
  Index := 0;
  (* Copy as much of One into OneTwo as possible. *)
```

LISTING 11-3   Continued

```
WHILE ((Index <= HIGH(One)) AND (One[Index] <> NULLChar)
      AND (Index <= HIGH(OneTwo))) DO
  OneTwo[Index] := One[Index];
  INC(Index);
END; (* WHILE *)
IF ((Index > HIGH(One)) OR (One[Index] = NULLChar)) THEN
  (* Succeeded in copying all of One into OneTwo. *)
  (* Now need to copy as much of Two as possible. *)
  NullInOneAt := Index;
  Index := 0;
  WHILE ((Index <= HIGH(Two)) AND (Two[Index] <> NULLChar)
        AND (Index + NullInOneAt <= HIGH(OneTwo))) DO
    OneTwo[Index + NullInOneAt] := Two[Index];
    INC(Index);
  END; (* WHILE *)
  IF (Index + NullInOneAt > HIGH(OneTwo)) THEN
    (* Ran out of room in OneTwo while copying Two. *)
    Done := ((Index > HIGH(Two) OR (Two[Index] = NULLChar));
  ELSE
    OneTwo[Index + NullInOneAt] := NULLChar;
  END; (* IF *)
ELSE (* Ran out of room in OneTwo while copying One. *)
  Done := ((One[Index] = NULLChar) AND (Two[0] = NULLChar));
END; (* IF *)
RETURN Done;
END CATENATEDStrings;

END StringStuff.
```

Other useful additions to the library started in Listings 11-2 and 11-3 might include: STRINGLessThan, for lexicographic ordering; STRINGLength, to return the length of the meaningful portion of an array of characters (i.e., the portion which precedes either the end of the array or the first null character, whichever comes first); FIRSTInstance, to return the index of the first instance of a particular character in an array of CHARs; and CAPITALIZEString, to capitalize all the characters in a string.

Of course, there are many other functions and procedures which might be equally useful. The reader is free to modify the library as he or she sees fit. In particular, a type STRING which is a pointer into some free string space managed by an appropriate module would be useful. This would lift the requirement that string variables be declared as fixed-length arrays of characters. Something like this is done in Listings 19-4 and 19-5. Ideally, the length of strings would be limited only by the size of the memory which is left over once the operating system and the currently executing program are given the space they require.

Initializing Arrays

Unfortunately, there is no way to initialize an arbitrary array without using separate assignment statements to make the individual assignments to each element. Except for strings such as

CONST ConstantCHARArray = "Hi, how are you?";

Modula-2 does not allow CONST declarations involving arrays, so one cannot initialize an array by assigning some previously declared constant array to it. If the value assigned to the Kth element of the array is a function of K, FOR loop(s) may be used for initialization:

```
FOR K := 1 TO 10 DO
   KSquared[K] := K*K;
END; (* FOR *)
```

But suppose one wishes to have an array whose elements hold the first few digits of pi. One cannot use anything such as:

PiArray := [3,1,4,1,5,9]; (* Illegal *)

Instead, a sequence of assignment statements must be used:

```
PiArray[1] := 3;
PiArray[2] := 1;
PiArray[3] := 4;
PiArray[4] := 1;
PiArray[5] := 5;
PiArray[6] := 9;
```

One may achieve the effect of a constant PiArray by making this sequence of assignments in the initialization portion of an implementation module which exports PiArray. A clear warning should be given in the corresponding definition module that PiArray is meant to be used in a read-only fashion. The same approach may be used to simulate constant records. An example of another way to make it easier to initialize large arrays is presented in the exercises.

Exercises

1. Write functions STRINGLessThan and STRINGLength which perform the jobs described for them in this chapter.

2. Write a function with the heading

InitializedCardinalArray(VAR CardinalArray: ARRAY OF CARDINAL;
                               InitialValues: ARRAY OF CHAR): BOOLEAN;

This function should try to fill a one-dimensional array of CARDINALs with the initial values listed in the string InitialValues. Assume the values are separated by commas. The function returns TRUE if the array matched to CardinalArray is large enough to hold all the values passed to InitialValues and returns FALSE otherwise. Thus, the statement

Done := InitializedCardinalArray(PiArray,"3,1,4,1,5,9");

should cause the same initialization of PiArray as this sequence of assignment statements:

PiArray[1] := 3;
PiArray[2] := 1;
PiArray[3] := 4;
PiArray[4] := 1;
PiArray[5] := 5;
PiArray[6] := 9;

Begin by writing a function with the heading

ASCIIToCardinal(String: ARRAY OF CHAR): CARDINAL;

which returns the CARDINAL value represented by String.

12

Records and Pointers

Declaring and Using Records

Record types, like array types, may be used to group together a number of logically related variables. Unlike arrays, however, the variables composing a record need not be all of the same type. The components of a record are known as its "fields." Each field may be of any legal Modula-2 type; this includes every type seen thus far except, of course, open arrays, which can only be used as formal parameters in subprograms. Given the following constant and enumeration type:

```
CONST NameSize = 20;
TYPE Facilities = (VAX780, Lilith, DEC20, PhotoLab, RoboticsLab);
```

it is possible to declare a record type such as this:

```
TYPE Employee = RECORD
                Name       : ARRAY[1..NameSize] OF CHAR;
                Seniority  : CARDINAL;
                AccessRights: SET OF Facilities;
                END; (* Employee RECORD *)
```

Once the type is declared, variables can be declared:

```
VAR AllEmployees: ARRAY[1..100] OF Employee;
    King        : Employee;
```

Type Employee has three fields: Name, Seniority, and AccessRights. The individual fields are selected by using dot notation:

```
King.Seniority := 1000;
```

Since the fields of a record can be arrays and the elements of arrays may be records, it is possible to build hierarchies of structures. This may lead to some confusion if one is not careful since the variable names involved bear some resemblance to one another:

AllEmployees is an array of Employee records.

AllEmployees[17] is a single Employee record with three fields.

AllEmployees[17].Seniority is a CARDINAL variable.

AllEmployees[17].Name is an array of CHAR variables.

AllEmployees[17].Name[2] is a single CHAR variable.

However, the dot notation used to refer to the fields of a record contrasts with the indexing method used to specify elements of an array, so with a little practice it is easy to see which types are involved in a statement. Assignment is defined for entire records, so

```
King := AllEmployees[17];
```

is legal. However, $=$, $<$, and the other nonassignment operators are not defined for entire records; recall that they are also illegal when used with entire arrays. Therefore

```
IF (King = AllEmployees[17]) THEN (* ILLEGAL *)
  WRITEString("King = AllEmployees[17]");
END;(* IF *)
```

is illegal. Note also that Modula-2 does not allow constant records; this is illegal:

```
CONST NullEmployee = RECORD (* ILLEGAL *)
                     Name        = "";
                     Seniority   = 0;
                     AccessRights = {};
                     END; (* ILLEGAL RECORD *)
```

Records are more general than arrays in that their components need not be all of the same type. On the other hand, records are less general because one may not use expressions to specify a field. The individual identifier for a field must be used each time the field is referenced. There is no equivalent to the FOR statement, which allows one to express operations on an array as repetitions of the same operation on the elements of the array. That is, there is no way to "step through" the fields of a record other than by explicitly listing the fields by name, one after another.

This restriction makes sense because the fields are quite probably of different types; it is unlikely that the same operation could be successfully applied to each field. To make an empty, or null, Employee record, for instance, one uses the empty string, the CARDINAL 0, and the empty set

```
King.Name := "";
King.Seniority := 0;
King.AccessRights := {};
```

One cannot simply say

```
King := Null;
```

and expect the compiler to fill in the details.

The WITH Statement

However, by using a WITH statement, it is possible to avoid prefacing each field name by the record's name in a sequence of operations on the fields:

```
WITH AllEmployees[17] DO
  Seniority := 0;
  Name[1] := "E";
  Name[2] := "Z";
  WRITEString(Name);
END; (* WITH *)
```

is equivalent to

```
AllEmployees[17].Seniority := 0;
AllEmployees[17].Name[1] := "E";
AllEmployees[17].Name[2] := "Z";
WRITEString(AllEmployees[17].Name);
```

Any indices or expressions that must be evaluated to determine which record a WITH statement refers to are evaluated only once, before the WITH statement is entered. Therefore, no attempt should be made to change which record a WITH statement refers to while control is still inside the WITH statement; code such as this should be avoided:

```
WITH AllEmployees[Index] DO
  FOR Index := 1 TO 100 DO
    Seniority := 0;
    Name[1] := "Z";
  END; (* FOR *)
END; (* WITH *)
```

The compiler cannot be relied upon to catch this kind of error. If the programmer fails to detect it, the result may be a very obscure bug in the program. The statement above should be rephrased so that the record referred to is fixed for the duration of the WITH statement:

```
FOR Index := 1 TO 100 DO
  WITH AllEmployees[Index] DO
    Seniority := 0;
    Name[1] := "Z";
  END; (* WITH *)
END; (* FOR *)
```

Declaring and Using Pointers

Records are often used together with pointers to create dynamic data structures such as linked lists and trees. For instance, a linked list of INTEGERs could be created by using these declarations:

```
TYPE PointerToListElement = POINTER TO ListElement;
TYPE ListElement = RECORD
                     Value: INTEGER;
                     Next : PointerToListElement;
                   END; (* RECORD *)
```

Notice that the declaration of a type which is pointed to, such as ListElement, may come after an earlier use of the type's name in the declaration of the corresponding pointer type.

It is assumed that the reader has some experience with the use of pointers; this section deals only with the particulars of using pointers in Modula-2. Several restrictions are placed on the use of pointers to help programmers avoid incomprehensible code. Pointer variables are only allowed to point to variables of a single type; the pointers are said to be "bound" to this type. For instance, if we declare

```
VAR One: POINTER TO INTEGER;
    Two: POINTER TO CHAR;
```

then

```
One := Two;
```

is illegal because of type incompatibility.

Note that while it is very common to use pointers in connection with records, one is not restricted to this usage. In the declaration

```
TYPE SomePointerType = POINTER TO SomeType;
```

SomeType may be any legal Modula-2 type. This includes the basic types such as INTEGER, REAL, or BITSET; subrange types; enumeration types; set types; array and record types; procedure types (these are discussed later in the book); and even other pointer types. The formal open array types are excluded; a declaration such as

```
TYPE String = POINTER TO ARRAY OF CHAR; (* ILLEGAL *)
```

is illegal. If we declare:

```
VAR FirstInList: PointerToListElement;
```

a new ListElement may be created by calling the standard procedure NEW. This call allocates space for a new ListElement and makes FirstInList "point to" that space:

```
NEW(FirstInList);
```

To free the space allocated for whichever record FirstInList currently points to, the standard procedure DISPOSE may be used:

```
DISPOSE(FirstInList);
```

This procedure must be used carefully to avoid "dangling pointers" which point to records whose storage has been freed for other uses. After executing

```
NEW(PointerOne);
PointerTwo := PointerOne;
```

PointerOne and PointerTwo both point to the same space in memory. If that space is released:

```
DISPOSE(PointerOne);
```

and an effort is made to use some value which was stored there:

```
MyVariable := PointerTwo ↑ .SomeField;
```

the results are unpredictable. There are some hidden steps here; the actual sequence of events might be something such as

```
NEW(PointerOne);
PointerTwo := PointerOne;
DISPOSE(PointerOne);
```

```
*Store something else in the space previously used by PointerOne ↑ ;*
*that space was made available again by the call to DISPOSE. The  *
*values previously stored in PointerOne ↑ are partially or         *
*completely overwritten, but PointerTwo has no way to know this,   *
*so it will go ahead and use the wrong values:                     *
MyVariable := PointerTwo ↑ .SomeField;
```

Before making a call to DISPOSE, one should be certain that the value(s) stored in the variable which is about to be disposed of are either useless or that they are preserved elsewhere for possible later use.

Some implementations require that any module which uses NEW or its companion procedure DISPOSE must include an import clause similar to

```
FROM Storage IMPORT ALLOCATE, DEALLOCATE;
```

The name of the module which handles storage allocation may be different on your system. Some systems provide several modules for different kinds of storage management.

Records and other variables created by calls on NEW have no names; they can only be referenced by using some pointer. A clear distinction is made between pointers and the variables they point to. No automatic type conversions are made. The entire variable created by the call to NEW is referred to by appending an up arrow to the pointer:

FirstInList is a pointer to a ListElement record.

FirstInList ↑ is the entire record pointed to by FirstInList.

FirstInList ↑ .Value is an INTEGER variable.

FirstInList ↑ .Next is another pointer to a ListElement record.

The predefined pointer value NIL is used to indicate explicitly that a pointer points nowhere. NIL is a reserved word. The value NIL may be assigned to any pointer variable:

```
FirstInList ↑ .Next := NIL;
```

Any expression involving Ptr ↑ makes no sense when Ptr = NIL:

```
FirstInList := NIL;
FirstInList ↑ .Next := SomeValue;
```

is illegal but will probably only be detected at run time. It is therefore a good idea to test a pointer to be certain it is not NIL before attempting to reference the variable the pointer points to.

The only operations applicable to a POINTER variable are the assignment of the value of another pointer of the same type, the assignment of the predefined value NIL, calls on NEW or DISPOSE, and "dereferencing" using ↑. Systems programmers should note that arithmetic can be done on ADDRESS variables (see Chapter 19) but not on POINTERs. This sort of pointer arithmetic is illegal:

FirstInList := FirstInList + 1; (* ILLEGAL *)

As an example of the use of pointers, Listings 12-1 and 12-2 contain the code for a pair of library modules which may be used to maintain a sorted list of names. The names are kept in a linked list. Part of the implementation is left as an exercise.

LISTING 12-1 *An example of the use of pointers to maintain a sorted linked list, part 1.*

```
DEFINITION MODULE NameListHandler;
   EXPORT QUALIFIED NAMELength, NAMEListElement,
                    ADDNameToList, DELETEName, PRINTList;

   CONST NAMELength = 20;
   TYPE  NAMEListElement;

   PROCEDURE ADDNameToList( NewName: ARRAY OF CHAR;
                   VAR NameTooLong: BOOLEAN;
                   VAR FirstInList: NAMEListElement );
   (* Maintains list of names, with lexicographically least name    *)
   (* pointed to by FirstInList.                                     *)

   PROCEDURE DELETEName( NameToDelete: ARRAY OF CHAR;
                   VAR NameFound: BOOLEAN;
                   VAR FirstInList: NAMEListElement );
   (* Deletes the specified name, if a name which matches it for the *)
   (* first K characters is found in the list. K is the minimum of   *)
   (* NAMELength and the number of meaningful characters in          *)
   (* NameToDelete.                                                  *)

   PROCEDURE PRINTList( FirstInList: NAMEListElement );
   (* Prints the indicated list of names. *)

END NameListHandler.
```

LISTING 12-2   *An example of the use of pointers to maintain a sorted linked list, part 2.*

```
IMPLEMENTATION MODULE NameListHandler;
  FROM StringStuff IMPORT COPIEDString, STRINGLessThan, STRINGSAreEqual;
  FROM Storage    IMPORT ALLOCATE, DEALLOCATE;

  TYPE NameType = ARRAY[1..NAMELength] OF CHAR;
  TYPE NAMEListElement = POINTER TO ListElement;
  TYPE ListElement = RECORD
                        Name: NameType;
                        Next: PointerToElement;
                        END; (* RECORD *)

  PROCEDURE ADDNameToList( NewName: ARRAY OF CHAR;
                           VAR NameTooLong: BOOLEAN;
                           VAR FirstInList: NAMEListElement );
    VAR NewElement, CurrentElement, CurrentButOne: NAMEListElement;
  (* Maintains list of names, with lexicographically least name      *)
  (* pointed to by FirstInList.                                      *)
  BEGIN (* AddedToList *)
    NEW(NewElement);
    NameTooLong := NOT COPIEDString(NewName, NewElement↑.Name);
    IF FirstInList <> NIL THEN
      (* List has at least one element. *)
      IF STRINGLessThan(NewName, FirstInList↑.Name) THEN
        (* Insert record pointed to by NewElement, which contains *)
        (* NewName, as the first element of the list.             *)
        NewElement↑.Next := FirstInList;
        FirstInList := NewElement;
      ELSIF (FirstInList↑.Next = NIL) THEN
        (* List has exactly one element. *)
        IF (STRINGLessThan(FirstInList↑.Name, NewName)) THEN
          (* New element belongs at end of list, as second element. *)
          FirstInList↑.Next := NewElement;
          NewElement↑.Next := NIL;
        END; (* IF *)
      ELSE (* List has more than one element. *)
        (* Search element by element through the list for the right *)
        (* place to insert the new element. Stop when an element is *)
        (* found with a name greater than or equal to the new name, *)
        (* or when the end of the list is reached.                  *)
        CurrentElement := FirstInList↑.Next;
        CurrentButOne := FirstInList;
        WHILE ((CurrentElement↑.Next <> NIL)
```

```
                AND (STRINGLessThan(CurrentElement↑.Name, NewName))) DO
          CurrentElement := CurrentElement↑.Next;
          CurrentButOne := CurrentButOne↑.Next;
        END; (* WHILE *)
        IF (CurrentElement↑.Next = NIL) THEN
          (* CurrentElement points to last element in list. *)
          IF (STRINGLessThan(NewName, CurrentElement↑.Name)) THEN
            (* New element should be next to last in list. *)
            CurrentButOne↑.Next := NewElement;
            NewElement↑.Next := CurrentElement;
          ELSIF (NOT STRINGSAreEqual(NewName, CurrentElement↑.Name)) THEN
            (* New element should be last in list. *)
            CurrentElement↑.Next := NewElement;
            NewElement↑.Next := NIL;
          END; (* IF *)
        ELSE (* CurrentElement points to element in middle of list. *)
          IF (NOT STRINGSAreEqual(NewName, CurrentElement↑.Name)) THEN
            CurrentButOne↑.Next := NewElement;
            NewElement↑.Next := CurrentElement;
          END; (* IF *)
        END; (* IF (CurrentElement↑.Next = NIL) *)
      END; (* IF STRINGLessThan(NewName, FirstInList↑.Name) *)
    ELSE
      FirstInList := NewElement;
      FirstInList↑.Next := NIL;
    END; (* IF FirstInList <> NIL *)
  END ADDNameToList;


  PROCEDURE DELETEName( NameToDelete: ARRAY OF CHAR;
                        VAR NameFound: BOOLEAN;
                        VAR FirstInList: NAMEListElement );
  (* Deletes the specified name, if a name which matches it for the *)
  (* first K characters is found in the list. K is the minimum of   *)
  (* NAMELength and the number of meaningful characters in          *)
  (* NameToDelete.                                                  *)
  BEGIN
    (* See the exercises. *)
  END DELETEName;


  PROCEDURE PRINTList( FirstInList: NAMEListElement );
  (* Prints the indicated list of names. *)
  BEGIN
    (* See the exercises. *)
  END PRINTList;


END NameListHandler.
```

Pointers as Value Parameters

If a pointer variable is matched to a formal value parameter in a subprogram call, the formal parameter will behave like a local variable which has been initialized with the current value of the pointer. This is what one would expect from the earlier discussion on value and variable parameters. Changing the value of a formal value parameter inside a subprogram will have no effect on the value of the corresponding actual parameter.

However, any change in the value of a variable pointed to by the formal parameter *will* change the value of the variable pointed to by the actual parameter because they both point to the same location in memory. Whether a pointer is matched to a variable or a value parameter, the variable it points to is always treated as a variable parameter. Listing 12-3 illustrates this point; the output from program Example will be 12345, not 11111.

LISTING 12-3 *Variables pointed to may be given new values inside subprogram calls even if their pointers were matched to value parameters.*

```
MODULE Example;
  FROM InOut IMPORT WRITEInteger;

  TYPE PointerToInteger = POINTER TO INTEGER;
  VAR  IntegerPointer: PointerToInteger;

  PROCEDURE ChangePointee(PointerValueFormal: PointerToInteger);
  BEGIN
    PointerValueFormal↑ := 12345;
  END ChangePointee;

BEGIN
  IntegerPointer↑ := 11111;
  ChangePointee(IntegerPointer);
  WRITEInteger(IntegerPointer↑,5);
END Example.
```

One implication of all this is that data structures such as linked lists and trees which are formed with pointers cannot be passed as value parameters by passing the pointer to their first element or root as a value parameter. Suppose some subprogram needs to manipulate a duplicate of the structure without changing the original. Only the pointer that is actually passed to the subprogram will be copied by the call; the rest of the structure must be explicitly copied to create a duplicate that can be modified without changing the original list or tree.

Exercise

1. Complete the implementation of NameListHandler begun in Listing 12-1 by writing the code for procedures DELETEName and PRINTList.

Chapter

13

Variant Records

Declaring and Using Variant Records

We have seen that pointers may be used to connect variables together in dynamically changing data structures such as linked lists. Modula-2 also allows individual variables of "variant" record types to change their size and composition while a program is executing. Over a period of time, different fields may be accessible in different variables of the same variant record type or in the same record variable. Like variable parameters in functions, variant records provide a powerful facility for programmers, but their use can lead to very obscure bugs if one is not careful.

Any record type declaration may contain zero or more variant fields, just as it may contain zero or more invariant fields:

```
TYPE EnumType = (Integer, Bitset);
TYPE VariantRecord = RECORD
                CASE Discriminator: EnumType OF
                Integer: IntegerField: INTEGER |
                Bitset  : BitsetField  : BITSET
                END; (* End of Variant field *)
                CharacterField: CHAR; (* Invariant field *)
                END; (* Variant RECORD *)

VAR First,
      Second: VariantRecord;
```

As shown, each variant field is declared using a statement whose syntax is similar but not identical to that of the CASE statement. In particular, an ELSE portion is allowed.

Any given value of a discriminator may have zero or more fields associated with it. In the example above, each of the possible Discriminator values Integer, Bitset has one field associated with it. These fields "exist" in the record, i.e., they are safely accessible only when the discriminator has the associated value. For instance, a VariantRecord variable such as First has the fields IntegerField and CharacterField when Discriminator has the value Integer.

Discriminators may be of any discrete type, including CHAR, INTEGER, CARDINAL; enumeration types; and subrange types. Discriminators are referenced using the dot notation, just as if they were a field in the record:

```
First.Discriminator := Integer;
```

Variant record variables may have different fields even though they are of the same type. One must check the value of the discriminator to avoid assuming that a variant record variable has some field which is not safely accessible at the present time:

```
IF First.Discriminator = Integer THEN
    First.IntegerField := 12345;
ELSE
    First.BitsetField := {2..7};
END; (* Legal IF *)
```

One cannot depend on the compiler to catch mistakes such as:

```
Second.Discriminator := Integer;
Second.BitsetField := {};
```

After the assignment to Second's discriminator, Second has no field named BitsetField; it has an INTEGER field named IntegerField and a CHAR field named CharacterField. In fact, errors such as this will not necessarily cause a program to crash when one tries to execute it. It is doubtful, however, that a program containing such errors could be relied upon to run correctly.

As a simple example of the use of variant records, suppose one wished to maintain an array of records containing data on some group of employees. If an employee is a boss, the record is to contain a pointer to a list of the people who are directly responsible to the employee. Whether an employee is a boss or not, the record for the employee is to contain a pointer to the employee's boss. Some type declarations such as the following could be used in such a situation; the data could be stored in an array of EmployeeRecords:

```
TYPE EmployeeRecordPointer = POINTER TO EmployeeRecord;
TYPE EmployeeRecord = RECORD
```

```
CASE IsABoss: BOOLEAN OF
   TRUE : Subordinates: NameListPointer |
   FALSE: (* Empty *)
END; (* Variant Field *)
Boss: EmployeeRecordPointer;
END; (* Variant EmployeeRecord *)
```

Before we consider a longer example of how variant records may be usefully applied, there are a few more prohibitions to note. Sequences of statements such as the following should be avoided:

```
First.Discriminator := Bitset;
Second.Discriminator := Integer;
First := Second;
```

The two record variables have been made incompatible by giving them different fields; illegal assignments such as the last one will probably not be discovered by the compiler.

The result of assigning a value to one variant of a field and then changing the discriminator so that the field containing the value no longer exists is implementation-dependent. One cannot assume any transfer of values from the old variant to the new one. For instance, after executing

```
First.Discriminator := Bitset;
First.BitsetField := {};
First.Discriminator := Integer;
```

one cannot safely make any assumptions about the value of the newly created IntegerField. It is also unsafe to assume that the value assigned to BitsetField will still be there if the field is recreated by reassigning the discriminator its original value of Bitset. Because Modula-2 compilers do recognize so many semantic and syntactic errors in programs, it is especially important to note that one cannot rely on the compiler to discover many of the inconsistencies in statements which involve variant records. This is because the fields associated with a given record variable may change during program execution as the discriminator assumes different values.

An Example: LISP Functions in Modula-2

To illustrate the power of variant records, Listings 13-1 and 13-2 show a Modula-2 implementation of some basic LISP data structures and functions. Readers unfamiliar with LISP may view it as a language which represents lists as trees and which manipulates lists by modifying the corresponding trees appropriately. The elements of a LISP list may be either lists or atoms. The only atoms are literal strings such as "foo," integer values, and two predefined values, t and nil. The values nil and t correspond roughly to Modula-2's FALSE and TRUE. However, nil is not only an atom, it is also the empty list: (). The LISP value nil should not be confused with Modula-2's NIL, the predefined value used to indicate that a pointer points nowhere. LISPNIL is a Modula-2 version of the LISP atom nil; LISPT represents the LISP value t.

LISTING 13-1   *A Modula-2 implementation of some basic* **LISP** *data structures and functions, part 1.*

```
DEFINITION MODULE LispInModula2;
  EXPORT QUALIFIED LISPT, LISPNIL, NULL, ATOM, LIST, CAR, CDR,
                   CONS, APPEND, INTEGERToAtom, STRINGToAtom,
                   PRINTAtom, PRINTList;
  TYPE NodePointer;
  VAR  LISPT, LISPNIL: NodePointer; (* These should be treated as *)
                                    (* READ-ONLY variables.       *)


  (* All functions which expect to be passed a pointer to a list write *)
  (* an error message if they are passed a pointer to an atom.         *)

  PROCEDURE NULL(Node: NodePointer): NodePointer;
  (* Returns LISPT if Node points to an empty list, LISPNIL otherwise.*)
  PROCEDURE ATOM(Node: NodePointer): NodePointer;
  (* Returns LISPT if Node points to an atom; returns LISPNIL if Node *)
  (* points to a list. Atoms and lists are the only LISP data        *)
  (* structures supported; no dotted pairs are allowed.              *)

  PROCEDURE LIST(Node: NodePointer): NodePointer;
  (* Returns the list containing what Node points to as its single *)
  (* element.                                                      *)
  PROCEDURE CAR(Node: NodePointer): NodePointer;
  (* Returns a pointer to the first element of the list pointed to *)
  (* by Node; if the list is empty, returns LISPNIL.              *)
  PROCEDURE CDR(Node: NodePointer): NodePointer;
  (* Returns a pointer to the list obtained by removing the first  *)
  (* element from the list pointed to by Node; if the list pointed *)
  (* to by Node is empty, returns LISPNIL.                        *)
  PROCEDURE CONS(One, Two: NodePointer): NodePointer;
  (* Returns a pointer to the list obtained by inserting the       *)
  (* element pointed to by One into the list pointed to by Two.   *)
  PROCEDURE APPEND(One, Two: NodePointer): NodePointer;
```

LISTING 13-1   Continued

```
(* Returns a pointer to the list obtained (for instance) by starting *)
(* with the last element of One, inserting it at the first of Two,    *)
(* then inserting the next to last element of One at the first of     *)
(* this new list, and so forth. In LISP, (append '(a b) '(c d))       *)
(* gives (a b c d).                                                   *)

PROCEDURE STRINGToAtom(Value: ARRAY OF CHAR): NodePointer;
(* Transfers a Modula-2 string into a LISP-like atom whose value is   *)
(* the given string. This function and INTEGERToAtom are implicit in  *)
(* the interpreter (for instance) in most full-scale implementations  *)
(* of LISP; the transfer is done automatically, and is invisible      *)
(* to most users.                                                     *)

PROCEDURE INTEGERToAtom(Value: INTEGER): NodePointer;
(* Transfers a Modula-2 INTEGER into a LISP-like atom whose value is  *)
(* the given INTEGER. See STRINGToAtom; this function is              *)
(* invisible to most users in a full-scale implementation of LISP.    *)

PROCEDURE PRINTAtom(ToPrint: NodePointer);
(* Prints the atom indicated; gives an error message if ToPrint does  *)
(* not point to a node which represents an atom.                      *)
PROCEDURE PRINTList(ToPrint: NodePointer);
(* Prints the list indicated; gives an error message if ToPrint does  *)
(* not point to the root of a tree representing a list.               *)

END LispInModula2.
```

LISTING 13-2   *A Modula-2 implementation of some basic* **LISP** *data structures and functions, part 2.*

```
IMPLEMENTATION MODULE LispInModula2;
  FROM Storage IMPORT ALLOCATE, DEALLOCATE;
  FROM InOut   IMPORT WRITECharacter, WRITEString, WRITEInteger;
  CONST NULLChar     = 0C;
        StringLength = 20;
  TYPE CellType    = (Integer, String, Pointer);
  TYPE StringType  = ARRAY[0..StringLength-1] OF CHAR;
  TYPE NodePointer = POINTER TO NodeRecord;
  TYPE NodeRecord  = RECORD (* Variant Record *)
                       CASE LeftCellIs: CellType OF
                         Integer: LeftInteger: INTEGER    |
                         String : LeftString : StringType |
                         Pointer: LeftPointer: NodePointer
```

```
                    END; (* CASE LeftCell *)
                    RightPointer: NodePointer;
                    END; (* Variant RECORD *)

PROCEDURE NULL(Node: NodePointer): NodePointer;
BEGIN
  IF (Node = LISPNIL) THEN
    RETURN LISPT;
  ELSIF (Node↑.LeftCellIs = Pointer) THEN
    IF ((Node↑.LeftPointer = NIL)
        AND (Node↑.RightPointer = NIL)) THEN
      RETURN LISPT;
    ELSE
      RETURN LISPNIL;
    END; (* IF *)
  ELSE
    WRITEString(" NULL was passed an atom ");
  END; (* IF *)
END NULL;

PROCEDURE ATOM(Node: NodePointer): NodePointer;
BEGIN
  IF ((Node = LISPT) OR (Node = LISPNIL)) THEN
    RETURN LISPT;
  ELSIF (Node↑.LeftCellIs = Pointer) THEN
    RETURN LISPNIL;
  ELSE
    RETURN LISPT;
  END; (* IF *)
END ATOM;

PROCEDURE LIST(Node: NodePointer): NodePointer;
  VAR TempPointer: NodePointer;
BEGIN
  NEW(TempPointer);
  TempPointer↑.LeftCellIs := Pointer;
  TempPointer↑.LeftPointer := Node;
  TempPointer↑.RightPointer := NIL;
  RETURN TempPointer;
END LIST;

PROCEDURE CAR(Node: NodePointer): NodePointer;
BEGIN
  IF (NULL(Node) = LISPT) THEN
    RETURN LISPNIL;
  ELSIF (ATOM(Node) = LISPT) THEN
    WRITEString(" CAR was passed an atom ");
```

LISTING 13-2   Continued

```
ELSE
  RETURN (Node↑.LeftPointer);
  END; (* IF *)
END CAR;

PROCEDURE CDR(Node: NodePointer): NodePointer;
BEGIN
  IF (Node↑.RightPointer = NIL) THEN
    RETURN LISPNIL;
  ELSIF (ATOM(Node) = LISPT) THEN
    WRITEString(" CDR was passed an atom ");
  ELSE
    RETURN (Node↑.RightPointer);
  END; (* IF *)
END CDR;

PROCEDURE CONS(One, Two: NodePointer): NodePointer;
  VAR TempPointer: NodePointer;
BEGIN
  IF (NULL(Two) = LISPT) THEN
    RETURN LIST(One);
  ELSE
    NEW(TempPointer);
    TempPointer↑.LeftCellIs := Pointer;
    TempPointer↑.LeftPointer := One;
    TempPointer↑.RightPointer := Two;
    RETURN TempPointer;
  END; (* IF *)
END CONS;

PROCEDURE APPEND(One, Two: NodePointer): NodePointer;
  VAR TempPointer: NodePointer;
BEGIN
  IF (NULL(One) = LISPT) THEN
    RETURN Two;
  ELSIF (NULL(Two) = LISPT) THEN
    RETURN One;
  ELSIF ((ATOM(One) = LISPT) OR (ATOM(Two) = LISPT)) THEN
    WRITEString(" APPEND was passed an atom ");
  ELSE
    TempPointer := One;
    WHILE (TempPointer↑.RightPointer <> NIL) DO
      TempPointer := TempPointer↑.RightPointer;
    END; (* WHILE *)
    TempPointer↑.RightPointer := Two;
    RETURN One;
```

```
  END; (* IF *)
END APPEND;

PROCEDURE INTEGERToAtom(Value: INTEGER): NodePointer;
  VAR TempPointer: NodePointer;
BEGIN
  NEW(TempPointer);
  TempPointer↑.LeftCellIs := Integer;
  TempPointer↑.LeftInteger := Value;
  TempPointer↑.RightPointer := NIL;
  RETURN TempPointer;
END INTEGERToAtom;

PROCEDURE STRINGToAtom(Value: ARRAY OF CHAR): NodePointer;
  VAR TempPointer: NodePointer;
      Index      : CARDINAL;
BEGIN
  NEW(TempPointer);
  TempPointer↑.LeftCellIs := String;
  Index := 0;
  (* Store as much of Value in the new NodeRecord as possible .*)
  WHILE ((Index <= StringLength-1) AND (Index <= HIGH(Value))
        AND (Value[Index] <> NULLChar)) DO
    TempPointer↑.LeftString[Index] := Value[Index];
    INC(Index);
  END; (* WHILE *)
  IF (Index <= StringLength-1) THEN
    TempPointer↑.LeftString[Index] := NULLChar;
  END; (* IF *)
  (* Assume the meaningful portion of any string stored *)
  (* in an array ends when either the end of the array  *)
  (* or a NULLChar is encountered.                       *)
  TempPointer↑.RightPointer := NIL;
  RETURN TempPointer;
END STRINGToAtom;

PROCEDURE PRINTAtom(ToPrint: NodePointer);
BEGIN
  IF (ATOM(ToPrint) = LISPNIL) THEN
    WRITEString(" PRINTAtom was passed a non-atom ");
  ELSIF (ToPrint = LISPNIL) THEN
    WRITEString(" LISPNIL ");
  ELSIF (ToPrint = LISPT) THEN
    WRITEString(" LISPT ");
  ELSE
    CASE ToPrint↑.LeftCellIs OF
      Integer: WRITEInteger(ToPrint↑.LeftInteger,6); |
      String : WRITEString(ToPrint↑.LeftString);
```

LISTING 13-2   Continued

```
    END; (* CASE *)
  END; (* IF *)
END PRINTAtom;

PROCEDURE PRINTList(ToPrint: NodePointer);
BEGIN
  IF (ATOM(ToPrint) = LISPT) THEN
    IF (ToPrint = LISPNIL) THEN
      WRITEString("()");
    ELSE
      WRITEString(" PRINTList was passed an atom ");
    END; (* IF *)
  ELSE
    WRITECharacter("(");
    IF (NULL(ToPrint) = LISPNIL) THEN
      PrintElements(ToPrint);
    END; (* IF *)
    WRITECharacter(")");
  END; (* IF *)
END PRINTList;

PROCEDURE PrintElements(ToPrint: NodePointer);
(* Used in a mutually recursive fashion by PRINTList *)
BEGIN
  IF (ATOM(CAR(ToPrint)) = LISPT) THEN
    PRINTAtom(CAR(ToPrint));
  ELSIF (ToPrint↑.LeftPointer <> NIL) THEN
    PRINTList(CAR(ToPrint));
  END; (* IF *)
  IF (ToPrint↑.RightPointer <> NIL) THEN
    PrintElements(CDR(ToPrint));
    END; (* IF *)
  END PrintElements;

BEGIN (* body of LispInModula2 *)
  (* Initialize LISPT, LISPNIL *)
  LISPT↑.LeftCellIs := Pointer;
  LISPT↑.LeftPointer := NIL;
  LISPT↑.RightPointer := NIL;

  LISPNIL↑.LeftCellIs := Pointer;
  LISPNIL↑.LeftPointer := NIL;
  LISPNIL↑.RightPointer := NIL;

END LispInModula2.
```

(12 34) (* List with two integer atom elements *)

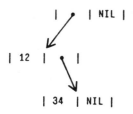

(foo (-2)) (* List with two elements, a string atom and a list *)

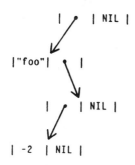

() (* List with no elements *)

| NIL | NIL |

one (* A string atom *)

|"one"| NIL |

Figure 13-1   Tree representations of some lists and atoms.

Figure 13-1 shows some LISP lists and atoms and their representations as trees. An atom is indicated by a string or integer without any enclosing parentheses since parentheses are used to enclose lists: 12345 is an atom and (12345) is a list with one element, the atom 12345.

The implementation shown in Listings 13-1 and 13-2 represents trees using records for nodes and pointers for branches. Nodes in the tree will be represented by record variables of type NodeRecord:

```
TYPE NodePointer = POINTER TO NodeRecord;
TYPE NodeRecord  = RECORD (* Variant Record *)
```

```
CASE LeftCellIs: CellType OF
    Integer: LeftInteger: INTEGER    |
    String : LeftString : StringType   |
    Pointer: LeftPointer: NodePointer
END; (* CASE LeftCell *)
    RightPointer: NodePointer;
END; (* Variant RECORD *)
```

For instance, the NodeRecord for node

|"foo"| NIL |

will have LeftCellIs = String, so the record variable has two fields: LeftString, of type StringType and RightPointer, of type NodePointer. LeftString will hold the character string "foo," and RightPointer will have the value NIL.

Notice in Figure 13-1 that the record fields which represent the left cells in the nodes will be required to hold a mixture of strings, INTEGER values, and pointers to other nodes. This may be implemented quite easily with variant records. The implementation assumes that right cells of nodes always hold pointers. All entities are either lists or atoms except for LISPNIL, which is both an atom and the empty list. Readers familiar with LISP will notice that dotted pairs are not supported. These readers are invited to determine the changes to modules LispInModula2 which would be necessary to provide such support.

The important things for readers unfamiliar with LISP to remember are that a particular variant record variable may have one group of fields at one point in time and another group of fields at another point in time and that different variables of the same variant record type may contain different fields at the same time.

Exercise

1. Write the declaration for a variant record type SuperType which contains the two record types below as special cases. That is, for appropriate values of the discriminator(s) of SuperType variables, one obtains variables with the same structure as SubTypeOne or SubTypeTwo.

```
TYPE SubTypeOne = RECORD
                OneA: INTEGER;
                OneB: CHAR;
                OneC: BOOLEAN;
                END; (* RECORD *)

TYPE SubTypeTwo = RECORD
                TwoA: BITSET;
                TwoB: INTEGER;
                TwoC: REAL;
                END; (* RECORD *)
```

Chapter

14

Opaque Types

Declaring and Using Opaque Types

At times it is neither necessary nor desirable for a module which imports a type to have access to the details of the type's representation in terms of Modula-2's basic types. For instance, one may wish to allow programmers to make use of data types and their associated subprograms without worrying about all the details involved. One would like, for instance, to be able to import a type FILEType and some "operators" such as READCharacter and OPENFile without needing to understand how files are stored on the disks. Hiding details also makes it possible to prevent novices from trying to make use of code they may not fully understand.

By declaring a type as an "opaque" type in a definition module, a programmer allows importing modules to declare variables of that type and to pass them as parameters; certain assignment statements are also legal. The only other operations applicable to variables of an opaque type are those defined by exported subprograms; these operations are generally the ones used most by importers. No statements which depend on the importer knowing how the opaque type is represented are allowed. That is, the type may be a pointer, a record, an array, or some mix of these and other types, but the importer cannot use this information even if the programmer who is writing the importer has access to all the source code associated with the opaque type.

Opaque type declarations contain nothing except the type's name:

```
DEFINITION MODULE FileHandler;
    EXPORT QUALIFIED FILEType, . . . , other exports . . . ;

    TYPE FILEType; (* Opaque type *)

    . . . other exports . . .
END FileHandler.
```

The description of the type's composition in terms of known types is hidden in the implementation module. We have already seen examples of opaque types and will see others later.

In Listings 12-1 and 12-2, for instance, NAMEListElement is declared as an opaque type. The only operations allowed on a NAMEListElement variable are assignment, test for equality, and calls to the procedures ADDNameToList, DELETEName, and PRINTList. Importers need to know what the effects of calls on these procedures are, but they should not be concerned with the details of how the list of names is maintained. Because the details are best hidden, it makes sense to declare NAMEListElement as an opaque type.

In Listings 16-8 and 16-9, a pair of CharSetHandler library modules is presented to remedy the fact that SET OF CHAR is not allowed on many systems. The type SETOfChar is declared as an opaque type since it is immaterial to other modules whether sets are represented using linked lists, arrays, or some other data structure. CharSetHandler exports an "abstract data type"; except for declaring SETOfChar variables and making certain assignments, the only operations defined for SETOfChar variables are those provided by the procedures and functions exported from CharSetHandler. For this reason, one must be careful to provide subprograms which perform all the operations an importer might reasonably require.

Modules LispInModula2, shown in Listings 13-1 and 13-2, provide a third example of the use of opaque types. It is not strictly necessary to declare NodePointer as an opaque type; since NodePointer is not exported, its details are already hidden outside LispInModula2. However, remember that definition modules are probably the most commonly used form of documentation in Modula-2. They should tell *what* can be done by exports without including any unnecessary details on *how* these actions are achieved. Declaring NodePointer as an opaque type allows us to avoid cluttering up the definition module with details which are of no interest to most programmers who use LispInModula2's exports.

Different systems will allow some or all of the following types to be used as opaque types: INTEGER, CARDINAL, BOOLEAN, CHAR, BITSET, WORD, ADDRESS, PROCESS, subrange, and set. Opaque pointer types are always allowed and should be favored to enhance portability. In the second version of Modula-2, compilers are only required to support pointers as opaque types; one will not necessarily be able to opaquely export subranges, enumerations, or any other non-pointer type.

To illustrate the relationships between export lists, opaque type definitions, and visibility, consider the following definition module:

```
DEFINITION MODULE Exporter;
    EXPORT   QUALIFIED TYPEOne, TYPEThree, TYPEFour;
       TYPE   TYPEOne; (* an exported opaque type *)
              TypeTwo;  (* another opaque type, not exported *)
              TYPEThree = ARRAY[0..10] OF BOOLEAN;
              TYPEFour  = POINTER TO TypeTwo;
END Exporter.
```

TYPEOne and TypeTwo have been defined as opaque types, so the details of their implementations reside in Exporter's implementation module:

```
IMPLEMENTATION MODULE Exporter;
    TYPE  RecordType = RECORD
                          FieldOne:INTEGER;
                          FieldTwo:CARDINAL;
                          END; (* RECORD *)
          TYPEOne   = POINTER TO RecordType;
          TypeTwo   = [2..7];
END Exporter.
```

TypeTwo is not exported, so it is not visible at all outside Exporter if the original version of Modula-2 is being used. As mentioned earlier, the second version of Modula-2 does not use export lists; everything in a definition module is exported. Appendix 5 contains more information on the newer version of Modula-2. TYPEOne is an exported opaque type, so it is visible outside Exporter, but its details are not visible outside Exporter. If some module Importer tries to use any of the implementation details of TYPEOne, the compiler will report an error:

```
MODULE Importer;
    FROM Exporter IMPORT TYPEOne, TYPEThree, TYPEFour;
       VAR One  : TYPEOne;
           Three: TYPEThree;
           Four : TYPEFour;
BEGIN
    One ↑ .FieldOne := −34; (* Will be marked as illegal *)
    Four ↑ := 12;           (* Will be marked as illegal *)
    Four := NIL;            (* Legal *)
    Three[2] := FALSE;      (* Legal *)
END Importer.
```

The first assignment in module Importer is illegal because it assumes that TYPEOne variables are pointers to records with an INTEGER field named FieldOne; this information is hidden in Exporter's implementation module where Importer cannot see it. TYPEFour is exported along with the fact that it is a pointer. However, none of the details of the object a TYPEFour variable points to are visible to importing modules since TYPEFour is a pointer to the opaque type TypeTwo. Thus, the second assignment in Importer is illegal. The compiler cannot determine whether 12 is a reasonable value for Four ↑ because Four ↑ is a variable of opaque TypeTwo. Four is known to be a pointer, so the third assignment in Importer is legal.

The details of exported TYPEThree are included in the definition module, so both the type and the details are exported. The fourth assignment statement in Importer would be illegal if the fact that TYPEThree variables are arrays of BOOLEANs were not included in definition module Exporter.

15

Software Engineering with Modula-2

What Are Desirable Program Qualities?

There is little or nothing in any computer language, including Modula-2, which forces the programmer to write good code. But it is easier to write clear programs in Modula-2 than it is to do so in other languages. This chapter suggests a number of techniques which may be used in connection with some of Modula-2's features to make reading, writing, understanding, modifying, debugging, and verifying programs easier. The subject of software engineering has grown dramatically over the past few years. There is room in this chapter to do little more than look briefly at some of the ideas available and to try to relate them to Modula-2.

The important software engineering questions one would like answered are "What good qualities should a program have?" and "How can these good qualities be given to a program?" Certainly an ideal program should work on all inputs, and it should produce the correct results quickly and efficiently. It should be easy to locate, understand, and fix problems in a program which does not work. Even if a program always works, the program should be easy to understand in case one wishes to modify it to perform a different task or to run on another machine. If one already has a program which does part of a necessary computation, it should be possible to use part or all of that existing code in a new program without a lot of trouble. Finally, all programs should be as easy to write as possible. Some of the desirable attributes of a program and some ways Modula-2 programs might be given these qualities are described in more detail below.

Understandability

Understandability is arguably the single most important property a program can have. Clearly written code is essential if a programmer is to convince anyone that a program will behave correctly since automated verification of a program's correctness is currently impractical in nearly all cases. If a program is ever to be modified to handle a more general or different task, the programmer who is responsible for making the changes must have a clear understanding of the program. The same is true of programs which are being ported to another machine.

Programmers who expect to receive any help debugging a program should try to make the code as clear as possible. The object of programming should not be to simply produce programs that run except perhaps in some programming classes. The object of writing a piece of software should be to help build up a library of software tools for repeated use in various forms and on different machines. Debugging, modifying, and porting a program will all be made easier if the program is clearly written.

The question still to be answered is "What is required to make a program clear?" Summary 15-1 lists some of the ways to contribute to a program's clarity. Most of the suggestions are self-explanatory, but Listing 15-1 is included as an example of the sixth point, which suggests that programmers avoid mixing source code which lies at different levels of abstraction. A reasonable approach to the use of comments is suggested in Summary 15-2.

SUMMARY 15-1   Ways to contribute to a program's clarity

1. Follow a consistent and reasonable style, which deals with the following points:
(a) Indentation
(b) Identification of global versus local objects
(c) Location and purpose of comments
(d) Indications of the extent of nested statements and subprograms
See Chapter 21 for a summary of the style used in this book.

2. Programs should provide a concise description of the kind of data expected whenever they ask a user for input, as well as clearly labelling any output. In both cases, the amount and type of data involved should be made clear.

3. Use descriptive identifiers, e.g., STRINGLength, CardinalArray, and ASCIIToCardinal are preferable to Length, CArr, and AToCard.

4. Avoid using identifiers which are easily confused, such as RunI and Run1 or TypeOne and typeOne.

5. Program modules should begin with a short message to the user which explains the program's purpose, enumerates its limitations if there is room for confusion, and tells the user who to contact with questions or problems if feasible.

6. Avoid mixing source code which lies at different levels of abstraction (see Listing 15-1 for an example). Of course, the decision that a given statement lies at a particular level of abstraction is a subjective one.

7. Do not include too much code in any of the different levels of abstraction. Introduce new subprograms and modules which handle some of the work whenever the body of a subprogram or module seems to be too long or too complex.

8. Take advantage of language constructs such as definition and implementation modules, opaque types, enumeration types, the various kinds of loops, and subprograms to make the flow of data and control as clear as possible. These constructs may be used to hide details which are unlikely to be of interest to a reader who is trying to understand the program by working his or her way down from the most abstract view of the program to its myriad details. The identifiers associated with these constructs should serve as summaries of the missing details.

9. Avoid functions with variable parameters, variant records, nesting to more than three or four levels, pointers to pointers, and other constructs which easily create confusion unless they are necessary and their use is well-documented in the program. In general, the simplest and clearest way of doing things is also the best way.

10. Keep definition modules small. All the exports should be clearly related. For instance, the same module should not export both of the types SETOfChar and SETOfString.

SUMMARY 15-2   A possible guide to the use of comments

1. Inside definition modules, the intended uses of each export, as well as any limitations on those uses, should be included in a comment near the export's definition.

2. The person to contact with questions and complaints should be given in a comment at the top of every module along with the appropriate version numbers, dates of creation, formal specifications, research references, names of related programs, and other similar information.

3. Whenever an unusual algorithm is used, a nearby comment should explain the algorithm, including an argument as to why it is correct and why it is applicable in this instance and a description of the way boundary conditions are handled. Alternatively, the comment could refer the reader to some other source of documentation.

4. The use of any machine- or implementation-dependent objects should be clearly noted in a nearby comment.

5. Each function or procedure heading should be followed by a comment which describes the purpose of the subprogram, its limitations, and its reaction to unexpected inputs.

6. Comments should be used to mark the ends of conditional and loop statements which are deeply nested or which extend over several lines.

7. In general, comments should be clear, concise, and not cryptic. They should not simply restate the code in English. The amount of commentary needed in any program, of course, depends on who is going to be reading the program (see Summary 15-3).

LISTING 15-1 *Example illustrating the mixture of code which lies at different levels of abstraction.*

```
(* This version mixes different levels of abstraction. The individual  *)
(* statements in the body of IntroduceProgram and the calls on         *)
(* WRITEStringAndLine lie at approximately equal levels of abstraction,*)
(* but the WRITEStringAndLine calls have been placed on the same level *)
(* as IntroduceProgram.                                                *)
WHILE (NextAction IN ActiveOptions) DO
   IntroduceProgram;
   WRITEStringAndLine("Your options are: C - Consult data base;");
   WRITEStringAndLine("                  M - Modify data base entry;");
   WRITEStringAndLine("                  H - Get help;");
   WRITEString("                  Any other letter - exit program.");
   READCharacter(NextAction);
   PerformAction(NextAction);
END;(* WHILE *)


(* In this version, the code which was at a lower level of   *)
(* abstraction has been moved into a new procedure, so that  *)
(* the mixture of different levels of abstraction is avoided.*)
WHILE (NextAction IN ActiveOptions) DO
   IntroduceProgram;
   GetNextAction(NextAction);
   PerformAction(NextAction);
END;(* WHILE *)
```

Note that the amount of clarity which is appropriate differs from program to program. No one would seriously suggest providing comments on register allocation in an object code version of a program. Comments which state or restate the obvious are not only unnecessary, they should be avoided. But what is obvious differs from situation to situation. The amount of effort spent on making a program clear depends on the answers to questions such as those in Summary 15-3.

SUMMARY 15-3   Questions to guide the efforts to make a program self-documenting

1. Will anyone ever need to understand this code once the program is running correctly? For instance,
 (a) Would this program ever be useful as the basis for a more powerful program or one which performs some slightly different task?
 (b) Would parts of this program ever be useful in another program?
 (c) Might this program ever need to be modified to run on a different machine?
 (d) Might I ever need help writing or debugging part of this program?

2. If anyone besides myself might ever need to make sense of this code,
 (a) What will likely be their level of expertise? Are they likely to understand the problem area involved, the algorithms employed, the library software used, and the specifics of the programming language?
 (b) How profound an understanding of the code will they need? Will they need to know precisely how things are done or only the end results?

3. Is this program code large enough or complex enough that special efforts must be made to keep it clearly organized and understandable even if I am the only one who will ever see it?

Correctness

A programmer can only convince herself or himself that a program does what it is intended to do if three things are true. First, the programmer must know exactly what it is that the program is supposed to do. The problem which the program is meant to solve must be clearly specified. Secondly, the programmer must know enough about the particular situation at hand to understand the tools available for use on the problem. These tools may include algorithms, special hardware, libraries of previously tested code, previous versions of the program, or other people who have an understanding of the problem area.

Finally, the program must be understandable so that the programmer can see that it actually uses the tools correctly to do the correct things. Automated verifications and formal proofs of correctness are generally impractical, so clearly written code is essential when one is trying to predict whether or not a program will run correctly.

Modifiability

At least two factors influence how easily a programmer may modify a given program. These factors are the difficulty the programmer has in gaining sufficient understanding of the way the program works and the degree to which the effects of a change in the code are localized. The first factor recalls once more the importance of writing clear code. The second factor might be taken to include the amount of recompilation required to reflect a change, as well as the amount of other changes which are necessary to preserve the program's correctness. Summary 15-4 shows some of the ways one can make programs easier to modify; the intent of the suggestions is to minimize the amount of work needed to create a new executable version of the program which reflects the changes made.

**SUMMARY 15-4   Ways to minimize the effects of a
                   change in a program**

1. Plan the contents of definition modules carefully. Changing the number or type of parameters in an exported subprogram, adding to the export list, or making other changes may require the recompilation of the definition module, the corresponding implementation module, and any modules which imported something from the old definition module. All the definition modules used in a program should be as close to their final, ideal state as possible before anyone starts working on implementation modules.

2. Place any details which are not needed in a definition module in the corresponding implementation module. Opaque types may be used to help do this. Include only the information which is associated with exports; there is no reason to include a subprogram heading in a definition module if the subprogram is not exported. Note that everything defined in the definition module will be exported if the second version of Modula-2 is being used.

3. Break large program modules into a smaller program module and one or more definition/implementation module pairs. The new library module pairs should export the objects which were previously found in the old monolithic program module so that the new smaller program module can use them. This confines the effects of many changes to one of the new smaller modules.

4. Within a given module, avoid unnecessary uses of global variables.

5. Do not depend on the visibility rules to define the mapping between identifiers and memory locations. That is, avoid using the same name for different variables even when the variables are at different visibility levels. Otherwise, renaming may be necessary if one of the procedures is moved to another level of nesting.

Efficiency

At first glance, there seems to be a conflict between making a program efficient and making it understandable. This is because a high-level language such as Modula-2 must be translated by a compiler into simple instructions which the machine can execute. The compilation itself consumes resources, and the compiled code may do some things in a more roundabout fashion than the code produced by an expert assembly or machine language programmer.

Therefore it would appear to be more efficient to use a low-level language which would not need to be compiled and which would make better use of the machine's registers, special instructions, and so forth. A good example is the trigonometric sine function. There can be an enormous difference in the efficiency of an expertly written machine language sine procedure and one produced by compiling source code from Modula-2 or another high-level language.

However, it should be recognized that there are at least two ways to be efficient. First, there is the ability to do things very quickly. Secondly, there is the ability to do only those things which are necessary. Expert programmers using assembly or machine language can produce programs which execute very quickly. But low-level languages do not give the programmer much help in designing the program as a whole, at a more abstract level. Moreover, in many programs execution time is not important enough to be worth the extra effort that low-level programming requires.

On the other hand, Modula-2 programs are relatively easy to understand and are therefore easier to write, read, test, and modify. This means that time and effort will likely be saved during the writing and debugging. Also it will be much easier to avoid including unnecessary work in the computations performed by even relatively small Modula-2 programs. The main cost paid for this ability to work at a higher level where one has a better idea of the overall structure of a program is the work required to compile the program. Small blocks of translated Modula-2 code may also run more slowly than functionally equivalent code written by a good low-level programmer.

Modula-2 helps programmers write programs which are efficient by making it easier to produce programs which are easy to understand and modify. Ideally, these programs are efficient because they do only the work that must be done to get the problem solved. It is much easier to spot a computation which could be pulled out of a loop, for instance, if one is programming in a high-level language. Programmers can concern themselves more with the algorithms applicable to a given problem and less with details particular to the machine. Porting programs is done more efficiently because it is much easier to modify a Modula-2 program that runs on one machine to run on another than it is to move a low-level program between different machines.

Durability

Ideally, a program should not simply terminate when an incorrect value arises during a computation. The program should be able to recover and continue execution. For instance, a program which solves quadratic equations by simply using the assignment Root1 := (−B + sqrt(B * B − 4.0 * A * C)) / 2.0 * A; will crash if A equals zero or if the quantity in the call to sqrt is negative. The solution, of course, is to test for these conditions before applying the formula. In general, it is a good idea to handle exceptional inputs like A = 0 separately whenever failure to do so could terminate the program midway through its execution. Summary 15-5 provides a list of ways to improve a program's durability, i.e., its ability to continue execution whenever possible.

SUMMARY 15-5   Ways to improve a program's
durability

1. Take advantage of Modula-2's short-circuit evaluation of logical expressions. Expressions which might not be defined should only be placed in positions in which their evaluation occurs only if a suitable "guardian" condition is satisfied. For instance, if String is a formal ARRAY OF CHAR parameter and Index is nonnegative, the evaluation of

((Index <= HIGH(String)) AND (String[Index] <> NULLChar))

will never result in an attempt to access an element whose index is out of bounds for the array String. Similarly, the evaluation of

((A = 0) OR (3.0/A <= MaxLength))

will never cause a run-time division by zero.

2. Try to trap improper values rather than proceeding with the computation and risking a run-time error or an incorrect result. See the functions Null, Car, Cdr in Listing 13-2 for an example.

3. Whenever a subprogram could fail, include a (BOOLEAN) parameter which indicates whether the call was successful. See COPIEDString in Listing 11-3 and ADDNameToList in Listing 12-2 for examples. Check the values of these parameters before proceeding with any computation which assumes that the subprogram calls were successful.

4. Whenever you have a program ask a user for input, make it clear what type of value is expected. This could be done by giving examples of appropriate values and/or describing the purpose of the input.

Associated with durability is the idea of error messages. You can save yourself a lot of grief during debugging if you try to include error prevention and detection throughout each program as you are writing it. Have the programs you write send you as explicit an error message as possible before they crash, especially if your debugger is not particularly sophisticated or easy to use. Trying to do this will also make you aware of errors that can be detected early enough to prevent a crash, such as pointers that might be NIL.

Portability

One of the best ways to improve portability is to program in a high-level language like Modula-2. The problem of producing object code which fits the quirks of a particular machine then becomes almost entirely the responsibility of the compiler. If it is easy to find and determine the purpose of machine- and implementation-dependent objects in a program, it will also be easier to port the program to a different machine. In particular, machine- or implementation-dependent values should not be embedded in the program. Instead, they should be given appropriate names and declared as constants at the top of the program. Also, some easily seen comments nearby should make it obvious that these values are system-dependent and should provide any appropriate additional information.

Most of the machine-dependent constructs in Modula-2 must be imported from the module SYSTEM, so any module which imports from SYSTEM should be considered to be machine-dependent. However, it is not necessary to import anything from SYSTEM in order to specify an absolute storage address for a variable. Any such declaration should be clearly marked by an appropriate comment. It might also be wise to note the machine-dependency at the top of the module. Note also that different machines may use a different number of bits to represent numeric values. Any program module which assumes a 32-bit representation for REAL, for instance, should be clearly commented to that effect. Finally, one should generally favor the use of pointers to implement opaque types. Although other types might be allowed on a particular system, pointers are the only types which will always be supported as opaque types.

Availability

Whenever a data structure, procedure, or function might be useful to programs other than the one being written, the programmer should consider pulling it out of the program or implementation module at hand and creating a new definition/implementation module pair which exports it for general use. Modula-2's lack of string-handling facilities is not a severe problem, for instance, because it is relatively easy to write whatever subprograms are desired and add them to a library which is available to all users. It would be foolish to embed the string-handling procedures in a single program or implementation module because there are so many programs which could make good use of them. See Listings 9-1, 9-2 and 9-3 for examples of what a monolithic program module looks like before and after being split into a smaller main module and some library module pairs.

16

An Example:
A Pattern Matcher

This chapter presents a practical example to illustrate the use of the Modula-2 constructs discussed so far. Using the algorithms published in Aho and Corasick (1975), a pattern matching program is fully implemented. This program accepts a finite list of key words and an arbitrary file of text as input. The program then scans the text file and informs the user of the positions at which key words are found in the text. With some minor changes, this program can be modified to perform a number of useful tasks. For instance, researchers at Bell Laboratories have used one such tailored program to locate all citations in a cumulative citation index which satisfy some boolean function of key words, e.g., to retrieve all titles which contain both of the key words "register" and "allocation."

The Algorithms

Aho and Corasick provide three algorithms which need to be implemented to build a pattern matching machine; these are shown in Figures 16-1, 16-2, and 16-3. They have been restated so that their resemblance to Modula-2 source code is much stronger than in Aho and Corasick (1975). Readers who are particularly interested in pattern matching should note that Wirth (1984) describes another text search algorithm which may be more efficient than Aho and Corasick's for long pieces of text.

The main program which scans the text and informs the user whenever a key word is found is an implementation of Algorithm 1 in Figure 16-1. The goto and failure functions referred to in Algorithm 1 may be constructed using Algorithms 2 and 3 in Figures 16-2 and 16-3, respectively. Construction of the output function used in Algorithm 1 is begun by Algorithm 2 and completed by Algorithm 3.

The behavior of the pattern matcher may be modeled using a finite state machine. Finite state machines consist of "states" and "transitions" and are often represented using "directed graphs" such as the one in Figure 16-4; this particular directed graph also represents a goto function constructed with Algorithm 2. The states of this particular finite state machine are numbered from 0 to 9. The transitions are represented by directed arcs which are labeled with characters. For instance, the arc labeled H from state 0 to state 1 in Figure 16-4 indicates that the finite state machine makes a transition to state 1 if it is given an H when it is in state 0. If it is given an S in state 0, this machine makes a transition to state 3. Any other letter causes a transition from state 0 back to itself.

The pattern matching machine implemented in Modula-2 processes a text string T by successively reading ASCII characters from the file containing T, making state transitions, and emitting output when appropriate. The goto and failure functions constructed with Algorithms 2 and 3 in Figures 16-2 and 16-3 are used by the pattern matching

```
Input:  A text string T, a goto function G, a failure function F,
   and an output function, as described in this chapter.
Output: The locations at which the key words represented by
   the goto and failure functions appear in the text string.
Pseudo-code:
   BEGIN
      State := 0;
      FOR each succesive symbol NextChar in T DO
         WHILE G(State, NextChar) = Fail DO
            State := F(State);
         END;
         State := G(State, NextChar);
         IF Output(State) <> empty THEN
            WRITE "Key word:";
            WRITE Output(State);
            WRITE "At position:";
            WRITE position;
         END; (* IF key word found *)
      END; (* loop through text string *)
   END; (* of search for key words in T *)
```

Figure 16-1   Algorithm 1, the pattern matching machine.

machine to determine which state to move into, given the current state and the next character in the text string.

State 0 is called the "starting state" since this is the state the pattern matching machine begins in. Figure 16-4 shows the functions used by a pattern matching machine for the set of key words {HE, SHE, HIS, HERS}. Suppose that T is the string "THIS IS HERS." The pattern matching machine will operate in the following fashion. It begins in state 0 and reads the first character in the text string. Since this is a

```
Input:  Set of key words
Output: Goto function G and a partially completed output
        function called Output.
Assumptions: Output(S) is empty when state S is first created;
        G(S, Char) is initially equal to Fail for all Char and all S.
Pseudo-code:
    PROCEDURE Enter(KeyWord);
    (* used in construction of goto function G *)
    BEGIN
      State := 0;
      J := 0;
      WHILE G(State, KeyWord[J]) <> Fail DO
        State := G(State, KeyWord[J]);
        INC(J);
      END; (* WHILE *)
      FOR P := J TO HIGH(KeyWord) DO
        INC(NewState);
        set G(State, KeyWord[P]) to NewState;
        State := NewState;
      END; (* FOR *)
      set Output(State) to KeyWord;
    END Enter;

    BEGIN (* construction of goto function G *)
      NewState := 0;
      FOR each key word KeyWord DO
        Enter(KeyWord);
      END;
      FOR every Char that could appear in the text string T DO
        IF G(0, Char) = Fail THEN
          set G(0, Char) to 0;
        END; (* IF *)
      END (* FOR *)
    END; (* of construction of goto function G *)
```

Figure 16-2   Algorithm 2, construction of the goto
function.

T and there is an arc from state 0 to state 0 in the goto graph for every letter except H and S, the machine "moves" to state 0. Output(0) is empty, so no output is emitted.

Next, the machine will read an H and move to state 1. Then the I will take the machine to state 6, and the S will take it to state 7. Since Output(7) is not empty, the machine will print HIS at this point. There are no transitions at all from state 7, so the goto function does not tell the machine what state to move to after reading the next character from T. Whenever the pattern matching machine reads a character for which there is no arc in the goto graph that leaves the current state, the machine consults the failure function to determine which state to

```
Input:   Goto function G and output function Output
         from Algorithm 2.
Output:  Failure function F and completed output function Output.
Pseudo-code:
  BEGIN
    Queue := empty;
    FOR each Char that could appear in the text string T DO
      S := G(0, Char);
      IF S <> 0 THEN
        add S to the end of the Queue;
        set F(S) to 0;
      END; (* IF *)
    END; (* FOR *)
    WHILE Queue <> empty DO
      let R be the state at the front of the Queue;
      remove R from the Queue;
      FOR each Char that could appear in the text string T DO
        S := G(R, Char);
        IF S <> Fail THEN
          add S to the end of the Queue;
          State := F(R);
          WHILE G(State, Char) = Fail DO
            State := F(State);
          END; (* WHILE *)
          set F(S) to G(State, Char);
          add Output(F(S)) to Output(S);
        END; (* IF *)
      END; (* FOR *)
    END; (* WHILE *)
  END; (* construction of the failure function *)
```

Figure 16-3   Algorithm 3, construction of the failure function.

Goto function:

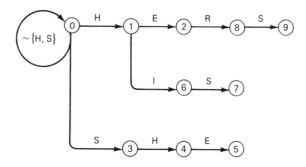

Failure function:

S	1	2	3	4	5	6	7	8	9
F(S)	0	0	0	1	2	0	3	0	3

Output function:

S	Output(S)
2	{HE}
5	{SHE, HE}
7	{HIS}
9	{HERS}

Figure 16-4   The pattern matching functions for keywords {HE, SHE, HIS, HERS}.

move to. For instance, after reading the first blank in "THIS IS HERS" and failing to find an arc labeled " " from state 7, the pattern matching machine moves to state F(7) = 3.

After this, the machine looks for an arc from state 3 labeled with a blank. When no such arc is found, the machine moves to state F(3) = 0. Here one of the "catchall" arcs is used; it is essential that an arc leaves state 0 for every possible character in the text string. The arc labeled I from state 0 leaves the machine in that state, but the S moves it to state 3. Then the second blank moves the machine back to state F(3) = 0. The final HERS will move the machine through states 1 and 2, where HE will be output, and then through states 8 and 9, where HERS will be output.

Dividing the Program into Modules

The first problem facing a programmer who is trying to implement Algorithms 1, 2, and 3 is how to represent the goto, failure, and output functions in Modula-2. Figure 16-4 suggests implementing the failure function by using a simple array of states, i.e., a variable FAILArray which is declared as an ARRAY[1..MAXVertices] OF CARDINAL. The failure function should return one of the array elements: F(State) will equal FAILArray[State]. MAXVertices is the maximum number of vertices the corresponding goto graph can have since one slot is needed in FAILArray for each state, i.e., for each vertex in the goto graph. The example of Figure 16-4 also points out that the output of a state is a set of strings, so the output function will be represented using an ARRAY [0..MAXVertices] OF SETOfString.

The goto function, however, is most easily viewed as a graph. Graphs may be represented as arrays of "adjacency lists." To do this, the vertices of the graph are numbered from 0 to MAXVertices. Conceptually, the Jth element of an array which represents a directed graph is a list of the vertices one can travel to directly from vertex J. In the present instance, the arcs of our graph are not only directed but also labeled with characters. Accordingly, the adjacency list for vertex J must include not only the number of each vertex adjacent to J but also the labels of the intervening arcs. An adjacency list representation of the subgraph that was obtained from the goto graph of Figure 16-4 by temporarily ignoring all the transitions from starting state 0 to itself is shown in Figure 16-5.

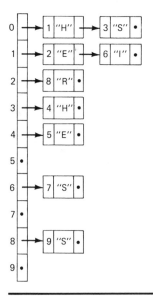

Figure 16-5 An adjacency list representation
of a subgraph of the goto graph in Figure 16.4.

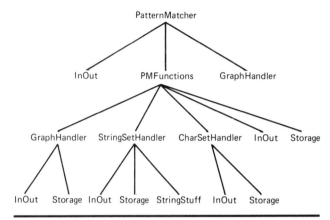

Figure 16-6   The import tree headed by PatternMatcher.

Once the representations of the main functions needed by the pattern matching machine have been chosen, it is possible to divide the program into a number of different modules. Skipping the trial and error portion of the programming task and moving directly to the results, the reader will find that the implementation presented consists of nine new modules. Use is also made of the common library modules InOut and Storage and the library module StringStuff, which was presented earlier. The main module, which is the program module at the root of the import tree shown in Figure 16-6, is called Pattern-Matcher. The code for PatternMatcher is shown in Listing 16-1. The other eight new modules are the definitions and implementations of PMFunctions, GraphHandler, StringSetHandler, and CharSet-Handler. PatternMatcher contains the implementation of the pattern matching machine described by Algorithm 1 in Figure 16-1.

LISTING 16-1   *An implementation of the pattern matching machine*
described by Algorithm 1 in Figure 16-1.

```
MODULE PatternMatcher;
    FROM InOut        IMPORT READCharacter, WRITEString, WRITELine,
                             INPUTFile, OPENInput, CLOSEInput, DONE,
                             WRITECardinal;
    FROM PMFunctions  IMPORT GOTO, FAILURE, FAIL, OUTPUTExists,
                             PRINTOutput;
    FROM GraphHandler IMPORT MAXVertices;

    CONST NEWLine = 36C;
    VAR STATE,
```

LISTING 16-1   Continued

```
      LINENumber,
      CHARNumber: CARDINAL;
      NEXTChar,
      CONTINUE   : CHAR;
      MOREText   : BOOLEAN;

   PROCEDURE OpenTextFile;
   BEGIN
     WRITELine;
     WRITEString("Which file should be scanned for key words?");
     OPENInput("");
     IF NOT DONE THEN
       WRITELine;
       WRITEString("Could not open text file");
     END; (* IF *)
   END OpenTextFile;

   PROCEDURE EmitOutput;
   BEGIN
     WRITELine;
     WRITEString("Key word: ");
     PRINTOutput(STATE);
     WRITELine;
     WRITEString(" Line Number: ");
     WRITECardinal(LINENumber, 6);
     WRITEString(" Character: ");
     WRITECardinal(CHARNumber,6);
     WRITELine;
   END EmitOutput;

BEGIN (* main body of pattern matching machine *)
   STATE := 0;
   CHARNumber := 0;
   LINENumber := 0;
     MOREText := TRUE;
     LOOP (* through text files *)
       OpenTextFile;
       WRITELine;
       WRITEString("Processing input...");
       READCharacter(NEXTChar);
       WHILE DONE DO (* more of current text file to scan *)
         IF NEXTChar = NEWLine THEN
           INC(LINENumber);
           CHARNumber := 0;
         END; (* IF new line *)
         WHILE GOTO(STATE, NEXTChar) = FAIL DO
```

```
         STATE := FAILURE(STATE);
      END; (* WHILE *)
      STATE := GOTO(STATE, NEXTChar);
      IF OUTPUTExists(STATE) THEN
         EmitOutput;
      END; (* IF *)
      READCharacter(NEXTChar);
      INC(CHARNumber);
    END; (* WHILE not at end of current text file *)
    CLOSEInput;
    WRITELine;
    WRITEString("Do you wish to scan another file ");
    WRITEString("for the same key words?");
    READCharacter(CONTINUE);
    IF ((CONTINUE <> "y") AND (CONTINUE <> "Y")) THEN
       WRITEString(" No.");
       EXIT;
    END; (* IF done scanning with current set of key words *)
  END; (* LOOP through some number of text files, scanning *)
      (* each for the key words provided by the user       *)
END PatternMatcher.
```

The code for PMFunctions is shown in Listings 16-2 and 16-3. The goto, failure, and output functions are created in PMFunctions during the initialization of its implementation module and exported so that they can be used in PatternMatcher. The fact that initializations of imported modules are executed before the importer begins to run is essential in this case. PMFunctions makes use of GraphHandler, StringSetHandler, and CharSetHandler while it builds the goto, failure, and output functions. All three of these pairs of library modules contain subprograms which are exported but not yet implemented. The reason for this is to minimize recompilations of their definition modules in the event that the unimplemented subprograms are needed in the future. The reader will recall that on some systems the recompilation of a definition module forces one to recompile all the modules which use imports from that definition module.

GraphHandler, shown in Listings 16-4 and 16-5, is used by procedure BuildGotoFunction in PMFunctions to build the graph which represents the goto function; BuildGotoFunction is the implementation of Algorithm 2 in Figure 16-2. The code for the StringSetHandler modules is shown in Listings 16-6 and 16-7. StringSetHandler is used both by BuildGotoFunction and by procedure BuildFailureFunction since construction of the output function is begun by the one and finished by the other. BuildFailureFunction is the implementation of Algorithm 3 in Figure 16-3.

LISTING 16-2 *An implementation of Algorithms 2 and 3 in Figures 16-2 and 16-3, respectively; exports goto, failure, and output functions used by pattern matching machines, part 1.*

```
DEFINITION MODULE PMFunctions;
  (* Exports functions for use by pattern matching machines *)
  FROM GraphHandler IMPORT MAXVertices;
  EXPORT QUALIFIED GOTO, FAILURE, FAIL, OUTPUTExists, PRINTOutput;

  CONST FAIL = (MAXVertices + 2);

  PROCEDURE GOTO(CurrentState: CARDINAL; Input: CHAR): CARDINAL;
  (* Tells the pattern matching machine which state to move to    *)
  (* after reading the next symbol from the text string which is  *)
  (* being scanned for key words.                                 *)
  PROCEDURE FAILURE(CurrentState: CARDINAL): CARDINAL;
  (* Must be used to determine state transitions when the GOTO    *)
  (* function returns FAIL.                                       *)
  PROCEDURE OUTPUTExists(CurrentState: CARDINAL): BOOLEAN;
  (* Returns TRUE when a key word has just been recognized.       *)
  PROCEDURE PRINTOutput(CurrentState: CARDINAL);
  (* Prints any key words which have been recognized as a result  *)
  (* of the pattern matching machine's transition to CurrentState.*)
END PMFunctions.
```

LISTING 16-3 *An implementation of Algorithms 2 and 3 in Figures 16-2 and 16-3, respectively; exports goto, failure, and output functions used by pattern matching machines, part 2.*

```
IMPLEMENTATION MODULE PMFunctions;
  FROM GraphHandler      IMPORT MAXVertices, GRAPH, INITGraph,
                                ADDEDArc, ARCExists;
  FROM CharSetHandler    IMPORT SETOfChar, INITCharSet, ISInCharSet,
                                ADDToCharSet;
  FROM StringSetHandler IMPORT SETOfString, INITStringSet, ISInStringSet,
                                ADDToStringSet, ADDStringSets,
                                NEXTStringSetElement, STRINGSetIsEmpty,
                                PRINTStringSetElement, MAXStringLength;
  FROM InOut             IMPORT INPUTFile, WRITELine, WRITEString,
                                READCharacter, OPENInput, CLOSEInput,
                                DONE, WRITECardinal;
  FROM Storage           IMPORT ALLOCATE, DEALLOCATE;

  CONST NULLChar = 0C; (* The ends of strings of length n which are  *)
```

```
                    (* stored in arrays of length m > n are always *)
                    (* marked by a final NULLChar.                  *)
VAR  GOTOGraph    : GRAPH;
     OUTPUTS      : ARRAY[0..MAXVertices] OF SETOfString;
     FAILArray    : ARRAY[1..MAXVertices] OF CARDINAL;
     WHITESpace   : SETOfChar;
     I            : CARDINAL; (* loop index *)
     CH           : CHAR;     (* loop index *)
     INITIALIZING: BOOLEAN;

PROCEDURE GreetUser;
BEGIN
  WRITELine;
  WRITEString("This program scans the text files indicated for any");
  WRITELine;
  WRITEString("of the key words in a list which is provided by");
  WRITELine;
  WRITEString("you. The key word and its position in the text are");
  WRITELine;
  WRITEString("output whenever a key word is found.");
  WRITELine;
END GreetUser;

PROCEDURE OpenKeyWordsFile;
BEGIN
  WRITELine;
  WRITEString("Which file contains the list of key words? ");
  OPENInput("");
  IF NOT DONE THEN
    WRITELine;
    WRITEString("Cannot open file of key words.");
    HALT;
  END; (* IF file not opened *)
END OpenKeyWordsFile;

PROCEDURE ReadKeyWord(VAR KeyWord: ARRAY OF CHAR);
(* Used by BuildGotoFunction to get key words from input file. *)
  VAR Ch: CHAR;
      I : CARDINAL;
BEGIN
  I := 0;
  READCharacter(Ch); (* Assumes input file containing key words has *)
              (* already been opened by a call to OpenKeyWordsFile.*)
  WHILE ((DONE) AND (ISInCharSet(Ch, WHITESpace))) DO
    READCharacter(Ch);
  END; (* WHILE not at the end of the file and there are more tabs, *)
      (* newline characters, and so forth to skip                  *)
```

LISTING 16-3   Continued

```
WHILE ((DONE) AND (NOT ISInCharSet(Ch, WHITESpace)) AND
       (I <= HIGH(KeyWord))) DO
    KeyWord[I] := Ch;
    INC(I);
    READCharacter(Ch);
END; (* WHILE more of current key word to read *)
IF I > HIGH(KeyWord) THEN
    WRITELine;
    WRITEString("Key word too long: ");
    WRITEString(KeyWord);
ELSE
    IF I < HIGH(KeyWord) THEN
        KeyWord[I] := NULLChar;
    END; (* IF end of key word should be marked by null char instead *)
            (* of by being the last element in the array KeyWord    *)
END; (* IF Key word too long *)
END ReadKeyWord;

PROCEDURE BuildGotoFunction;
(* Implementation of Algorithm 2 in Figure 16-2 in the text.    *)
    VAR NewState   : CARDINAL;
        Ch         : CHAR;
        NextKeyWord: ARRAY[1..MAXStringLength] OF CHAR;
        TransitionAdded: BOOLEAN;

    PROCEDURE Enter(KeyWord: ARRAY OF CHAR);
    (* Used by BuildGotoFunction to add a path corresponding to *)
    (* KeyWord to the GOTOGraph.                                *)
        VAR TransitionAdded: BOOLEAN;
            J, P, State   : CARDINAL;
    BEGIN
        IF KeyWord[0] <> NULLChar THEN (* KeyWord is not empty *)
            State := 0;
            J := 0;
            WHILE (GOTO(State, KeyWord[J]) <> FAIL) DO
                State := GOTO(State, KeyWord[J]);
                INC(J);
            END; (* WHILE *)
            P := J;
            WHILE ((P <= HIGH(KeyWord)) AND (KeyWord[P] <> NULLChar)) DO
                INC(NewState);
                TransitionAdded:=ADDEDArc(State,NewState,GOTOGraph,KeyWord[P]);
                IF NOT TransitionAdded THEN
                    WRITELine;
                    WRITEString("PMFunctions.Enter: could not add arc ");
```

```
              HALT;
            END; (* IF *)
          State := NewState;
          INC(P);
        END; (* WHILE more of KeyWord to enter in GOTOGraph *)
        ADDToStringSet(KeyWord, OUTPUTS[State]);
      END; (* IF KeyWord array contains string of length > 0 *)
  END Enter;

BEGIN (* BuildGotoFunction *)
  NewState := 0;
  ReadKeyWord(NextKeyWord);
  WHILE DONE DO
    Enter(NextKeyWord);
    ReadKeyWord(NextKeyWord);
  END; (* WHILE not at end of file *)
  (* Add 'catch-all' transitions from starting state 0 to itself *)
  FOR Ch := 0C TO 127C DO
    IF GOTO(0, Ch) = FAIL THEN
      TransitionAdded := ADDEDArc(0, 0, GOTOGraph, Ch);
      IF NOT TransitionAdded THEN
        WRITELine;
        WRITEString("PMFunctions.BuildGotoFunction: ");
        WRITEString("could not add 'catch-all' arc ");
        HALT;
      END; (* IF NOT TransitionAdded *)
    END; (* IF no arc labelled Ch leaves state 0 *)
  END; (* FOR all ASCII characters *)
END BuildGotoFunction;

PROCEDURE GOTO(CurrentState: CARDINAL; Input: CHAR): CARDINAL;
(* Tells the pattern matching machine which state to move to    *)
(* after reading the next symbol from the text string which is  *)
(* being scanned for key words.                                 *)
  VAR I: CARDINAL;
BEGIN
  I := 0;
  WHILE ((I <= MAXVertices) AND
         (NOT ARCExists(CurrentState, I, GOTOGraph, Input))) DO
    INC(I);
  END;
  IF I > MAXVertices THEN
    IF ((CurrentState = 0) AND (NOT INITIALIZING)) THEN
      RETURN 0;
    ELSE
      RETURN FAIL;
    END; (* IF *)
  ELSE
```

LISTING 16-3   Continued

```
    RETURN I;
    END;
END GOTO;

PROCEDURE BuildFailureFunction;
(* Implementation of Algorithm 3 in Figure 16-3 in the text.    *)
(* The following two types are used in the maintenance of the    *)
(* Queue of state which is called for.                           *)
  TYPE PtrToStateQEntry = POINTER TO StateQEntry;
  TYPE StateQEntry      = RECORD
                           Value: CARDINAL;
                           Next : PtrToStateQEntry;
                           END; (* StateQEntry *)

  VAR Queue, Temp,
      LastAdded  : PtrToStateQEntry;
      NextChar   : CHAR;
      S, R, State: CARDINAL;

  PROCEDURE AddSToStateQueue;
  (* Uses variables declared in BuildFailureFunction *)
  BEGIN
    NEW(Temp);
    Temp↑.Next := NIL;
    Temp↑.Value := S;
    IF LastAdded <> NIL THEN
      LastAdded↑.Next := Temp;
    END; (* IF Queue is not empty *)
    IF Queue = NIL THEN
      Queue := Temp;
    END; (* IF Queue is empty put newly created element at front *)
    LastAdded := Temp;
  END AddSToStateQueue;

BEGIN (* BuildFailureFunction *)
  Queue := NIL;
  LastAdded := NIL;
  FOR NextChar := 0C TO 127C DO
    S := GOTO(0, NextChar);
    IF S <> 0 THEN
      AddSToStateQueue;
      FAILArray[S] := 0;
    END; (* IF S <> 0 *)
  END; (* FOR each ASCII character *)
  WHILE Queue <> NIL DO
```

```
        (* get the next state from the Queue *)
        Temp := Queue;
        R := Queue↑.Value;
        Queue := Queue↑.Next;
        DISPOSE(Temp);
        FOR NextChar := 0C TO 127C DO
          S := GOTO(R, NextChar);
          IF S <> FAIL THEN
            AddSToStateQueue;
            State := FAILArray[R];
            WHILE GOTO(State, NextChar) = FAIL DO
              State := FAILArray[State];
            END; (* WHILE *)
            FAILArray[S] := GOTO(State, NextChar);
            ADDStringSets(OUTPUTS[S], OUTPUTS[FAILArray[S]]);
          END; (* IF  S <> FAIL *)
        END; (* FOR each ASCII character *)
      END; (* WHILE Queue <> NIL *)
  END BuildFailureFunction;


  PROCEDURE FAILURE(CurrentState: CARDINAL): CARDINAL;
  (* Must be used to determine state transitions when the GOTO    *)
  (* function returns FAIL.                                       *)
  BEGIN
    RETURN FAILArray[CurrentState];
  END FAILURE;


  PROCEDURE OUTPUTExists(CurrentState: CARDINAL): BOOLEAN;
  (* Returns TRUE when a key word has just been recognized.       *)
  BEGIN
    RETURN (NOT STRINGSetIsEmpty(OUTPUTS[CurrentState]));
  END OUTPUTExists;


  PROCEDURE PRINTOutput(CurrentState: CARDINAL);
  (* Prints any key words which have been recognized as a result  *)
  (* of the pattern matching machine's transition to CurrentState.*)
    VAR NextString: SETOfString;
  BEGIN
    NextString := OUTPUTS[CurrentState];
    WHILE (NOT STRINGSetIsEmpty(NextString)) DO
      PRINTStringSetElement(NextString);
      NextString := NEXTStringSetElement(NextString);
    END; (* WHILE more elements of OUTPUTS[CurrentState] to print *)
  END PRINTOutput;

BEGIN (* Main body of module Functions *)
  INITIALIZING := TRUE;
```

LISTING 16-3   Continued

```
GreetUser;
INITGraph(GOTOGraph);
INITCharSet(WHITESpace);
FOR I := 0 TO MAXVertices DO
  INITStringSet(OUTPUTS[I]);
END; (* initialize output sets to be empty *)
FOR CH := 0C TO " " DO
  ADDToCharSet(CH, WHITESpace);
END; (* FOR *)
OpenKeyWordsFile;
WRITELine;
WRITEString("Building goto function...");
BuildGotoFunction;
WRITELine;
WRITEString("Building failure function...");
BuildFailureFunction;
CLOSEInput; (* closes file containing list of key words *)
INITIALIZING := FALSE;
END PMFunctions.
```

LISTING 16-4 *Library module which exports data type* **GRAPH** *and some associated subprograms, part 1.*

```
DEFINITION MODULE GraphHandler;
  EXPORT QUALIFIED MAXVertices, GRAPH, INITGraph, ADDEDArc,
                   ARCExists, PRINTGraph;
  TYPE GRAPH;
  CONST MAXVertices = 250;

  PROCEDURE INITGraph( VAR SomeGraph: GRAPH );
  (* Initializes SomeGraph to the empty graph; all GRAPHs should *)
  (* be initialized before use.                                  *)
  PROCEDURE ADDEDArc( FromVertex, ToVertex: CARDINAL;
                            VAR InGraph: GRAPH;
                              ArcLabel: CHAR ): BOOLEAN;
  (* Tries to add an arc as indicated. Returns FALSE if either  *)
  (* vertex number is greater than MAXVertices.                 *)
  PROCEDURE ARCExists( FromVertex, ToVertex: CARDINAL;
                             InGraph: GRAPH;
                           WithLabel: CHAR ): BOOLEAN;
  (* Returns TRUE if the arc indicated exists in InGraph.  *)
  (* Returns FALSE otherwise.                              *)
  PROCEDURE PRINTGraph( SomeGraph: GRAPH );
  (* Prints the indicated graph; see implementation for format. *)
END GraphHandler.
```

LISTING 16-5 *Library module which implements data type GRAPH and some associated subprograms, part 2.*

```
IMPLEMENTATION MODULE GraphHandler;
  FROM Storage IMPORT ALLOCATE;
  FROM InOut   IMPORT WRITELine, WRITEString;


  CONST NULLChar = 0C;


  TYPE NODEPointer = POINTER TO NODE;
  TYPE NODE        = RECORD
                        VertexID: CARDINAL;
                        InArcID : CHAR;
                        Next    : NODEPointer;
                     END; (* NODE RECORD *)
  TYPE ONESizeOfGraph = ARRAY[0..MAXVertices] OF NODEPointer;
  TYPE GRAPH          = POINTER TO ONESizeOfGraph;


  PROCEDURE INITGraph( VAR SomeGraph: GRAPH );
  (* Initializes SomeGraph to the empty graph; all GRAPHs should *)
  (* be initialized before use.                                  *)
    VAR I: CARDINAL;
  BEGIN
    NEW(SomeGraph);
    FOR I := 0 TO MAXVertices DO
      SomeGraph↑[I] := NIL;
    END; (* FOR *)
  END INITGraph;


  PROCEDURE ADDEDArc( FromVertex, ToVertex: CARDINAL;
                      VAR InGraph: GRAPH;
                      ArcLabel: CHAR ): BOOLEAN;
  (* Tries to add an arc as indicated. Returns FALSE if either *)
  (* vertex number is greater than MAXVertices.                *)
    VAR Temp, TempTwo: NODEPointer;
  BEGIN
    IF ((FromVertex > MAXVertices) OR (ToVertex > MAXVertices)) THEN
      WRITELine;
      WRITEString("GraphHandler.ADDEDArc: Vertex out of range");
      RETURN FALSE;
    ELSE (* check to see if the arc is already in the graph *)
      IF InGraph↑[FromVertex] <> NIL THEN
        Temp := InGraph↑[FromVertex];
        IF ((Temp↑.VertexID = ToVertex) AND
            (Temp↑.InArcID = ArcLabel)) THEN
           (* arc to add is already in graph, represented by the *)
           (* first element of FromVertex's adjacency list       *)
```

LISTING 16-5 Continued

```
    RETURN TRUE;
    ELSE (* Look for the arc in the rest of the adjacency list *)
      WHILE ((Tempt.Next <> NIL) AND
             ((Tempt.VertexID <> ToVertex) OR
              (Tempt.InArcID <> ArcLabel))) DO
        Temp := Tempt.Next;
      END; (* WHILE still looking and not at end of list *)
      IF Tempt.Next = NIL THEN (* have reached end of list *)
        IF ((Tempt.VertexID <> ToVertex) OR
            (Tempt.InArcID <> ArcLabel)) THEN
          (* arc is not represented by last element of list, so it *)
          (* is not in the graph; go ahead and add it              *)
          NEW(TempTwo);
          Tempt.Next := TempTwo;
          TempTwot.VertexID := ToVertex;
          TempTwot.InArcID := ArcLabel;
          TempTwot.Next := NIL;
          RETURN TRUE;
        ELSE (* arc is last in list *)
          RETURN TRUE;
        END; (* IF arc is not last in list *)
      ELSE (* must have found arc in list *)
        RETURN TRUE;
      END; (* IF at end of list *)
    END; (* IF arc is at first of adjacency list *)
  ELSE (* add arc as first in FromVertex's adjacency list *)
    NEW(Temp);
    Tempt.VertexID := ToVertex;
    Tempt.InArcID := ArcLabel;
    Tempt.Next := NIL;
    InGrapht[FromVertex] := Temp;
    RETURN TRUE;
  END; (* IF there are any arcs leaving FromVertex *)
  END; (* IF Vertex out of range *)
END ADDEDArc;

PROCEDURE ARCExists( FromVertex, ToVertex: CARDINAL;
                                 InGraph: GRAPH;
                               WithLabel: CHAR ): BOOLEAN;
(* Returns TRUE if the arc indicated exists in InGraph.     *)
(* Returns FALSE otherwise.                                  *)
  VAR Temp: NODEPointer;
BEGIN
  IF InGrapht[FromVertex] = NIL THEN
    (* there are no arcs at all leaving FromVertex in InGraph *)
```

```
      RETURN FALSE;
    ELSE (* check the arcs which leave FromVertex *)
       Temp := InGrapht[FromVertex];
       WHILE ((Tempt.Next <> NIL) AND
              ((Tempt.VertexID <> ToVertex) OR
               (Tempt.InArcID <> WithLabel))) DO
          Temp := Tempt.Next;
       END; (* WHILE not at end of list and have not found desired arc *)
       IF Tempt.Next = NIL THEN (* at end of list *)
          IF ((Tempt.VertexID <> ToVertex) OR
              (Tempt.InArcID <> WithLabel)) THEN
             (* arc is not represented by last element of list *)
             RETURN FALSE;
          ELSE
             RETURN TRUE;
          END; (* IF arc is not last in list *)
       ELSE (* must have found arc in list before reaching end *)
          RETURN TRUE;
       END; (* IF at end of list *)
    END; (* IF there are any arcs leaving FromVertex *)
  END ARCExists;

  PROCEDURE PRINTGraph( SomeGraph: GRAPH );
  BEGIN
    WRITELine;
    WRITEString("GraphHandler.PRINTGraph not implemented");
  END PRINTGraph;

END GraphHandler.
```

LISTING 16-6 *Library module which exports data type* SETOfString *and some associated subprograms, part 1.*

```
DEFINITION MODULE StringSetHandler;
  EXPORT QUALIFIED SETOfString, INITStringSet, ISInStringSet,
                   ADDToStringSet, TAKEFromStringSet, ADDStringSets,
                   INTERSECTStringSets, NEXTStringSetElement,
                   STRINGSetIsEmpty, PRINTStringSetElement,
                   MAXStringLength;

  TYPE SETOfString; (* Implemented using unsorted linked lists; see   *)
                    (* NEXTStringSetElement and PRINTStringSetElement.*)

  CONST MAXStringLength = 15;
```

LISTING 16-6   Continued

```
PROCEDURE INITStringSet(VAR SomeSet: SETOfString);
(* Initializes SomeSet to the empty set; all SETOfString variables  *)
(* should be initialized before use.                                *)
PROCEDURE ISInStringSet( String: ARRAY OF CHAR;
                         SomeSet: SETOfString ): BOOLEAN;
(* Returns TRUE if String is an element of SomeSet; FALSE otherwise.*)
PROCEDURE ADDToStringSet( String: ARRAY OF CHAR;
                          VAR SomeSet: SETOfString );
(* Adds String to SomeSet.                                          *)
PROCEDURE TAKEFromStringSet( String: ARRAY OF CHAR;
                             VAR SomeSet: SETOfString );
(* Removes String from SomeSet.                                     *)
PROCEDURE ADDStringSets( VAR AddedTo: SETOfString;
                         NewElements: SETOfString );
(* Performs AddedTo := AddedTo + NewElements; where "+" denotes set *)
(* union.                                                           *)
PROCEDURE INTERSECTStringSets( VAR Result: SETOfString;
                              SomeSet: SETOfString );
(* Performs Result := Result*SomeSet; where "*" denotes set inter-  *)
(* section.                                                         *)
PROCEDURE NEXTStringSetElement( Previous: SETOfString ): SETOfString;
(* Returns (a pointer to) the next element after Previous in the    *)
(* same set Previous belongs to. Returns NIL if Previous is the     *)
(* "last" element of the set.                                       *)
PROCEDURE STRINGSetIsEmpty( SomeSet: SETOfString ): BOOLEAN;
PROCEDURE PRINTStringSetElement( SomeSet: SETOfString );
(* Prints the first element of SomeSet. To print all elements, call *)
(* PRINTStringSetElement repeatedly until STRINGSetIsEmpty = TRUE,  *)
(* using NEXTStringSetElement to get the (pointers to) successive   *)
(* elements which are passed to PRINTStringSetElement.              *)
END StringSetHandler.
```

LISTING 16-7 *Library module which implements data type* **SETOfString** *and some associated subprograms, part 2.*

```
IMPLEMENTATION MODULE StringSetHandler;
  FROM StringStuff IMPORT STRINGSAreEqual, COPIEDString;
  FROM Storage    IMPORT ALLOCATE;
  FROM InOut      IMPORT WRITELine, WRITEString;

  TYPE SETOfString = POINTER TO SETElementRecord;
  TYPE SETElementRecord = RECORD
                          Element: ARRAY[1..MAXStringLength] OF CHAR;
```

```
                Next   : SETOfString;
                END; (* SETElementRecord *)


PROCEDURE INITStringSet(VAR SomeSet: SETOfString);
(* Initializes SomeSet to the empty set; all SETOfString variables *)
(* should be initialized before use.                               *)
BEGIN
  SomeSet := NIL;
END INITStringSet;


PROCEDURE ISInStringSet( String: ARRAY OF CHAR;
                         SomeSet: SETOfString ): BOOLEAN;
(* Returns TRUE if String is an element of SomeSet; FALSE otherwise.*)
  VAR Temp: SETOfString;
BEGIN
  IF SomeSet = NIL THEN (* SomeSet is empty *)
    RETURN FALSE;
  ELSE
    Temp := SomeSet;
    WHILE ((Temp↑.Next <> NIL) AND
           (NOT STRINGSAreEqual(Temp↑.Element, String))) DO
      Temp := Temp↑.Next;
    END; (* WHILE String not found and not at end of element list *)
    IF Temp↑.Next = NIL THEN (* at end of linked list of elements *)
      IF STRINGSAreEqual(Temp↑.Element, String) THEN
        RETURN TRUE;
      ELSE
        RETURN FALSE;
      END; (* IF String is last element of SomeSet *)
    ELSE (* must have found String in list of elements *)
      RETURN TRUE;
    END; (* IF at end of element list *)
  END; (* IF SomeSet is empty *)
END ISInStringSet;


PROCEDURE ADDToStringSet( String: ARRAY OF CHAR;
                          VAR SomeSet: SETOfString );
(* Adds String to SomeSet.                                 *)
  VAR Temp, TempTwo: SETOfString;
      StringCopied : BOOLEAN;
BEGIN
  IF SomeSet = NIL THEN (* SomeSet is empty *)
    NEW(Temp);
    StringCopied := COPIEDString(String, Temp↑.Element);
    IF NOT StringCopied THEN
      WRITELine;
      WRITEString("StringSetHandler.ADDToStringSet: ");
```

LISTING 16-7   **Continued**

```
      WRITEString("SomeSet is empty; String not copied> ");
      WRITEString(String);
      HALT;
    END; (* IF NOT StringCopied *)
    Temp↑.Next := NIL;
    SomeSet := Temp;
  ELSE (* check to see if String is already an element of SomeSet *)
    Temp := SomeSet;
    WHILE ((Temp↑.Next <> NIL) AND
           (NOT STRINGSAreEqual(Temp↑.Element, String))) DO
      Temp := Temp↑.Next;
    END; (* WHILE String not found and not at end of element list *)
    IF Temp↑.Next = NIL THEN (* at end of linked list of elements *)
      IF NOT STRINGSAreEqual(Temp↑.Element, String) THEN
        (* must add String as last element of SomeSet *)
        NEW(TempTwo);
        StringCopied := COPIEDString(String, TempTwo↑.Element);
        IF NOT StringCopied THEN
          WRITELine;
          WRITEString("StringSetHandler.ADDToStringSet:
          WRITEString("String not copied> ");
          WRITEString(String);
          HALT;
        END; (* IF NOT StringCopied *)
        TempTwo↑.Next := NIL;
        Temp↑.Next := TempTwo;
      END; (* IF String is not last element of SomeSet *)
      (* ELSE must have found String in SomeSet *)
    END; (* IF at end list *)
  END; (* IF SomeSet is empty *)
END ADDToStringSet;


PROCEDURE TAKEFromStringSet( String: ARRAY OF CHAR;
                            VAR SomeSet: SETOfString );
(* Removes String from SomeSet.                              *)
BEGIN
  WRITELine;
  WRITEString("StringSetHandler.TAKEFromStringSet not implemented");
END TAKEFromStringSet;


PROCEDURE ADDStringSets( VAR AddedTo: SETOfString;
                         NewElements: SETOfString );
(* Performs AddedTo := AddedTo + NewElements; where "+" denotes set *)
(* union.                                                     *)
  VAR TempOne,
```

```
          TempTwo: SETOfString;
          Found  : BOOLEAN;
BEGIN
   IF AddedTo = NIL THEN
      AddedTo := NewElements;
   ELSIF NewElements = NIL THEN
      (* AddedTo := AddedTo;/ *)
      RETURN;
   ELSE (* neither set is empty *)
      TempOne := AddedTo;
      LOOP (* check each string in AddedTo to see if it is in   *)
           (* NewElements. If it is not, then add it to AddedTo.*)
         IF TempOne = NIL THEN EXIT; END; (* IF *)
         TempTwo := NewElements;
         Found := FALSE; (* assume string not yet found in NewElements *)
         IF STRINGSAreEqual(TempOne↑.Element, TempTwo↑.Element) THEN
            Found := TRUE;
         ELSE
            LOOP (* through NewElements *)
               IF TempTwo↑.Next = NIL THEN EXIT; END; (* IF *)
               IF STRINGSAreEqual(TempOne↑.Element, TempTwo↑.Element) THEN
                  Found := TRUE;
                  EXIT;
               ELSE
                  TempTwo := TempTwo↑.Next;
               END; (* IF current element of AddedTo found in NewElements *)
            END; (* LOOP through NewElements *)
         END; (* IF current element of AddedTo equals first element *)
              (* of NewElements.                                   *)
         IF NOT Found THEN
            ADDToStringSet(TempTwo↑.Element, AddedTo);
         END; (* IF NOT Found *)
         TempOne := TempOne↑.Next;
      END; (* LOOP through elements of AddedTo *)
   END; (* IF AddedTo is empty *)
END ADDStringSets;

PROCEDURE INTERSECTStringSets( VAR Result: SETOfString;
                                   SomeSet: SETOfString );
(* Performs Result := Result*SomeSet; where "*" denotes set inter-  *)
(* section.                                                         *)
BEGIN
   WRITELine;
   WRITEString("StringSetHandler.INTERSECTStringSets not implemented");
END INTERSECTStringSets;

PROCEDURE NEXTStringSetElement( Previous: SETOfString ): SETOfString;
```

LISTING 16-7   Continued

```
(* Returns (a pointer to) the next element after Previous in the    *)
(* same set Previous belongs to. Returns NIL if Previous is the     *)
(* "last" element of the set.                                       *)
BEGIN
  IF Previous = NIL THEN
    RETURN NIL;
  ELSE
    RETURN (Previous↑.Next);
  END; (* IF Previous is last element in set *)
END NEXTStringSetElement;


PROCEDURE STRINGSetIsEmpty( SomeSet: SETOfString ): BOOLEAN;
BEGIN
  RETURN (SomeSet = NIL);
END STRINGSetIsEmpty;


PROCEDURE PRINTStringSetElement( SomeSet: SETOfString );
(* Prints the first element of SomeSet. To print all elements, call *)
(* PRINTStringSetElement repeatedly until STRINGSetIsEmpty = TRUE,   *)
(* using NEXTStringSetElement to get the (pointers to) successive    *)
(* elements which are passed to PRINTStringSetElement.               *)
BEGIN
  WRITELine;
  WRITEString(SomeSet↑.Element);
END PRINTStringSetElement;


END StringSetHandler.
```

CharSetHandler, shown in Listings 16-8 and 16-9, is used by PM-Functions to create and work with sets of characters. This pair of library modules is interesting for two reasons. First, it implements a useful data type which one might have hoped would already exist, namely SET OF CHAR. Unfortunately, CHAR contains too many elements for SET OF CHAR to be legal on most systems, but CharSet-Handler helps remedy this problem. CharSetHandler is also worth notice because of its close resemblance to StringSetHandler (in Ada the two could be instantiations of the same generic package). Once the code for type SETOfString and its associated subprograms is written, a module which manages type SETOfChar is easy to produce because the algorithms and most of the actual implementation are the same as for SETOfString. PMFunctions makes use of a SETOfChar called WHITESpace, which contains ASCII characters that should be skipped while the list of key words is being read from the appropriate file.

LISTING 16-8 *Library module which exports data type* **SETOfChar** *and some associated subprograms, part 1.*

```
DEFINITION MODULE CharSetHandler;
    EXPORT QUALIFIED SETOfChar, INITCharSet, ISInCharSet,
                     ADDToCharSet, TAKEFromCharSet, ADDCharSets,
                     INTERSECTCharSets, NEXTCharSetElement,
                     CHARSetIsEmpty, PRINTCharSet;
    TYPE SETOfChar;

    PROCEDURE INITCharSet(VAR SomeSet: SETOfChar);
    (* Initializes SomeSet to the empty set; all SETOfChar variables    *)
    (* should be initialized before use.                                *)
    PROCEDURE ISInCharSet( Char: CHAR;
                           SomeSet: SETOfChar ): BOOLEAN;
    (* Returns TRUE if Char is an element of SomeSet; FALSE otherwise.   *)
    PROCEDURE ADDToCharSet( Char: CHAR;
                            VAR SomeSet: SETOfChar );
    (* Adds Char to SomeSet.                                            *)
    PROCEDURE TAKEFromCharSet( Char: CHAR;
                               VAR SomeSet: SETOfChar );
    (* Removes Char from SomeSet.                                       *)
    PROCEDURE ADDCharSets( VAR AddedTo: SETOfChar;
                           NewElements: SETOfChar );
    (* Performs AddedTo := AddedTo + NewElements; where "+" denotes set *)
    (* union.                                                           *)
    PROCEDURE INTERSECTCharSets( VAR Result: SETOfChar;
                                 SomeSet: SETOfChar );
    (* Performs Result := Result*SomeSet; where "*" denotes set inter-  *)
    (* section.                                                         *)
    PROCEDURE NEXTCharSetElement(Previous: CHAR; SomeSet: SETOfChar): CHAR;
    (* Returns the next element after Previous in SomeSet. Returns NIL  *)
    (* if Previous is the "last" element.                               *)
    PROCEDURE CHARSetIsEmpty( SomeSet: SETOfChar ): BOOLEAN;
    PROCEDURE PRINTCharSet( SomeSet: SETOfChar );
    (* Prints the elements of SomeSet.                                 *)
END CharSetHandler.
```

LISTING 16-9 *Library module which implements data type* **SETOfChar** *and some associated subprograms, part 2.*

```
IMPLEMENTATION MODULE CharSetHandler;
  FROM Storage     IMPORT ALLOCATE;
  FROM InOut       IMPORT WRITECharacter, WRITELine, WRITEString;

  TYPE SETOfChar = POINTER TO SETElementRecord;
  TYPE SETElementRecord = RECORD
                            Element: CHAR;
                            Next   : SETOfChar;
                          END; (* SETElementRecord *)

  PROCEDURE INITCharSet(VAR SomeSet: SETOfChar);
  (* Initializes SomeSet to the empty set; all SETOfChar variables   *)
  (* should be initialized before use.                               *)
  BEGIN
    SomeSet := NIL;
  END INITCharSet;

  PROCEDURE ISInCharSet( Char: CHAR;
                         SomeSet: SETOfChar ): BOOLEAN;
  (* Returns TRUE if Char is an element of SomeSet; FALSE otherwise.  *)
    VAR Temp: SETOfChar;
  BEGIN .
    IF SomeSet = NIL THEN (* SomeSet is empty *)
      RETURN FALSE;
    ELSE
      Temp := SomeSet;
      WHILE ((Temp↑.Next <> NIL) AND (Temp↑.Element <> Char)) DO
        Temp := Temp↑.Next;
      END; (* WHILE Char not found and not at end of list of elements *)
      IF Temp↑.Next = NIL THEN (* at end of linked list of elements *)
        IF Temp↑.Element = Char THEN
          RETURN TRUE;
        ELSE
          RETURN FALSE;
        END; (* IF Char is last element of SomeSet *)
      ELSE (* must have found Char in list of elements *)
        RETURN TRUE;
      END; (* IF at end of element list *)
    END; (* IF SomeSet is empty *)
  END ISInCharSet;

  PROCEDURE ADDToCharSet( Char: CHAR;
                          VAR SomeSet: SETOfChar );
```

```
(* Adds Char to SomeSet.                                              *)
   VAR Temp, TempTwo: SETOfChar;
BEGIN
   IF SomeSet = NIL THEN (* SomeSet is empty *)
      NEW(Temp);
      Temp↑.Element := Char;
      Temp↑.Next := NIL;
      SomeSet := Temp;
   ELSE (* check to see if Char is already an element of SomeSet *)
      Temp := SomeSet;
      WHILE ((Temp↑.Next <> NIL) AND (Temp↑.Element <> Char)) DO
         Temp := Temp↑.Next;
      END; (* WHILE Char not found and not at end of list of elements *)
      IF Temp↑.Next = NIL THEN (* at end of linked list of elements *)
         IF Temp↑.Element <> Char THEN
            (* must add Char as last element of SomeSet *)
            NEW(TempTwo);
            TempTwo↑.Element := Char;
            TempTwo↑.Next := NIL;
            Temp↑.Next := TempTwo;
         END; (* IF Char is not last element of SomeSet *)
         (* ELSE must have found Char in SomeSet *)
      END; (* IF at end list *)
   END; (* IF SomeSet is empty *)
END ADDToCharSet;

PROCEDURE TAKEFromCharSet( Char: CHAR;
                           VAR SomeSet: SETOfChar );
(* Removes Char from SomeSet.                                         *)
BEGIN
   WRITELine;
   WRITEString("CharSetHandler.TAKEFromCharSet not implemented");
END TAKEFromCharSet;

PROCEDURE ADDCharSets( VAR AddedTo: SETOfChar;
                       NewElements: SETOfChar );
(* Performs AddedTo := AddedTo + NewElements; where "+" denotes set *)
(* union.                                                           *)
BEGIN
   WRITELine;
   WRITEString("CharSetHandler.ADDCharSets not implemented");
END ADDCharSets;

PROCEDURE INTERSECTCharSets( VAR Result: SETOfChar;
                             SomeSet: SETOfChar );
(* Performs Result := Result*SomeSet; where "*" denotes set inter-  *)
(* section.                                                         *)
```

LISTING 16-9   Continued

```
BEGIN
  WRITELine;
  WRITEString("CharSetHandler.INTERSECTCharSets not implemented");
END INTERSECTCharSets;


PROCEDURE NEXTCharSetElement(Previous: CHAR; SomeSet: SETOfChar): CHAR;
(* Returns the next element after Previous in SomeSet. Returns NIL  *)
(* if Previous is the "last" element.                               *)
BEGIN
  WRITELine;
  WRITEString("CharSetHandler.NEXTCharSetElement not implemented");
END NEXTCharSetElement;

PROCEDURE CHARSetIsEmpty( SomeSet: SETOfChar ): BOOLEAN;
BEGIN
  RETURN (SomeSet = NIL);
END CHARSetIsEmpty;

PROCEDURE PRINTCharSet( SomeSet: SETOfChar );
(* Prints the elements of SomeSet.                                  *)
BEGIN
  WRITELine;
  WRITEString("CharSetHandler.PRINTCharSet not implemented");
END PRINTCharSet;

END CharSetHandler.
```

Incidentally, it is possible to significantly improve the performance of the pattern matcher by moving the code for GraphHandler into implementation module PMFunctions and replacing the function GOTO in Listing 16-3 by this version:

```
PROCEDURE GOTO(CurrentState: CARDINAL; Input: CHAR): CARDINAL;
  VAR Temp : NODEPointer;
      Found: BOOLEAN;
BEGIN
  Found := FALSE;
  Temp := GOTOGraph[CurrentState];
  WHILE ((NOT Found) AND (Temp <> NIL)) DO
    IF (Temp ↑.InArcID = Input) THEN
      Found := TRUE;
    ELSE
      Temp := Temp ↑.Next;
    END; (* IF *)
```

```
END; (* WHILE *)
IF NOT Found THEN
    IF ((CurrentState = 0) AND (NOT INITIALIZING)) THEN
        RETURN 0;
    ELSE
        RETURN FAIL;
    END; (* IF *)
ELSE
    RETURN (Temp ↑ .VertexID);
END;
END GOTO;
```

The code above assumes that type GRAPH is declared as

```
TYPE GRAPH = ARRAY[0..MAXVertices] OF NODEPointer;
```

This optimization has not been made in the listings shown because it decreases execution time at the expense of readability; the machinery for manipulating graphs is at a lower level of abstraction than the code which implements Algorithms 2 and 3. Also, the type GRAPH and its associated subprograms are useful enough to deserve their own pair of library modules.

17

Procedure Types

Values Which "Do" Versus Values Which "Say"

One of Modula-2's most distinctive and powerful features is the ability to declare variables whose values are subprograms. All the variables seen thus far do nothing except store information. Even the more complex types which are defined in terms of records, arrays, and pointers have been filled only with static data which cannot operate on other data. These kinds of values do not "do" anything; instead, they "say" things such as "The number of words in this line is 12" or "The set of positive odd numbers less than 8 is {1,3,5,7}."

Procedure types, on the other hand, allow programmers to assign values which do something. Procedure variables take procedures and functions as their values. Procedure types are useful because certain programs and procedures are known to depend on other procedures, but the specific dependencies are not known until run time. Procedure variables may be used in two ways: as independent variables and as formal subprogram parameters.

First we consider some examples of independent procedure variables:

```
TYPE RealFunction    = PROCEDURE(REAL): REAL;
     OutputProcedure = PROCEDURE(ARRAY OF CHAR);
VAR  WeightFunction: RealFunction;
     CurrentOutput : OutputProcedure;
```

A declaration of a procedure type must specify the number, mode, and types of the parameters that a procedure must have in order to be a legal value for variables of the procedure type. If the procedure variables are to take functions as their values, the type returned by these functions must also be specified in the procedure type's declaration.

The standard type PROC denotes a parameterless procedure; it may be considered to have the declaration

TYPE PROC = PROCEDURE;

Any procedure or function whose parameters match those declared for a given procedure type may be assigned as the value of a variable of that type. There are two exceptions: neither subprograms which are declared locally to another subprogram nor standard procedures and functions such as ODD, INCL, and DEC may be assigned as the value of a procedure variable. In any case, the parameters of a subprogram must match the declaration of a procedure type both in type and mode for the subprogram to be assigned to a variable of the procedure type. For instance, if WRITEInteger has the heading

PROCEDURE WRITEInteger(Value: INTEGER; DigitsToUse: CARDINAL);

then the assignment

CurrentOutput := WRITEInteger;

is illegal because CurrentOutput is a procedure variable of type:

TYPE OutputProcedure = PROCEDURE(ARRAY OF CHAR);

However, if WRITEString has the heading

PROCEDURE WRITEString(Message: ARRAY OF CHAR);

then

CurrentOutput := WRITEString;

is legal because CurrentOutput is of type OutputProcedure, and the declaration of OutputProcedure specifies that any (nonstandard, non-nested) procedure that expects one ARRAY OF CHAR value parameter can be assigned to any OutputProcedure variable.

Suppose that the declarations for RealFunction and WeightFunction are visible and that functions with the following headings are also visible:

PROCEDURE Fudger(y: INTEGER): REAL;
PROCEDURE Cheeky(VAR z: REAL): REAL;

```
PROCEDURE Nested(z: REAL): REAL;
PROCEDURE sin(z: REAL): REAL;
PROCEDURE cos(z: REAL): REAL;
```

Then this assignment is legal:

```
WeightFunction := sin;
```

The assignment

```
WeightFunction := cos + sin; (* ILLEGAL *)
```

is illegal because one can only assign a single subprogram to an independent procedure variable such as WeightFunction. This assignment is also illegal:

```
WeightFunction := ORD; (* ILLEGAL *)
```

One is not allowed to assign any of Modula-2's standard subprograms to a procedure variable. Also, one cannot assign subprograms which are declared locally to another subprogram, so this assignment is illegal if function Nested is declared locally to some other subprogram:

```
WeightFunction := Nested; (* ILLEGAL *)
```

Note finally that the assignments

```
WeightFunction := Cheeky; (* ILLEGAL *)
WeightFunction := Fudger; (* ILLEGAL *)
```

are illegal because the parameter modes and types declared for Cheeky and Fudger do not match those of WeightFunction.

Using Independent Procedure Variables

Suppose a programmer wishes to write a data retrieval program for the executives of a multinational corporation. The program must run in a wide range of different modes, depending on the experience and native language of the user. The program must communicate only in the natural language chosen by the user from among five or six possibilities. New users may require extensive, time-consuming help with errors. More experienced users may either request very concise error messages or suppress the messages entirely. Code for the top level of such a program is shown in Listing 17-1.

LISTING 17-1 *An example illustrating one use of independent procedure variables.*

```
MODULE AdaptiveDataRetrieval;
  FROM InOut IMPORT WRITEString, READCardinal;

  TYPE Languages    = (English, French, Spanish, German, Italian);
  TYPE UserType     = (New, Occasional, Experienced);
  TYPE MessageType  = ( ToGetUserType, ToGetID, ToGetQuery,
                                ToShowData, ToCloseSession );
  TYPE WriteSomeUser      = PROCEDURE(MessageType);
  TYPE QueryErrorHandler = PROCEDURE;
  TYPE QuestionAnswerer  = PROCEDURE;


  VAR  WriteUser      : WriteSomeUser;
       FixQueryError  : QueryErrorHandler;
       GiveHelp       : QuestionAnswerer;
       LanguageNumber : CARDINAL;
       UserTypeNumber : CARDINAL;
       CurrentLanguage: Languages;
       CurrentUserType: UserType;


  (* Code for procedures mentioned below, such as WriteEnglishUser,*)
  (* GiveLongAnswers, could be given here, or could be imported.   *)

  BEGIN (* AdaptiveDataRetrieval main body *)
    WRITEString("?? 1> English; 2> Francais; 3> Espanol; ");
    WRITEString("4> Deutsch; 5> Italiano ??");
    READCardinal(LanguageNumber);
    CurrentLanguage := VAL(Languages,LanguageNumber);
    CASE CurrentLanguage OF
      English: WriteUser := WriteEnglishUser;  |
      French : WriteUser := WriteFrenchUser;   |
      Spanish: WriteUser := WriteSpanishUser;  |
      German : WriteUser := WriteGermanUser;   |
      Italian: WriteUser := WriteItalianUser;
    END; (* CASE *)
    WriteUser(ToGetUserType);
    ReadCardinal(UserTypeNumber);
    CurrentUserType := VAL(UserType,UserTypeNumber);
    CASE CurrentUserType OF
      New        : FixQueryError := AskIsThisTheQuestion;
                   GiveHelp         := GiveLongInstructions;|
      Occasional : FixQueryError := GiveQuerySyntax;
                   GiveHelp         := AskIfUserWantsHelp;  |
      Experienced: FixQueryError := SayReenterPlease;
```

LISTING 17-1   Continued

```
           GiveHelp        := DoNothing;
END; (* CASE *)
(* The rest of AdaptiveDataRetrieval goes here. *)
END AdaptiveDataRetrieval.
```

Of course, there are other ways to achieve the effect of independent procedure variables such as WriteUser and GiveHelp without using procedure types (see Ogilvie, 1984). However, most other methods would require the use of tests throughout the rest of the program to decide which of the language and error-handling procedures should be used. The implementation in Listing 17-1, which uses procedure variables, settles the question once and for all and then gets on with the work to be done.

Procedure variables are most useful when a program makes heavy use of some members of a family of procedures or functions and it is not known until run time which member(s) of the family should be used. The family of subprograms may be very small; procedure types are still useful if a large number of calls are made on elements of the family.

As another example, suppose that a compiler has two options: time optimization and space optimization. That is, the compiler can either produce code which executes very quickly but uses a lot of storage space or else it can produce code which executes more slowly but uses very little space. The decision between the two optimizations is made at run time, and it would be inconvenient to fill the compiler with tests of the form

```
IF TimeSpaceOption = MuchTimeLittleSpace THEN
    DoSomething;
ELSE
    DoSomethingElse;
END; (* IF *)
```

The compiler writer could avoid the need for most of these tests by using procedure variables as shown in Listing 17-2.

LISTING 17-2   *Another example of the use of independent procedure variables.*

```
TYPE ExpressionCodeGenerator = PROCEDURE(Expression);
VAR  GenExpressionCode: ExpressionCodeGenerator;

PROCEDURE GenCodeInMinimalTime(Source: Expression);
(* body goes here *)
```

```
PROCEDURE GenCodeInMinimalSpace(Source: Expression);
(* body goes here *)
    .
    .
    .
BEGIN (* initialization of compiler *)
  CASE TimeSpaceOption OF
    MuchTimeLittleSpace: GenExpressionCode := GenCodeInMinimalSpace; |
    LittleTimeMuchSpace: GenExpressionCode := GenCodeInMinimalTime;
  END; (* CASE *)
  (* Inside the compiler's body, one need only call GenExpressionCode;*)
  (* there is no need for repeated tests to determine the value of    *)
  (* TimeSpaceOption.                                                  *)
    .
    .
    .
```

Other families of related procedures which might be represented using procedure types include the tree-traversal routines (pre-order, in-order, and post-order), tree-search procedures (e.g., depth-first, breadth-first), sorting routines (bubble-sort, quick-sort), and the trigonometric functions. Of course, there are many other families as well.

Procedures as Parameters

Procedures or functions may also be used as actual parameters when other Modula-2 subprograms are called. Listing 17-3 shows part of a simple database retrieval system which uses a single procedure Print-ChosenDataOffList to traverse a list and print certain information from each element in the list. One of the parameters to PrintChosen-

LISTING 17-3   *An illustration of the use of procedures as parameters.*

```
TYPE PointerToData = POINTER TO DataRecord;
TYPE DataRecord = RECORD
                   Name     : ARRAY[1..20] OF CHAR;
                   Seniority: CARDINAL;
                   IsABoss  : BOOLEAN;
                   Next: PointerToData;
                  END; (* RECORD *)
TYPE DataPrinters = PROCEDURE(PointerToData);

PROCEDURE PrintAllInfo(OfRecordAt: PointerToData);
```

LISTING 17-3   Continued

```
BEGIN
  WRITEString(OfRecordAt↑.Name);
  WRITEString(" Seniority Level: ");
  WRITECardinal(OfRecordAt↑.Seniority);
  IF OfRecordAt↑.IsABoss THEN
    WRITEStringAndLine(" Management ");
  ELSE
    WRITEStringAndLine(" Not in management ");
  END; (* IF *)
END PrintAllInfo;

PROCEDURE PrintNameIfABoss(OfRecordAt: PointerToData);
BEGIN
  IF OfRecordAt↑.IsABoss THEN
    WRITEStringAndLine(OfRecordAt↑.Name);
  END; (* IF *)
END PrintNameIfABoss;

(* Neither PrintAllInfo nor PrintNameIfABoss need to be *)
(* declared as DataPrinters; they are values, just as   *)
(* 12, 0, and -342 are INTEGER values, and do not need  *)
(* to be declared as such.                              *)

PROCEDURE PrintChosenDataOffList(First: PointerToData;
                      SomeDataPrinter: DataPrinters );
BEGIN
  IF First <> NIL THEN
    SomeDataPrinter(First);
    WHILE (First↑.Next <> NIL) DO
      First := First↑.Next;
      SomeDataPrinter(First);
    END; (* WHILE *)
  END; (* IF *)
END PrintChosenDataOffList;
          .
          .
          .

BEGIN
  (* A possible use of PrintChosenDataOffList *)
  CASE DataDesired OF
    All   : PrintChosenDataOffList(SomeList, PrintAllInfo);  |
    Bosses: PrintChosenDataOffList(SomeList, PrintNameIfABoss);
  ELSE
```

```
    WRITEStringAndLine("Sorry, that set of data is not available.");
END;  (* CASE *)
        .
        .
        .
```

DataOffList is the printing procedure which is to be executed for each element in the list. For instance, the call

PrintChosenDataOffList(SomeList, PrintAllInfo);

produces a list of employees' names and seniorities along with indications of whether or not the employees are in management. The call

PrintChosenDataOffList(SomeList, PrintNameIfABoss);

produces a list of managers' names.

Chapter

18

Processes

Coroutines and Concurrency

One may divide all programs into three categories. Programs which execute at the same time on different central processing units (CPUs) are said to be "concurrent processes." Programs which take turns running on the same CPU are known as "coroutines." All the programs seen thus far in this book fall into a third category since they stop running only when they reach completion or when a run-time error occurs. None of the programs seen so far can be suspended in order to allow another program to run and then be resumed later. Modula-2 supports coroutines by way of a system-dependent type called "PROCESS." The name chosen is unfortunate because process is generally used to mean concurrent process, not coroutine. PROCESS and coroutine are used as synonyms in this chapter.

At any point in time, a Modula-2 PROCESS may be executing, it may be suspended, or it may be terminated. Only one PROCESS may run at a time on any machine which has only one CPU. A program or procedure which has been made into a PROCESS may be suspended in mid-execution. Control is then passed to another PROCESS which is specified by the one being suspended. PROCESSes may only suspend themselves. All suspensions occur as the result of a call to the procedure TRANSFER, which transfers control from one PROCESS to another. The second PROCESS may in turn be suspended when control is passed to a third PROCESS, and so forth. If a suspended PROCESS is given control of the CPU, it continues execution right where it left off, as though it had always controlled the CPU.

Coroutines terminate when they have executed the last statement in their code or when the program which spawned them terminates. A program which contains a coroutine will terminate when any of its coroutines terminate. It is *not* safe to assume that execution will continue at the point after a transfer of control if the coroutine to which control was transferred terminates; there is no automatic return from coroutines the way there is from procedures. All transfers of control between coroutines should be explicitly programmed using calls on TRANSFER.

A coroutine consists of two parts: code and state information. The code defines the coroutine's behavior just as the code in the body of a subprogram or an implementation module defines the behavior of those constructs. The state information includes the values of all of the coroutine's local variables and an instruction pointer which can be used to determine the point at which execution should be resumed after a call is made on TRANSFER. All of a coroutine's state information is preserved while the coroutine is suspended.

Coroutines Versus Subprograms

The main difference between coroutines and subprograms is that coroutines may be suspended while some other computation runs on the CPU and then resumed later, with all local variables intact, at the point of suspension. Once a subprogram is called, there are only a few crude ways to stop it from executing each of its statements in order and continuing straight through to the end of its body: stop the execution by crashing the program and returning control to the operating system, hold up execution indefinitely by refusing to supply necessary input or by entering an infinite loop, or hold up execution temporarily by calling another subprogram which must finish execution before the original subprogram can terminate.

When the execution of a subprogram is stopped by any method except the last one, namely, a call to another subprogram, it is not possible to resume execution at the point of suspension after doing something else. A subprogram is indeed suspended when it makes a call, just as though it were a coroutine, but there are differences nonetheless between the two methods of suspending execution with the intent of resuming it later.

In the case of a subprogram call, control has been passed to a second subprogram and execution of the original calling subprogram will be resumed at the statement following the call, with all local variables intact. However, suppose one wishes to suspend the execution of the called subprogram and return control for a time to the caller, the first subprogram. If the second subprogram calls the first, control will pass to a new instantiation of the first. In this new instantiation, the values of the local variables in the original instantiation of the first are unknown. The call to the original caller results in the creation of a new activation record, with new variables.

Figures 18-1 and 18-2 illustrate the differences between subprogram calls and transfers between coroutines. In Figure 18-1, each of two coroutines makes an assignment to a local variable, transfers control to the other coroutine, tests the value of the local variable, transfers control once again, and then terminates when control is returned to it. In Figure 18-2, each of two subprograms makes an assignment to a local variable, calls on the other subprogram, and then becomes tangled in an infinite mutual recursion.

Creating Coroutines

Modula-2 allows a programmer to make any parameterless procedure into a PROCESS, i.e., into a coroutine. A new coroutine is created by a call to NEWPROCESS. This procedure is often imported from module SYSTEM but might be available from other modules on a given system. On many systems, NEWPROCESS has a heading such as this:

```
PROCEDURE NEWPROCESS( Code: PROC;
              WorkspaceAddress: ADDRESS;
              WorkspaceSize: CARDINAL;
              VAR NewProcess: PROCESS );
```

A call to NEWPROCESS creates the new coroutine NewProcess, using the parameterless procedure Code, and the storage area of size WorkspaceSize which starts at location WorkspaceAddress in memory. The standard module SYSTEM exports the types PROCESS and ADDRESS, as well as the procedures NEWPROCESS and TRANSFER. Your system may require different parameters than those shown, especially for NEWPROCESS since PROCESSes are implementation-dependent. In particular, your system might automatically allocate a workspace for the new PROCESS.

An appropriate value for WorkspaceAddress may be obtained by calling ALLOCATE; if this is not done, critical areas of memory may be overwritten when NewProcess is created. The procedure ALLOCATE is generally available from module Storage, and it has a heading such as:

```
PROCEDURE ALLOCATE(VAR Address: ADDRESS; Size: CARDINAL);
```

ALLOCATE allocates an area of the given size and returns its starting address in Address. If no space is available, the calling program

First, execute some initial transfer from CoroutineMain to CoroutineOne;

In CoroutineOne
  start execution
  at top of code;
  x is undefined;
  do x:= 1;
  transfer to Two;

                        In CoroutineTwo
                          start execution
                          at top of code;
                          y is undefined;
                          do y := 2;
                          transfer to One;

In CoroutineOne
  continue execution
  with statement
  following transfer;
  (x = 1) is TRUE;
  transfer to Two;

                        In CoroutineTwo
                          continue execution
                          with statement
                          following transfer;
                          (y = 2) is TRUE;
                          transfer to One;

In CoroutineOne
  finish execution;
  return control to
  point of call in Two
  with an explicit
  transfer; otherwise
  execution of all
  coroutines stops at
  this point,

                        In CoroutineTwo
                          finish execution;
                          transfer control back
                          to point of original
                          transfer to One,
                          in CoroutineMain, or
                          execution of all
                          coroutines stops
                          at this point;

Figure 18-1   The first diagram of two, illustrating some differences between coroutines and subprograms.

First, make some initial call to SubprogramOne;

```
In Instance 1
Of SubprogramOne
   start execution
   at top of code;
   x is undefined;
   do x:= 1;
   call Two;
                                In Instance 1
                                Of SubprogramTwo
                                   start execution
                                   at top of code;
                                   y is undefined;
                                   do y := 2;
                                   call One;
In Instance 2
Of SubprogramOne
   start execution
   at top of code;
   x is undefined;
   do x:= 1;
   call Two;
                                In Instance 2
                                Of SubprogramTwo
                                   start execution
                                   at top of code;
                                   y is undefined;
                                   do y := 2;
                                   call One;
In Instance 3
Of SubprogramOne
   start execution
   at top of code;
   x is undefined;
   do x:= 1;
   call Two;



   try to execute infinite mutual recursion
```

**Figure 18-2 The second diagram of two,
illustrating some differences between coroutines
and subprograms.**

may be terminated; this depends on the implementation. For this reason, some implementations also include a procedure

PROCEDURE AVAILABLE(Size: CARDINAL): BOOLEAN;

which can be used before calls on ALLOCATE to determine whether or not the desired amount of memory is available.

The state information associated with the coroutine will be stored in the workspace of size WorkspaceSize which starts at the location WorkspaceAddress in memory. Your system may define a minimal value for WorkspaceSize. There must be enough room in the workspace of a PROCESS to hold the subprogram call information and the local variables of any subprogram called by the PROCESS.

Since a coroutine may easily invoke system library modules, directly or indirectly, determining the proper size of the workspace may be a very difficult task. The results of allocating a workspace which is too small or which overlaps areas of memory used for another purpose are unpredictable. Although you will probably receive an error message similar to "stack overflow" or "attempt to read beyond allocated memory" if the workspace designated in a call to NEWPROCESS is too small, you cannot depend on the system to provide a warning if attempts are made to put part of a coroutine's workspace into locations which are already being used. If one wishes to avoid simply allocating huge chunks of memory in the hope that they will suffice, one may use a testing procedure such as the one shown in Listing 18-1. By trying different values and seeing whether the program runs to completion or causes a run-time memory error, it is usually possible to determine how much space a given coroutine requires.

LISTING 18-1 *A procedure which may be used to determine by trial and error what size workspace is needed by a process.*

```
IMPLEMENTATION MODULE CoroutineHandler;
    FROM InOut   IMPORT WRITEString, WRITELine, READCardinal;
    FROM Storage IMPORT ALLOCATE;
    FROM SYSTEM  IMPORT NEWPROCESS, TRANSFER, PROCESS, ADDRESS;

    PROCEDURE TryWorkspaceSizeGuess(Procedure: PROC);
        VAR Process, TryGuess: PROCESS; (* Procedure will be made into the *)
                                        (* coroutine Process; TryGuess is  *)
                                        (* the coroutine created from      *)
                                        (* TryWorkspaceSizeGuess.          *)
            WorkspaceAddress : ADDRESS;
```

LISTING 18-1   Continued

```
    WorkspaceSize    : CARDINAL;
  BEGIN (* TryWorkspaceSizeGuess *)
    WRITELine;
    WRITEString(" Make a guess for the workspace size> ");
    READCardinal(WorkspaceSize);
    ALLOCATE(WorkspaceAddress, WorkspaceSize); (* Use ALLOCATE to     *)
    (* obtain an area which may safely be used as a workspace, to avoid*)
    (* writing over some part of memory which is already in use.       *)
    NEWPROCESS(Procedure, WorkspaceAddress, WorkspaceSize, Process);
    TRANSFER(TryGuess, Process);
  END TryWorkspaceSizeGuess;
END CoroutineHandler.
```

The procedure asks for a guess from the user for the size of workspace which will be needed to turn parameterless Procedure into a working coroutine. If the guess is too small, it is assumed that the transfer of control to the newly created Process will cause a run-time memory overflow, and the user will be informed of this error by the operating system. If execution proceeds normally, the size of the workspace was either just adequate or larger than necessary.

If a program which involves PROCESSes neither gives an error message nor executes, but simply "hangs" as if it is waiting for input or is stuck in an infinite loop, try giving the PROCESSes larger workspaces. On some systems, programs may halt rather than transfer control to a PROCESS that has a workspace that is too small. As indicated in Listing 18-1, control is transferred between coroutines by calls to the SYSTEM procedure TRANSFER:

PROCEDURE TRANSFER(VAR Source, Destination: PROCESS);

A call to TRANSFER suspends execution of the current coroutine and saves it in Source. If TRANSFER is called from inside a subprogram or module body, that subprogram or module will probably also be saved as a suspended process. However, a particular system might only support TRANSFER calls made from within coroutines.

The coroutine designated by Destination is identified before the assignment to Source is made, so the two actual parameters may be identical. Control of the CPU passes to Destination, which resumes execution where it left off or else begins at its first statement if it has not previously controlled the CPU. Destination must have been assigned a coroutine by an earlier call to TRANSFER or NEWPROCESS.

All transfers of control between coroutines must be made explicitly; control does not automatically return to the point after the last transfer when a coroutine terminates. This is an important difference between coroutines and subprograms; all subprograms contain an implicit or explicit RETURN statement. If CoroutineOne transfers control to CoroutineTwo, which then terminates, the entire program will terminate. CoroutineTwo must contain an explicit TRANSFER back to CoroutineOne if that coroutine is to continue execution past the point of the transfer to CoroutineTwo.

An Example of the Use of Coroutines

Listing 18-2 contains an example of the use of coroutines. Program TextProcessor asks the user for the name of a file which contains text and formatting commands and sends the contents of the file to a printer after interpreting the formatting commands. The program expects the character @ to be used only in formatting commands, three of which are available.

LISTING 18-2   *A simple text processor which uses coroutines.*

```
MODULE TextProcessor;
    FROM SYSTEM  IMPORT PROCESS, ADDRESS, NEWPROCESS, TRANSFER;
    FROM Storage IMPORT ALLOCATE;
    FROM InOut   IMPORT WRITEString, WRITEStringAndLine, READCharacter,
                        OPENInputFile, CLOSEInputFile, INPUTFile;
    FROM PrinterInterface IMPORT SENDCharToPrinter, SENDStringToPrinter,
                        FONTS;
    FROM ModulaDefinitions IMPORT RESERVEDWord, CARDINALToString;


    CONST TextProcessSize = 325;    (* These values work on the Lilith *)
          SectionsProcessSize = 300;(* machine. They were determined   *)
          ChaptersProcessSize = 300;(* by using TryWorkspaceSizeGuess; *)
          ProgramsProcessSize = 375;(* see Listing 18-1. They are      *)
          MaxWordSize = 30;         (* somewhat conservative.          *)
          NULLChar = 0C;
          Blank = " ";
          CarriageReturnLineFeed = 36C;

    VAR NextChar: CHAR;
        TextProcess,
        ChapterHeadingsProcess,
        SectionHeadingsProcess,
```

LISTING 18-2   Continued

```
ProgramExamplesProcess,
Initialization        : PROCESS;
Address               : ADDRESS;

PROCEDURE ProcessText;
  VAR Command: ARRAY[1..4] OF CHAR;
      Index  : CARDINAL;
BEGIN
  WRITEStringAndLine(" Processing text... ");
  READCharacter(NextChar);
  WHILE (NOT INPUTFile.EndOfFile) DO
    IF NextChar <> "@" THEN
      SENDCharToPrinter(NextChar, NormalFont);
    ELSE
      FOR Index := 1 TO 4 DO
        READCharacter(Command[Index]);
      END; (* FOR *)
      IF (STRINGSAreEqual(Command, "Chap")) THEN
        TRANSFER(TextProcess, ChapterHeadingsProcess);
      ELSIF (STRINGSAreEqual(Command, "Sect")) THEN
        TRANSFER(TextProcess, SectionHeadingsProcess);
      ELSIF (STRINGSAreEqual(Command, "Prog")) THEN
        TRANSFER(TextProcess, ProgramExamplesProcess);
      ELSE
        WRITEString(" Unknown command found in text: ");
        WRITEStringAndLine(Command);
      END; (* IF *)
    END; (* IF *)
    READCharacter(NextChar);
  END; (* WHILE *)
  WRITEString(" Finished processing text. ");
  CLOSEInputFile;
END ProcessText;

PROCEDURE ProcessChapterHeadings;
  VAR Chapter : CARDINAL;
      NextChar: CHAR;
BEGIN
  Chapter := 0;
  LOOP
    INC(Chapter);
    SENDStringToPrinter(CARDINALToString(Chapter), BoldFont);
    READCharacter(NextChar);
    WHILE (NextChar <> "@") DO
      SENDCharToPrinter(NextChar, BoldFont);
```

```
        READCharacter(NextChar);
      END; (* WHILE *)
      TRANSFER(ChapterHeadingsProcess, TextProcess);
    END; (* LOOP *)
END ProcessChapterHeadings;

PROCEDURE ProcessSectionHeadings;
  VAR Section: CARDINAL;
BEGIN
  Section := 0;
  LOOP
    INC(Section);
    SENDStringToPrinter(CARDINALToString(Section), UnderlinedFont);
    READCharacter(NextChar);
    WHILE (NextChar <> "@") DO
      SENDCharToPrinter(NextChar, UnderlinedFont);
      READCharacter(NextChar);
    END; (* WHILE *)
    TRANSFER(SectionHeadingsProcess, TextProcess);
  END; (* LOOP *)
END ProcessSectionHeadings;

PROCEDURE ProcessProgramExamples;
  VAR Example : CARDINAL;
      Index   : CARDINAL;
      NextWord: ARRAY[1..MaxWordSize]OF CHAR;

  PROCEDURE IsWhiteSpace(Char: CHAR): BOOLEAN;
  BEGIN
    RETURN ((Char = Blank) OR (Char = CarriageReturnLineFeed));
  END IsWhiteSpace;

BEGIN (* ProcessProgramExamples *)
  Example := 0;
  LOOP
    INC(Example);
    READCharacter(NextChar);
    (* See if there is more to the program example being processed.*)
    WHILE (NextChar <> "@") DO
      (* Send any white space to the printer. *)
      WHILE (IsWhiteSpace(NextChar)) DO
        SENDCharToPrinter(NextChar, NormalFont);
        READCharacter(NextChar);
      END; (* WHILE *)
      (* Read the characters which form the next identifier, *)
      (* expression, delimiter, etc., into NextWord array.   *)
      Index := 1;
```

LISTING 18-2   Continued

```
WHILE ((Index <= MaxWordSize)
       AND (NOT IsWhiteSpace(NextChar))) DO
  NextWord[Index] := NextChar;
  READCharacter(NextChar);
  INC(Index);
END; (* WHILE *)
IF (Index <= MaxWordSize) THEN
  NextWord[Index] := NULLChar;
END; (* IF *)
SENDCharToPrinter(NextChar, NormalFont);
(* Check to see if NextWord contains a reserved word. If *)
(* so, print it in boldface; if not, use the normal font.*)
IF ((Index > MaxWordSize) AND (NOT IsWhiteSpace(NextChar))) THEN
  WRITEString(" Maximum number of characters without ");
  WRITEString("intervening white space exceeded; ");
  WRITEString("the printout may be incorrect.");
ELSIF (RESERVEDWord(NextWord)) THEN
  Index := 1;
  WHILE ((Index <= MaxWordSize)
         AND (NextWord[Index] <> NULLChar)) DO
    SENDCharToPrinter(NextWord[Index], BoldFont);
    INC(Index);
  END; (* WHILE *)
ELSE
  Index := 1;
  WHILE ((Index <= MaxWordSize)
         AND (NextWord[Index] <> NULLChar)) DO
    SENDCharToPrinter(NextWord[Index], NormalFont);
    INC(Index);
  END; (* WHILE *)
END; (* IF *)
READCharacter(NextChar);
  END; (* WHILE *)
  TRANSFER(ProgramExamplesProcess, TextProcess);
  END; (* LOOP *)
END ProcessProgramExamples;

PROCEDURE InitializeAndExecute;
BEGIN
  (* Get file name from user, open file, and get ready to read it. *)
  WRITEString("Enter name of file to be printed: ");
  OPENInputFile;
  (* Create the four main processes used, plus one for the *)
  (* initialization; then transfer control to TextProcess. *)
  ALLOCATE(Address, TextProcessSize);
```

```
NEWPROCESS(ProcessText, Address, TextProcessSize, TextProcess);
ALLOCATE(Address, SectionsProcessSize);
NEWPROCESS( ProcessSectionHeadings, Address,
                    SectionsProcessSize, SectionHeadingsProcess );
ALLOCATE(Address, ChaptersProcessSize);
NEWPROCESS( ProcessChapterHeadings, Address,
                    ChaptersProcessSize, ChapterHeadingsProcess );
ALLOCATE(Address, ProgramsProcessSize);
NEWPROCESS( ProcessProgramExamples, Address,
                    ProgramsProcessSize, ProgramExamplesProcess );
(* The transfer below to TextProcess starts execution; it also     *)
(* creates an Initialization coroutine as an unneeded side effect.*)
TRANSFER(Initialization, TextProcess);
END InitializeAndExecute;

BEGIN (* Body of TextProcessor *)
    InitializeAndExecute;
END TextProcessor;
```

Including "@Chap Modula-2's Version of Private Types@" in the file, for instance, causes the chapter title "Modula-2's Version of Private Types" to be printed in a bold font, prefaced by an appropriate chapter number. "@Sect Opaque Types and Visibility@" causes the section title "Opaque Types and Visibility" to be printed in an underlined font, prefaced by an appropriate section number. Finally, program examples which lie between @Prog and @ are printed in the same font as normal text except that reserved words are printed in boldface.

Module Priorities

It is convenient at times to implement some method for coroutines to communicate with each other. One approach is to use shared variables. It is good programming practice to hide shared variables inside special modules which are known as "monitors." A monitor is a module which can be accessed by only one process at a time so that the integrity of the module's local data is ensured. The data should be made accessible only by way of calls on the monitor's exported subprograms. Any process which calls the monitor while another process is executing one of the monitor's subprograms will be temporarily delayed until the execution of the subprogram is completed. This guarantees the mutual exclusion of any processes which are trying to access the monitor's data.

Since Modula-2 assumes an underlying machine with a single CPU, the ideas surrounding monitor modules are mainly of theoretical interest. On a uniprocessor system, every module is a monitor. However, it is possible nonetheless to explicitly label a module as a monitor by specifying a priority in the module's heading, e.g.,

MODULE BufferData[1];

The priority must be a constant expression. Any value will serve to mark the module as a monitor. If you find yourself using module priorities, Modula-2's creator, Nicklaus Wirth, suggests that it would probably be best to define only two levels of priority: interruptable and uninterruptable. See Wirth (1983) for some examples. Although one should never depend on module priorities to determine the order in which a group of coroutines will be executed, they may be useful when certain modules need a higher execution priority. For example, one could give a system's laser printer driver higher priority than the screen driver so that output can be printed rapidly at the expense of some flicker in the screen.

Exercise

1. Given the two procedures

```
PROCEDURE One;
BEGIN
    WRITEString("Inside One");
END One;
PROCEDURE Two;
BEGIN
    WRITEString("Inside Two");
END Two;
```

determine the results of trying to execute

```
TryWorkspaceSizeGuess(One);
TryWorkspaceSizeGuess(Two);
```

Assume that WRITEString and TryWorkspaceSizeGuess are visible wherever they are needed.

Modula-2's Low-Level Features

Modula-2 provides a number of low-level facilities which are examined individually below. These features make use of information which varies from machine to machine and from implementation to implementation. For this reason, you must be particularly careful when using them; it is easy to make errors which are detected neither by you nor by your compiler. For this reason (among others), many high-level languages simply do not make available any low-level features such as the ones described in this chapter.

Many of Modula-2's low-level features are exported from the pseudo-module SYSTEM, which is not actually a separate pair of library modules but is effectively part of the compiler. Any module which imports something from SYSTEM may be system-dependent; changes may be necessary before such a module will run correctly on another implementation of Modula-2. Unlike all other library modules, SYSTEM does not have a separate definition module, but it can be used as though it had the one shown in Listing 19-1.

LISTING 19-1 *Definition Module for* **SYSTEM,** *which is actually not a separate module but is effectively part of the compiler.*

```
DEFINITION MODULE SYSYTEM
  EXPORT QUALIFIED WORD, ADDRESS,
                   ADR, SIZE, TSIZE,
                   PROCESS, NEWPROCESS, TRANSFER;
                   (* There may be other exports,     *)
                   (* depending on the implementation *)
                   (* used; type BYTE is fairly common.*)
```

LISTING 19-1   Continued

```
TYPE WORD;     (* Discussed in this chapter.*)
     ADDRESS; (* Discussed in this chapter.*)
     PROCESS;  (* Discussed in Chapter 18.  *)


(* See discussions in this chapter for details on these: *)
PROCEDURE ADR(SomeVariable: AnyType): ADDRESS;
PROCEDURE SIZE(VAR SomeVariable: AnyType): CARDINAL;
PROCEDURE TSIZE(AnyTypeName): CARDINAL;


(* See Chapter 18 for details on these two procedures: *)
PROCEDURE NEWPROCESS( Code: PROC;
            WorkspaceAddress: ADDRESS;
            WorkspaceSize: CARDINAL;
            VAR NewProcess: PROCESS );
PROCEDURE TRANSFER(VAR Source, Destination: PROCESS);
END SYSTEM.
```

Storage Information and Allocation

Module SYSTEM exports the types WORD and ADDRESS and the
functions ADR, SIZE, and TSIZE. The type ADDRESS allows programmers to refer to specific locations in a particular computer's memory. Memory is viewed as a sequence of so-called words, each with its
own index in the sequence, i.e., its own address. The number of bits in a
word will vary from machine to machine. The type ADDRESS is defined by the declaration

TYPE ADDRESS = POINTER TO WORD;

The type WORD is discussed separately below; one implication of its
rather unusual properties is that any pointer type will match a formal
parameter which is of type ADDRESS. One may do arithmetic with
ADDRESS values just as if they were CARDINAL values. This is
useful when one is writing compilers or other system software.

The function ADR may be taken to have the heading

PROCEDURE ADR(SomeVariable: AnyType): ADDRESS;

This function returns the starting address of any variable of any type.

The function SIZE may be used to determine how many words of
memory a variable uses; this function has the heading

PROCEDURE SIZE(VAR SomeVariable: AnyType): CARDINAL;

SIZE probably will not accept open array parameters as arguments, so this will not serve to provide the storage requirements of the actual parameter which is matched to a formal open array parameter:

```
PROCEDURE SizeOfActual(FOAP: ARRAY OF ElementType): CARDINAL;
BEGIN
   RETURN SIZE(FOAP);
END SizeOfActual;
```

Instead, one must do something such as:

```
PROCEDURE SizeOfActual(FOAP: ARRAY OF ElementType): CARDINAL;
BEGIN
   RETURN ((HIGH(FOAP)+1)*SIZE(ElementType));
END SizeOfActual;
```

SIZE returns the correct value for procedure variables, not for the workspaces required by their current value; since the procedure variables may be implemented as pointers, executing

```
PROCVariable := ParameterlessProcedure;
WorkspaceSize := SIZE(PROCVariable);
ALLOCATE(WorkspaceAddress, WorkspaceSize);
```

will probably not allocate a space large enough to hold the compiled version of ParameterlessProcedure.

TSIZE returns the number of words used to hold any variable of the indicated type. This function's heading is

```
PROCEDURE TSIZE(AnyTypeName): CARDINAL;
```

TSIZE(INTEGER), for instance, returns the number of storage units used to hold INTEGER values. When either SIZE or TSIZE is asked for information about the size of a variant record variable or variant record type, respectively, the value returned depends on the implementation used. With both SIZE and TSIZE, the storage unit assumed (bytes, words, bits, etc.) is system-dependent.

As noted in Chapter 5, it is possible to override the compiler's storage allocation scheme by designating an absolute starting address for a variable. No import from SYSTEM is required to do this, so it is particularly important that any use of the override facility be clearly marked in the code. The declaration

```
VAR Status [51243B]: BITSET; (* ABSOLUTE ADDRESS USED *)
(* THIS PROGRAM IS MEANT TO RUN ON THE GREEN MACHINE! *)
```

indicates, for instance, that Status is to be stored at location 51243B in memory on the Green machine. The address given must be a constant integer expression, which will be interpreted as a decimal, octal, or hexadecimal number, depending on the system used. Obviously, this facility must be used very carefully if one is not to overwrite critical storage areas. Wirth (1983) indicates that implementations of Modula-2 do not have to provide this facility, so it might not be available on your system. If the override facility is used for some variable X, then X's value will be stored in the N memory locations which start at the specified address. The variable N, which depends on X's type, is equal to TSIZE(XType), when X has been declared to be of type XType.

Any statements involving absolute addresses or type ADDRESS must be considered to be implementation-dependent for at least three reasons. First, the actual amount of memory differs from machine to machine, so certain absolute addresses used on one system may simply not exist on another system. Second, the regions of memory which are set aside for the operating system, for dynamic allocation, to hold the run-time stack, or to be used in I/O operations are different on different systems. Finally, the addressing scheme used may differ: one system might use a simple linear address space where another uses paging and therefore refers to addresses as pairs (PageNumber, WordNumber).

The Type WORD

The type WORD is also exported from module SYSTEM. WORD may be used whenever one wishes to avoid interpreting the contents of some memory word as being of some particular type, e.g., INTEGER, BITSET, and CHAR. No operators except assignment and transfer to one of the known types are allowed on WORD variables. Use of this type makes a program highly machine-dependent since versions of Modula-2 now run both on 16-bit and 32-bit machines.

A formal parameter of type WORD is compatible with any type of actual parameter as long as that type occupies a single word of memory. The list of single-word types will differ from system to system, but it generally includes: INTEGER, CARDINAL, BOOLEAN, BITSET, CHAR, enumeration types, set types, subrange types, opaque types, and pointer types. A formal parameter of type ARRAY OF WORD will match any actual parameter, structured or unstructured; this includes records. Certain implementations of Modula-2 also provide other low-level types such as BYTE, but WORD is the only one called for by the language's specification. The specification does not dictate the number of bits contained in a WORD.

Listings 19-2 and 19-3 contain the code for a pair of EasyOutput modules which take advantage of the ability of WORD to match all the basic types except REAL on the Lilith machine. REAL requires two words of storage on the Lilith. The EasyOutput modules export procedures which combine the various other more specialized procedures such as WRITECharacter, WRITEString, WRITEStringAndLine, WRITELine, WRITECardinal, and WRITEInteger into a family of similar procedures. By using the different members of this family, nearly any mixture of single-word types can be passed in a single procedure call.

LISTING 19-2 *An example illustrating the use of type* **WORD**, *part 1.*

```
DEFINITION MODULE EasyOutput;
  FROM SYSTEM IMPORT WORD; (* WRITTEN FOR THE LILITH MACHINE UNDER *)
  (* VERSION 4 OF THE MEDOS OPERATING SYSTEM. SYSTEM-DEPENDENT!   *)

  EXPORT QUALIFIED WRITE0, WRITE1, WRITE2, WRITE3;
  (* Others may be added as necessary, using these for patterns. *)

  PROCEDURE WRITE0( String: ARRAY OF CHAR );
  PROCEDURE WRITE1( String: ARRAY OF CHAR; FirstInsert: WORD );
  PROCEDURE WRITE2( String: ARRAY OF CHAR; FirstInsert,
                                 SecondInsert: WORD );
  PROCEDURE WRITE3( String: ARRAY OF CHAR; FirstInsert,
                                 SecondInsert, ThirdInsert: WORD );
  (* The markers allowed in the string include "%N" for the insertion *)
  (* of a carriage return-line feed, "%A" for an ASCII CHAR value,    *)
  (* "%I" for an INTEGER value, "%C" for a CARDINAL, "%B" for a       *)
  (* BITSET, and "%G" (for the "G" in "George Boole") for a BOOLEAN   *)
  (* value.                                                           *)
END EasyOutput.
```

LISTING 19-3 *An example illustrating the use of type* **WORD**, *part 2.*

```
IMPLEMENTATION MODULE EasyOutput;
  (* Allows up to 3 values to be mixed between parts of an output  *)
  (* string. Even this limit is not absolute, since procedures WRITE4,*)
  (* WRITE5, etc., can be easily written using those below as models. *)

  FROM SYSTEM IMPORT WORD; (* WRITTEN FOR THE LILITH MACHINE *)
  FROM InOut  IMPORT WRITECharacter, WRITEInteger, WRITECardinal;
```

LISTING 19-3   Continued

```
CONST  WORDLength    = 16;  (* On Lilith machine; SYSTEM-DEPENDENT! *)
       LeftSetBrace  = "{";
       RightSetBrace = "}";
       Delete        = 177C;
       Comma         = ",";
       CarriageReturn= 15C;
       LineFeed      = 12C;
       Null          = 0C;  (* Terminates the meaningful characters *)
                            (* in an array of CHAR which is larger  *)
                            (* than the meaningful part of the      *)
                            (* string it contains.                  *)

PROCEDURE WriteBitSet(Set: BITSET);
  VAR Index: CARDINAL;
BEGIN
  WRITECharacter(LeftSetBrace);
  FOR Index := 0 TO WORDLength-1 DO
    IF Index IN Set THEN
      WRITECardinal(Index,3);
      WRITECharacter(Comma);
    END; (* IF *)
  END; (* FOR *)
  IF Set <> {} THEN
    WRITECharacter(Delete);   (* Get rid of extra comma *)
  END; (* IF *)
  WRITECharacter(RightSetBrace);
END WriteBitSet;

PROCEDURE WRITE0(String: ARRAY OF CHAR);
  VAR Char : CHAR;
      Index: CARDINAL;
BEGIN
  Index := 0;
  LOOP
    Char := String[Index];
    IF Char = Null THEN
        EXIT;
      ELSIF Char <> "%" THEN
        WRITECharacter(Char);
      ELSIF String[Index+1] = "N" THEN
        WRITECharacter(CarriageReturn);
        WRITECharacter(LineFeed);
        INC(Index);
      ELSIF String[Index+1] = "%" THEN
        WRITECharacter("%");
```

```
      INC(Index);
    ELSE
      WRITE0("%NUnknown Command in WRITE0%N");
      EXIT;
    END; (* IF *)
    INC(Index);
    IF (Index > HIGH(String)) THEN
      EXIT;
    END; (* IF *)
  END; (* LOOP *)
END WRITE0;


PROCEDURE WRITE1( String: ARRAY OF CHAR; FirstInsert: WORD );
BEGIN
  (* May be derived from WRITE2 in a straight-forward manner. *)
END WRITE1;


PROCEDURE WRITE2( String: ARRAY OF CHAR; FirstInsert,
                                         SecondInsert: WORD );
CONST NumberOfInserts = 2;
VAR   Char               : CHAR;
      Index, InsertNumber: CARDINAL;
      Inserts            : ARRAY[1..NumberOfInserts] OF WORD;
BEGIN
  Inserts[1] := FirstInsert;
  Inserts[2] := SecondInsert;
  Index := 0;
  InsertNumber := 1;
  LOOP
    Char := String[Index];
    IF Char <> "%" THEN
      WRITECharacter(Char);
    ELSE
      CASE String[Index+1] OF
        "A" : WRITECharacter(CHR(CARDINAL(Inserts[InsertNumber])));
              INC(Index);
              INC(InsertNumber);                    |
        "C" : WRITECardinal(CARDINAL(Inserts[InsertNumber]),6);
              (* The 6 indicates the number of digits to used. *)
              INC(Index);
              INC(InsertNumber);                    |
        "I" : WRITEInteger(INTEGER(Inserts[InsertNumber]),6);
              INC(Index);
              INC(InsertNumber);                    |
        "N" : WRITECharacter(CarriageReturn);
              WRITECharacter(LineFeed);
              INC(Index);                           |
```

LISTING 19-3   Continued

```
    "%" : WRITECharacter("%");
          INC(Index);                           |
    "B" : WriteBitSet(BITSET(Inserts[InsertNumber]));
          INC(Index);
          INC(InsertNumber);                    |
    "G" : IF BOOLEAN(Inserts[InsertNumber]) THEN
            WRITE0("TRUE");
          ELSE
            WRITE0("FALSE");
          END; (* IF *)
          INC(Index);
          INC(InsertNumber);
  ELSE
    WRITE0("%NUnknown Command in WRITE2%N");
    EXIT;
  END; (* CASE String[Index+1] *)
END; (* IF Char <> "%" *)
INC(Index);
IF (Index > HIGH(String)) THEN
  EXIT;
END; (* IF *)
  END; (* LOOP *)
END WRITE2;

PROCEDURE WRITE3( String: ARRAY OF CHAR;  FirstInsert,
                         SecondInsert, ThirdInsert: WORD );
BEGIN
  (* May be derived from WRITE2 in a straight-forward manner. *)
END WRITE3;

END EasyOutput.
```

The procedure WRITE2 accepts a string and two parameters whose values are to be printed at the indicated points in the string. The string contains text which is to be printed as is; any number of %N's, which indicate the insertion of a carriage return-line feed into the output stream; and markers which indicate the location and type of variables or constant values which are to be inserted in the output as it is printed. These inserted values are passed as additional parameters.

WRITE2 expects two values to be inserted, WRITE3 expects three values, and so forth. The results are unpredictable if the type indicated in the string for the Kth inserted value is not the same as the type of the (K + 1)th parameter (the string is the first parameter):

WRITE2("This is not wise: %G", CardinalVariable);

The markers allowed in the string include %N for the insertion of a carriage return-line feed, %A for an ASCII CHAR value, %I for an INTEGER value, %C for a CARDINAL value, %B for a BITSET value, and %G (for the G in George Boole) for a BOOLEAN value. For instance,

```
WRITEString("Outer Loop = ");
WRITECardinal(IndexOne,6);
WRITEString(" , Inner Loop = ");
WRITECardinal(IndexTwo,6);
WRITELine;
```

could be combined into the single call:

WRITE2("Outer Loop = %C , Inner Loop = %C%N", IndexOne, IndexTwo);

Sidestepping Type Compatibility

By using the type transfer function associated with each data type, the standard type conversion functions such as FLOAT and TRUNC, or functions written by the programmer, it is possible to avoid almost entirely the restrictions imposed by Modula-2's strong typing. Of these, type transfers must be considered implementation-dependent.

It is useful at times to be able to change values of one type to "corresponding" values of another type. The correspondence between values of the types concerned must be made clear to the compiler. This may be done in several ways. It might happen that the correspondence is obvious, such as that between type INTEGER and any subrange of INTEGER. In this case, for instance, the compiler takes it for granted that the subrange value −2 corresponds to the INTEGER value −2, and no explicit description of the correspondence is required from the programmer.

If the correspondence between the values is not obvious or if the types involved are programmer-defined, type transfer, type coercion, or type conversion functions must be used. One may see the terms "type transfer," "type coercion," and "type conversion" used as synonyms, but this is not really correct. Although type transfer and type coercion are synonymous, type conversion means something quite different. A conversion normally implies that the compiler generates some code to produce the new value from the old one, whereas a coercion or transfer involves nothing more than reinterpreting a bit representation as a value of another data type. It is understood that one can only make coercions between types which use the same number of bits to represent their values.

For instance, if BOOLEANs are implemented using single bits, one could convert a BOOLEAN value to a CARDINAL (0 or 1, say), but one could not coerce or transfer BOOLEANs to CARDINALs on such a system. Any data type name may also be used as the name of a type transfer function. No code from the programmer is required to define transfer or coercion functions since the transfer involves nothing more than reinterpreting an existing bit representation. A number of conversion functions such as FLOAT, ORD, and CHR are also predefined. Of course, if the system does not provide a desired conversion function, the programmer is free to write one.

The use of transfer functions will be illustrated using the following declarations:

```
TYPE StructuredOne   = ARRAY[1..100] OF CHAR;
     StructuredTwo   = ARRAY[1..100] OF CHAR;
     StructuredThree = StructuredOne;
     StructuredFour  = ARRAY[1..50] OF CHAR;
```

The fact that these types are created by the programmer makes it necessary to explicitly transfer the value of a variable ArrayOne of type StructuredOne, for instance, to a value of type StructuredTwo. Transfers between StructuredThree and StructuredOne variables are not necessary because those two types are declared to be equal. Statements involving the transfer of values from a variable of one type to a variable of some other type are implementation-dependent if only because of the assumption that both types use the same number of bits to represent a value. If ArrayTwo is of type StructuredTwo, the statement

```
ArrayTwo := ArrayOne; (* ILLEGAL *)
```

is not legal since it mixes incompatible types. However, the statement

```
ArrayTwo := StructuredTwo(ArrayOne);
```

is legal. The last assignment statement means "interpret the value in ArrayOne as a value of type StructuredTwo and then assign this value to the variable ArrayTwo." To assign one array to another in this way, three conditions must be met. First of all, the arrays must be the same size. They do not need to have the same index type. Secondly, the arrays' types must be made compatible. This may involve the use of a type transfer function. Finally, the assignment can only be made if the elements of the arrays are of compatible types.

If a variable ArrayFour was of the type StructuredFour, the statement

ArrayFour := StructuredFour(ArrayOne);

would have unpredictable results. It is not clear what should be done with the values in Cells 51..100 of ArrayOne. Since the compiler does not know how to make the conversion, the assignment is illegal. Similarly, if one tries to execute

ArrayOne := StructuredOne(ArrayFour);

it is not clear what values should be assigned to cells 51..100 of Array-One.

In order for a variable to receive the value returned by a type transfer function, the variable's type must have a name. This is because the name of the variable's type is also the name of the only transfer function which can return values compatible with the variable. For instance, consider the variables VariableOfNamedType and Anonymous declared as

VAR VariableOfNamedType: StructuredOne;
    Anonymous   : ARRAY[1..100] OF CHAR;

One can assign the value of Anonymous to VariableOfNamedType with the statement

VarOfNamedType := ArrayType(Anonymous);

However, one cannot assign the value of VariableOfNamedType to Anonymous. The statement

Anonymous := VariableOfNamedType;

is illegal because it involves a type incompatibility. Anonymous is not of a named type, so there is no way to use type transfers to avoid the incompatibility. The assignment to Anonymous must be made element by element. From the standpoint of type transfers, therefore, the following two versions of SomeVariable's declaration are not equivalent:

```
TYPE ArrayType = ARRAY[1..5] OF CHAR;
VAR  SomeVariable: ArrayType;

VAR  SomeVariable: ARRAY[1..5] OF CHAR;
```

The easiest way to avoid difficulties is to make sure that all data types used in a program have names. Assignments to individual elements of structured types present no similar problems since the types of the elements are known. Type conversion functions may be used whether a type transfer is legal or not since the programmer can define his or her own conversion functions if necessary. For instance, on a machine which uses 32 bits to represent REALs and 16 bits to represent INTEGERs, one cannot transfer REAL values into INTEGER values. Instead, type conversion functions such as TRUNC or ROUND-TowardZero which are provided by the system or the programmer may be used.

As another example, consider the mapping between CARDINAL and CHAR values. In this case, Modula-2 provides the standard functions CHR(CardinalVariable) and ORD(CharacterVariable). The conversions are made according to the ASCII ordering given in Table 4-3. Note that ORD returns a decimal CARDINAL value, not an octal number. Thus, CHR(80) = P, and ORD("P") = 80. The standard functions CAP, CHR, FLOAT, ORD, TRUNC, and VAL may all be viewed as type conversion functions. Modula-2 compilers do not normally perform any conversions since doing so would probably introduce machine-dependencies which are hidden from most programmers. The conversions provided by Modula-2's standard functions are generally portable, so they should be used instead of transfer functions whenever possible. For instance, one should prefer

```
Card := ORD(Char);
```

to

```
Card := CARDINAL(Char);
```

An Example: Dynamic String Handling

Given the availability of the types ADDRESS and WORD; the Storage subprograms AVAILABLE, ALLOCATE, and DEALLOCATE; and a few type transfer functions, it is possible to improve on the string-handling facilities presented in Listings 11-2 and 11-3. Listings 19-4 and 19-5 contain a pair of library modules which export a dynamically allocated STRING type along with subprograms ASSIGNEDSTRING, WRITESTRING, DELETESTRING, and DYNAMICArray. ASSIGNEDSTRING calls DYNAMICArray to obtain HIGH(Value) + 2 spaces in memory. Recall that the indices of a formal open array parameter FOAP which is matched to an actual parameter with N elements will run from 0 to HIGH(FOAP) = N − 1. ASSIGNED-STRING needs space for N + 1 = HIGH(Value) + 2 CHAR values; the extra space is for a null character which marks the end of the string.

LISTING 19-4 *The basis for a pair of library modules which manage dynamically allocated* **STRING** *variables, part 1.*

```
DEFINITION MODULE STRINGHandler;
    (* This pair of library modules uses type transfers and assumptions *)
    (* about the size of CHAR variables; these may be different on a    *)
    (* system other than the Lilith under MEDOS V4. The type STRING and *)
    (* the associated subprograms allow one to work with strings        *)
    (* dynamically. To ensure that the best use is made of the system's *)
    (* memory resources, one should explicitly call DELETESTRING on     *)
    (* STRINGs which are no longer needed.                              *)
    FROM SYSTEM IMPORT ADDRESS;
    EXPORT QUALIFIED STRING, ASSIGNEDSTRING, WRITESTRING, DELETESTRING,
                     DYNAMICArray;

    TYPE STRING;
    PROCEDURE ASSIGNEDSTRING( VAR StringVariable: STRING;
                                  Value: ARRAY OF CHAR ): BOOLEAN;
    (* Tries to assign the array of characters in Value to the      *)
    (* StringVariable;returns FALSE if there is not enough memory to *)
    (* make the necessary dynamic storage allocation.               *)
    PROCEDURE WRITESTRING( StringVariable: STRING );
    (* Writes the characters stored in the StringVariable; assumes that *)
    (* they were put there by a use of ASSIGNEDSTRING. Writes nothing if *)
    (* the STRING is empty.                                            *)
    PROCEDURE DELETESTRING( VAR StringVariable: STRING );
    (* Releases the space which was dynamically allocated to hold the   *)
    (* characters in StringVariable, so it can be used by something else.*)
    (* DELETESTRING also marks the STRING as empty.                    *)
    PROCEDURE DYNAMICArray( NumberOfVariables,
                            WordsPerVariable: CARDINAL ): ADDRESS;
    (* Allocates NumberOfVariables*WordsPerVariable words in memory, if *)
    (* a block that size is available, and returns the block's starting *)
    (* address. Returns NIL otherwise.                                 *)
END STRINGHandler.
```

LISTING 19-5   *The basis for a pair of library modules which manage dynamically allocated* **STRING** *variables, part 2.*

```
IMPLEMENTATION MODULE STRINGHandler;
  FROM Storage IMPORT ALLOCATE, DEALLOCATE, AVAILABLE;
  FROM SYSTEM  IMPORT ADDRESS, WORD;
  FROM InOut   IMPORT WRITECharacter;

  CONST WORDSPerCHAR = 1;
        NULLChar     = 0C;
  TYPE  STRING       = POINTER TO StringRecord;
  TYPE  StringRecord = RECORD
                         FirstCharAt: ADDRESS;
                         WordsUsed  : CARDINAL;
                       END; (* RECORD *)

  PROCEDURE DYNAMICArray( NumberOfVariables,
                          WordsPerVariable: CARDINAL ): ADDRESS;
    VAR StartingAddress: ADDRESS;
  BEGIN
    IF AVAILABLE(NumberOfVariables*WordsPerVariable) THEN
      ALLOCATE(StartingAddress, NumberOfVariables*WordsPerVariable);
      RETURN StartingAddress;
    ELSE
      RETURN NIL;
    END; (* IF *)
  END DYNAMICArray;

  PROCEDURE ASSIGNEDSTRING( VAR StringVariable: STRING;
                                Value: ARRAY OF CHAR ): BOOLEAN;
    VAR Index      : CARDINAL;
        NextAddress: ADDRESS;
  BEGIN
    StringVariable↑.FirstCharAt :=
            STRING( DYNAMICArray( HIGH(Value)+2, WORDSPerCHAR ));
    IF StringVariable↑.FirstCharAt <> NIL THEN
      FOR Index := 0 TO HIGH(Value) DO
        NextAddress := StringVariable↑.FirstCharAt
                       + ADDRESS(Index*WORDSPerCHAR);
        NextAddress↑ := WORD(Value[Index]);
      END; (* FOR *)
      NextAddress := StringVariable↑.FirstCharAt
                     + ADDRESS((HIGH(Value)+1)*WORDSPerCHAR);
      NextAddress↑ := WORD(NULLChar);
      StringVariable↑.WordsUsed := (HIGH(Value)+2)*WORDSPerCHAR;
      RETURN TRUE;
    ELSE
```

```
    RETURN FALSE;
    END; (* IF *)
END ASSIGNEDSTRING;

PROCEDURE WRITESTRING( StringVariable: STRING );
    VAR Index      : CARDINAL;
        NextAddress: ADDRESS;
BEGIN
    Index := 0;
    NextAddress := StringVariable↑.FirstCharAt;
    IF NextAddress <> NIL THEN
        WHILE (CHAR(NextAddress↑) <> NULLChar) DO
            WRITECharacter(CHAR(NextAddress↑));
            INC(Index);
            NextAddress := StringVariable↑.FirstCharAt
                         + ADDRESS(Index*WORDSPerCHAR);
        END; (* WHILE *)
    END; (* IF *)
END WRITESTRING;

PROCEDURE DELETESTRING( VAR StringVariable: STRING );
BEGIN
    IF StringVariable↑.FirstCharAt <> NIL THEN
        DEALLOCATE(StringVariable↑.FirstCharAt,StringVariable↑.WordsUsed);
        StringVariable↑.FirstCharAt := NIL;
    END; (* IF *)
END DELETESTRING;

END STRINGHandler.
```

DELETESTRING must be called to release the space allocated to a STRING variable when that variable is no longer needed. If STRING had been provided as a standard type, such as BITSET or INTEGER, the system would take care of this for the user. It is a serious mistake to call DEALLOCATE with arguments that have been modified since they were passed to ALLOCATE or that were never passed to ALLO-CATE at all. This is one reason for hiding calls to ALLOCATE and DEALLOCATE inside ASSIGNEDSTRING and DELETESTRING. Notice that the approach taken in STRINGHandler could be extended to provide dynamically allocated arrays of element types other than CHAR.

20

Debugging Modula-2 Programs

Causes of Programming Errors

Programming errors may be divided into three general categories: syntactic and semantic errors, code generation errors, and logic errors. These categories are discussed briefly below. Summaries 20-1, 20-2, and 20-3 contain lists of some errors which are possible when one is programming in Modula-2 and suggestions of ways to repair or avoid these mistakes. The numbers given in parentheses refer to the chapters in which the associated topics are discussed. Most compile-time errors are not listed in this chapter because such a list is normally provided as part of a system's documentation.

The reader should also be aware that two versions of Modula-2 compilers exist. A number of revisions and amendments to Modula-2 were agreed upon by Wirth and several of Modula-2's other implementors a few months before the final version of this book was submitted to the publisher. If you have tried everything else, you should check Appendix 5 to see whether your problem is caused by the differences between the original and revised language definitions.

Syntactic and semantic errors are usually detected by the compiler before it begins to produce object code. Examples include missing reserved words such as END, THEN, or DO; misspelled identifiers; a mismatch between the subprogram headings found in a definition module and its implementation module; use of objects which are neither declared nor imported; mismatched parentheses; and perhaps 200 other mistakes. Some semantic errors involving type compatibility may be missed by the compiler when WORD or variant records are used.

SUMMARY 20-1   Causes of some common errors

1. Open comments. Recall that comments may be nested, so one must keep track of the nesting depth when checking for this error. (5)

2. Trying to reference an array element whose index is out of range. If the array concerned is a formal open array parameter, HIGH should be used to test the index before referencing an element. (11)

3. Variables whose values are used before they are initialized. One cannot count on the compiler to catch these. No declarations of Modula-2 variables include initialization.

4. Infinite loops. (6)

5. Unexpected value in a global variable. Either test the value before using it and/or make the variable less global.

6. FOR loop indexing errors. Print the values being used to see if they are the same as you thought they were. (6)

7. Infinite recursion. See Figure 18-2 and Listing 7-9 for examples. Provide an escape hatch so that some call to a recursively called subprogram will not result in another recursive call. (7)

8. Expressions involving Pointer ↑ when Pointer has the value NIL. Test the value of Pointer before trying to reference Pointer ↑ . (12)

9. Failure to respect Modula-2's case sensitivity; BOOLEAN, Boolean, and boolean are three distinct identifiers, for instance.

SUMMARY 20-2   Causes of some strange errors

1. Trying to change which record a WITH statement refers to inside the WITH statement. Do not do this. (12)

2. Failing to account for the side effects caused by functions with variable parameters. (7)

3. Assuming the wrong value for a discriminator in a variant record. Test the value if it is in doubt. (13)

4. Trying to change the range of a FOR loop inside the loop or trying to make assignments to the control variable there. Do not do either. (6)

5. Leaving dangling pointers, destroying the wrong variable with DISPOSE, or changing pointer values in such a way that a dynamically created variable no longer has any pointer pointing to it. (12)

6. Confusing similar variable names. Avoid similar names.

7. Assuming that Pointer = NIL after executing DISPOSE(Pointer).

8. Failing to provide large enough workspaces for coroutines. If a program hangs as if it is in an infinite loop or terminates instead of executing a TRANSFER, this may be the problem. (18)

9. Attempting to TRANSFER control to a PROCESS which has not been assigned a coroutine by an earlier call to TRANSFER or NEWPROCESS. (18)

10. Trying to use code which assumes that the parameters passed to a subprogram are evaluated in a certain order. The order of evaluation is not defined by the Modula-2 language standard, and programs should not assume that a particular order is used.

11. Trying to use code which assumes that library module initializations are done in a particular order. Control runs through all the bodies of the implementation modules imported by a given module, taking the exporting modules in a system-dependent order, before passing to the first statement in the body of the module which did the importing.

12. Passing DEALLOCATE parameters which were never passed to ALLOCATE or which have been modified since the call to ALLOCATE.

SUMMARY 20-3 Main causes of run-time errors

1. Trying to access an array element whose index is out of bounds. (11)

2. Trying to access an enumeration value whose ordinal number is out of bounds. (10)

3. Attempted division by zero.

4. Other overflows and underflows including assignment of a negative value to a CARDINAL variable and a call to INCL or EXCL with a variable whose value is out of range for the set passed.

5. Stack, heap, or other memory shortage caused by too much recursion, variables requiring too much memory, too much dynamic allocation, too many modules need to be loaded, an expression which is too long or too complicated, or subprograms with too many parameters.

6. Calls to READInteger which are fed CHAR or REAL values, and similar type clashes caused by ignorant or malevolent users. (5, 7)

7. Attempts to execute an undefined instruction. Examples include CASE statements with no ELSE portion and no label containing the value of the controlling expression (6), requests to override the compiler's allocation scheme which ask for a variable to be stored at a nonexistent address or one which is protected (19), attempts to access Pointer ↑ when Pointer = NIL (12), and functions which are not terminated by a RETURN statement (7).

8. Attempts to link in an incompatible or nonexistent module just before running a program; see your system's documentation.

9. Program execution may also be deliberately stopped by a call on the standard procedure HALT, a hardware interrupt which is triggered by <control>-C, <control>-Z, or some other "stop" key.

Object code generation errors are also detected by the compiler. Most of these will be implementation restrictions such as too many identifiers used, scope table overflow, FOR step too large, boolean expression too long, expression too complicated, or too many parameters.

The symptoms of most logic errors in a program do not appear until the program is running. Some logic errors cause incorrect output which is noticed after the program has finished execution. Other logic errors are simply never detected. Examples of logic errors include

Failures to trap unusual inputs (e.g., to avoid division by zero)

Assumptions that a procedure has succeeded when it has not (see Listing 11-3)

Missed boundary conditions (see DELETEName in Listing 12-2)

Infinite loops

Infinite recursions

Overflows in numeric types

Range errors in enumeration types or array indices

Improper or missing transfer of control between coroutines

Even people who are experienced with a particular programming language will make some mistakes because of unfamiliarity with various details of the language. Before spending too much time looking for obscure causes of a stubborn bug, it makes sense to see whether or not the constructs involved are actually meant to do what they are being used for. A quick review of material presented earlier in this book or of associated entries in the glossary could save a lot of time. Programmers familiar with other languages might waste a lot of time in Modula-2, for instance, if they incorrectly assume that pointer variables are initialized to NIL.

Debugging Techniques

Debugging is currently an art form. However, there are a number of factors whose presence can greatly aid a programmer who is trying to determine why his or her program is not working. Some of the helpful factors are a good knowledge of the language and the system being used, a clear understanding of the problem area and the algorithms which are being used, source code which is easy to understand and which takes advantage of ways to localize code (e.g., procedures, functions, modules, opaque types), clear statements about any important assumptions made while coding, the availability of a good debugger which will allow one to trace selected portions of the program as it steps through its execution, and intuition. Many of these factors increase with thoughtful experience.

If a debugger is not available, one can still trace the execution of selected parts of a program by inserting write statements at various points in the code. These statements may print the current values of certain variables which the programmer thinks might be different than he or she had supposed. Write statements can also mark the flow of control as calls are made on subprograms or as different branches of IF statements and CASE statements are taken. Try to make the output from these write statements as clear as possible. For instance, a message such as "Null was passed an atom" is preferable to "bad param" or, worse yet, garbage or an operating system message such as "address overflow." Since all this output is used mainly for debugging, the programmer may wish to embed the write statements inside conditionals similar to this one:

```
IF Debug THEN
    WRITE0("%NEntering ProcedureTwo");
END; (*IF Debug *)
```

The program could read a value for Debug as soon as it starts, or Debug could be a constant BOOLEAN.

The fact that Modula-2 comments may be nested makes it very easy to comment out a portion of code, including its associated comments, so that it does not affect the program. This is sometimes useful when one is trying to localize the area in which a problem lies. Since a suspicious block of code can be made invisible to the compiler by enclosing it in a single pair of comment delimiters, several different versions of the code can be tried without deleting anything. This may save the programmer a substantial amount of editing time.

Chapter

21

A Modula-2
Programming Style

Programs interact with people in two basic ways. While a program is being written, debugged, modified, or ported to another machine, people must work extensively with the program in its source code form. When one is testing or running a program, one interacts with the object code version by way of the English and numeric expressions which the object code produces and accepts while running. A good programming style is important in both situations. This chapter summarizes the stylistic rules used throughout the book.

Comments

Comments should be clear, concise, and not cryptic. Try to use complete sentences in comments which are more than a few words long. Do not simply restate the code. Differentiate between what belongs in comments and what belongs in messages sent to users while the program is executing. Avoid abbreviations unless they are necessary. Programmers should consider placing comments in the following positions:

At the beginning of each module

With constant, type, variable, and procedure declarations

Near any unusual or complex algorithms or data structures

Near calls to procedures whose names do not tell the full story of what they do

Following the reserved word END

Near any machine- or implementation-dependent objects

Comments could be used at the beginning of a module to tell the following:

What the module's purpose is

Who wrote the module

When it was written

Any books, articles, or programmers that were used as sources for the algorithms and/or data structures in the module

Comments could be placed near constant, type, variable, and procedure declarations to do the following:

Make the object's intended purpose clear, especially if the identifier used is at all cryptic

Expand on the meaning of any abbreviated names used

Enumerate any limitations on the object's use which are not obvious

Note that the comments in a definition module should usually be all that one needs to read in order to decide whether or not one wishes to import something from that module.

Comments may be used near any unusual or complex algorithms or data structures to list any sources outside the program which provide further explanation. One might also consider providing an English or pseudocode version of the algorithm or structure.

Comments may be useful near calls on procedures or functions whose names do not tell the full story of what they do. This is especially important in connection with functions that produce side effects by using variable parameters.

Comments are useful following the reserved word END because they help clarify two items: the kind of statement which has just ended (i.e., IF, CASE, FOR, WHILE, REPEAT..UNTIL, LOOP, or WITH) and which particular statement of that kind has just ended. If a statement covers only a few lines, its key word is enough to tell a reader both these things. But for longer statements or ones which are deeply nested, more clarification is often required.

Comments should be used to clearly mark any machine- or implementation-dependent objects. Examples of these objects include

Imports from SYSTEM

Variables stored at an absolute address specified by the program

Constants such as ScreenWidth or NumberOfDiskSectors

Uses of type transfer functions should normally be marked since it is usually possible for the correspondence between the values of the two types to be defined differently on different systems.

Of course, not every program requires the same amount of commentary. The reader is urged to consult Summaries 15-1, 15-2, and 15-3 for further suggestions.

Identifiers

Descriptive names are preferable to short, cryptic ones. Note, however, that length does not necessarily imply great descriptive power. Names which begin to differ in the first six or eight letters are also preferable, i.e., pairs like LocalModuleOne and LocalModuleTwo should be avoided to improve readability and portability. In this book, global objects and exports and imports have usually been indicated by capitalizing all the letters in the first word in their identifiers, e.g., WRITEString.

Format

The following conventions for laying out source code may be used to make Modula-2 programs easier to read:

1. Put at most one statement per line. The only exception to this is that you may wish to think of the code for exiting a LOOP loop as a single statement, i.e., put "IF SomeCondition THEN EXIT; END;" on one line instead of three. Do not try to save space by putting two or three assignment statements or procedure calls, no matter how short, on a single line. The gain in legibility is well worth the cost of the extra paper.

2. Use consistent indentation. Each level of nesting should be indented the same amount; this book used two spaces per level. Use blank lines whenever doing so will make the source code easier to read.

3. Keep certain special characters and words lined up. These include: | in case statements, : in declarations and case statements, and = in constant and type declarations. Leave blanks around certain (groups of) characters including :=, =, and perhaps + and −. Line up the key words in import lists.

4. Carry long procedure declarations over onto several lines. For in-

```
PROCEDURE ManyParameters ( VAR SomeLongName: INTEGER;
                               AnotherLongName: BOOLEAN;
                               ADifferentLongName: CARDINAL;
                           VAR LastLongName: BOOLEAN );
```

Notice how the colons are lined up and the opening and closing parentheses are clearly visible. Capitalized reserved words such as VAR are easy to spot even though the parameter names are of different lengths.

5. Do not use expressions of the form

```
Boolean Variable = TRUE
```

or

```
Boolean Variable = FALSE
```

For instance, suppose we have declared

```
VAR SystemIsUp : BOOLEAN;
```

Rather than writing

```
IF SystemIsUp = TRUE THEN
   DoSomething;
END; (* IF *)
```

write

```
IF SystemIsUp THEN
   DoSomething;
END; (* IF *)
```

Similarly, "IF NOT SystemIsUp THEN . . ." is in a better style than "IF SystemIsUp = FALSE THEN . . . ."

Object Code Style

Whenever a user is expected to provide input, make the range of acceptable values clear by giving examples and/or descriptions. Label all output clearly and in such a way that the user will notice if output is missing. Have programs introduce themselves to the user if this is appropriate. The introduction could include the following:

The program's name

The intended purpose of the program

The way a user can gracefully exit the program if this is desired

Any limitations on the use or effectiveness of the program which are not obvious

The name of the person the user should contact with problems or questions

Error messages are also very important. If anything frustrates program users more than obscure error messages such as "internal error: unexpected value 109 at line 7," it is a crash with no error message at all. Ideally, of course, the program should not simply terminate when an incorrect value arises during a computation. It should be durable enough to recover and continue execution. The next best thing is to terminate with an error message that tells the user how to fix the error if possible or whom to contact if professional help is required; how to avoid the same error in the future; what damage is likely to have been caused by the error; and how to repair the damage.

22

A Discussion of
Modula-2's Shortcomings

Disclaimer

Like all programming languages, Modula-2 does have some problems. The complaints discussed in this chapter have been compiled from several sources, including my own experience; my discussions with other programmers; Spector (1982); and Powell ("Using Modula-2 for System Programming with UNIX"). I make no claims that this chapter discusses all of Modula-2's shortcomings. This discussion is not meant to discourage people from using Modula-2, which is one of the best programming languages currently available. However, I also believe it is better, whenever possible, to know ahead of time what problems to expect.

Ways to handle some of these problems are presented at the appropriate places earlier in the text or are given in this chapter. Making the changes necessary to handle others would involve rewriting the compiler, the operating system, or both. Readers are encouraged to look at Appendix 5, which contains a summary of the changes to Modula-2 that have been approved by Nicklaus Wirth as of March 1984, since several of the problems discussed in this chapter have been addressed.

Problems Hardly Worth Mentioning

Summary 22-1 contains a list of very minor annoyances. I consider these problems hardly worth mentioning for two reasons. First, these shortcomings do not have very important consequences. For instance, the legibility of almost any Modula-2 program would be improved very little by rewriting it using identifiers which contain underscores. Second, they are easy to get around. It is no real trouble at all to write your own SystemConstants module, for instance, and all of the problems listed could be solved completely by using a fairly simple preprocessor before compilation.

**SUMMARY 22-1   Some very minor problems with
Modula-2**

1. One cannot include both apostrophes and quotes in the same character literal string. The solution, of course, is to use more than one string.

2. The EXIT command only passes control out of the current LOOP loop; nested loops require one EXIT per nesting level.

3. Exported variables cannot be made read only; we must initialize such variables in the exporting module and rely on the user to change their value only by making calls on subprograms which have been exported with the variables.

4. Identifiers cannot contain underscores.

5. Conditional, loop, and WITH statements do not end in key phrases such as END IF and END LOOP, but just with END. Although the same effect can be achieved for human readers by using comments, this approach does not enable compilers to check for proper nesting.

6. The number of bits per word, MaxCard, maximum size of a BITSET, and other implementation constants are not always available as imports from some module SystemConstants.

7. Tests for equality and inequality between entire arrays or records are not allowed.

Some Truly Annoying Problems

Summary 22-2 contains a list of some of Modula-2's more serious shortcomings. I consider these problems to be more than minor annoyances because their ideal solutions are beyond the reach of the ordinary Modula-2 programmer. This is because the solutions involve the definition of language standards and the implementation of compilers which support these standards. These problems would not have been difficult to remedy if they had been foreseen by Modula-2's implementors.

The first problem is the incompatibility of CHAR values and formal ARRAY OF CHAR parameters. One solution is to assign the CHAR value concerned to a variable which was declared as an ARRAY [1..1] OF CHAR; then the compatible array variable may be passed. This annoyance has been fixed in the second version of Modula-2. The sec-

---

SUMMARY 22-2   Serious problems with Modula-2

1. The type CHAR is not compatible with a formal parameter ARRAY OF CHAR

2. Not enough is said about string handling; a basic type STRING of unconstrained length would be a useful addition to the language.

3. There is no standard set of library modules which every implementation is required to support. This helps contribute to the awkwardness of the I/O procedures presented in Wirth's reports on the language.

4. Only one precision is supported for each of the numeric types INTEGER, CARDINAL, and REAL. There is no double precision arithmetic as there is in FORTRAN.

5. The behavior of the standard procedures INC and DEC at the boundaries of enumeration types should be specified. It is unclear whether they wrap around, raise a run-time constraint error, or just assign some garbage value. Also, what should CAP do with nonalphabetic characters?

6. Only one-dimensional open arrays are available as formal parameters. An ARRAY OF INTEGER formal parameter, for instance, only matches actual parameters which are one-dimensional arrays of INTEGER; it would be more useful if such a formal parameter would match any array of INTEGER with one or more dimensions.

7. Some confusion is possible since HIGH(FOAP) = 0 whether the open array formal parameter FOAP was matched to literal string "" or to a string of length one, "B" for example.

8. The results of division by zero, arithmetic overflow, referencing through a pointer which is NIL, and other erroneous operations are not defined. There is no exception mechanism to handle run-time errors.

9. Compilers should be required to allow SET OF CHAR and other sets with more than just a few elements.

---

ond problem, Modula-2's lack of string-handling facilities, is much more serious. I have tried to provide a partial solution in Chapters 11 and 19, but even the best such solution is likely to have limited portability because of the differences between libraries.

Similarly, the lack of a standardized library and of support for double precision arithmetic would have been solved best by providing appropriate standards when the language was released to the public. The same is true of the fifth problem, the lack of any common definition of the behavior of Modula-2's standard subprograms in extreme circumstances. In Wirth's second public version of Modula-2, the identifiers LONGCARD, LONGINT, and LONGREAL denote predefined types, but implementations are still not required to support these types. The best solution I have seen to the sixth problem, the lack of multidimensional open array parameters, is described in Wiener (1983).

The seventh problem listed in Summary 22-2 could have been avoided by assuming that the lowest index of any formal open array parameter is 1, not 0. Then if FOAP was a formal ARRAY OF CHAR parameter which was passed the empty string "", HIGH(FOAP) would be 0. If "B" was passed to FOAP, HIGH(FOAP) would be 1. As things stand (at least on the Lilith machine running the original ETH compiler), it is necessary to compare FOAP[0] with OC to see whether the actual parameter passed was the empty string.

When I suggest in item 8 of Summary 22-2 that the results of division by zero and other erroneous operations should have been defined as part of the language, the obvious question is "What should the results be defined as?" The easiest thing to do would be to simply terminate a program which tries to execute one of these operations. The problem with this is that it removes all opportunity for error recovery. I would suggest therefore that the standard procedure HALT should have been placed in SYSTEM and that the result of any attempt to divide by zero, etc., would be a call to HALT.

On a given system, HALT might do nothing more than print a cursory error message such as "CARDINAL overflow" and then return control to the operating system. A more sophisticated version of HALT might also cause a memory dump so that a postmortem symbolic debugger could be used. In the most general case, HALT could pass some sort of description of the error to an exception-handling routine provided by the user as part of the program. In this last case, it is reasonable to expect control to be returned to the main program after the error-handling routine finishes execution.

Are These Really Shortcomings?

We turn now to Summary 22-3, a list of some complaints which I believe have been made unfairly about Modula-2.

The first complaint listed in Summary 22-3 seems to be based mainly on an aversion to typing. This "problem" is solved in Ada, in which programmers can do the equivalent of "import everything from module M" without listing each import from M separately. The problem with this is that it is not always possible to look at an Ada package and tell immediately where a given identifier was imported from.

In Modula-2, we never need to look further than the surrounding declarations and import lists to determine where an object's declara-

---

**SUMMARY 22-3   Unjustified complaints about
Modula-2**

1. It is not possible to import everything from a module without either listing each import separately or else prefacing each use of an import by the name of the exporting module.

2. The predefined name FLOAT is inconsistent with the name REAL.

3. Capitalizing reserved words such as END makes them seem more important than they are. Case sensitivity is generally more trouble than it is worth.

4. Comments require four bracket characters, (* and *). In addition, many programmers will add two spaces to improve legibility. Ada's use of -- or Pascal's use of single braces { and } is better. The best solution would be to have a comment start with single comment character and extend either to the next comment character or end of line, whichever comes first.

---

tion is located. If we see an identifier of the form

NameOne.NameTwo

and the surrounding module asks to

IMPORT NameOne;

we know immediately that the code defining NameTwo may be found in module NameOne. The same is true, of course, if we see an import list such as

FROM NameOne IMPORT NameTwo;

If neither of these import lists is found, NameOne must be a record with a field called NameTwo, and we must look for the declaration or importation of NameOne.

If Modula-2's import rules were like Ada's, something like "Import A, B, C, D, E;" might appear at the top of a module in which SomeName was referred to; assume also that we are not required in this instance to use a qualifying module name, i.e., the reference is to SomeName, not C.SomeName or something similar. Now suppose I want to know more about SomeName. I have no idea which module it was imported from, so I am forced to check the definition modules for A, B, C, D, and E until I find an export called SomeName. Then I must be sure that I have the right export called SomeName, since there is no rule against using the same name for different exports. Modula-2's approach is clearly better.

The second unjustified complaint listed in Summary 22-3 is that the predefined name FLOAT is inconsistent with the name REAL. The very good reason for using this name is that FLOAT is a type conversion function whereas REAL is the name of a type transfer function. Consider an example. On a 16-bit machine which uses two words to represent REAL values, FLOAT takes one word which represents, say, the CARDINAL value 12345 and produces a two-word representation of 12345.0E0. REAL, on the other hand, simply tries to reinterpret any given 32 bits as a REAL value. The difference in behavior justifies the names used.

The third unjustified complaint involves case sensitivity and is probably one of the most common complaints against Modula-2. This is a matter of personal opinion, but I would argue first that reserved words are important enough to deserve capitalization. For instance, the fact that VAR is in caps makes it much easier to distinguish variable parameters in subprogram headings. No one would argue seriously that we should *ignore* case in natural language texts such as the one you are reading now, would they? Case sensitivity therefore fits in very well with Modula-2's design philosophy that programs should be easy to read.

The fourth complaint, that too many characters are needed to bracket comments, also seems to be based on an aversion to typing. I would argue that Modula-2's approach serves very well to separate comments from source code. Single braces with no spaces are fine for compilers, but the human reader does better with bolder delineations. The problem with the "best solution," which would have comments start with a single character and extend to the next comment character or end of line, whichever comes first, is that it deprives programmers of the very useful ability to nest comments.

1

Modula-2's Standard Subprograms

Standard Functions

ABS(x)	Returns the absolute value of x. The type of the result will be the same as the type of the argument. The results are implementation-dependent if x is not an INTEGER or a REAL.
CAP(ch)	If ch is a lowercase character, returns the corresponding uppercase character. If ch is already uppercase, returns ch. If ch is not an alphabetic character, the value returned is implementation-dependent.
CHR(x)	Returns the character with the ordinal number x. Different systems may expect x in different bases, e.g., octal x on one system, decimal x on another.
FLOAT(x)	Returns the REAL value which corresponds to x. Usually x is assumed to be a CARDINAL; some systems may allow x to be an INTEGER.
HIGH(FOAP)	Returns the high index bound of the actual array which was matched to the formal open array parameter FOAP.
ODD(x)	Returns (x MOD 2 <> 0).
ORD (x)	Returns the CARDINAL value which is the ordinal number of x in the set of values defined for x's type T; T may be an enumeration type, CHAR, INTEGER, or CARDINAL. For instance, if
	TYPE StopLight = (Green, Yellow, Red);
	ORD(Green) = 0, ORD(Yellow) = 1, and ORD(Red) = 2.

| TRUNC(x) | Returns the CARDINAL value obtained by truncating the REAL x. May return an INTEGER on some systems. |
| VAL(T,x) | Returns the value with ordinal number x in the set of values defined for type T; T may be an enumeration type, CHAR, INTEGER, or CARDINAL. VAL(T,ORD(x)) = x if x is of type T. |

Standard Procedures

DEC(x)	Decrements x by one; could be replaced by x := x − 1 if x is of a numeric type. DEC might not accept REAL values for x on your system. DEC is always defined for enumeration types and results in the replacement of the current value of x by the predecessor of that value. The result of trying to DEC some variable X whose value satisfies ORD(X) = 0 differs from system to system.
DEC(x,n)	Causes the same action as n consecutive calls on DEC(x); could be replaced by x := x − n if x is of a numeric type.
EXCL(s,i)	Causes the same action as s := s − {i}.
HALT	Terminates program execution. The program is not suspended; execution can only be resumed at the top of the program. On many systems, HALT causes the current state of the program (i.e., the values of all variables and the history of calls which were made leading into the subprogram that called HALT) to be dumped for later use by a postmortem debugger.
INC(x)	Increments x by one; could be replaced by x := x + 1 if x is of a numeric type. INC might not accept REAL values for x on your system. INC is always defined for enumeration types and results in the replacement of the current value of x by the successor of that value. The result of trying to INC some variable whose value is already the greatest value defined for the variable's type differs from system to system.
INC(x,n)	Causes the same action as n consecutive calls on INC(x); could be replaced by x := x + n if x is of a numeric type.
INCL(s,i)	Causes the same action as s := s + {i}.

Calls on NEW and DISPOSE are textually translated into calls on ALLOCATE and DEALLOCATE. These last two procedures are usually provided in library module Storage and must be compatible with the procedure type defined by PROCEDURE(VAR ADDRESS, CARDI-

NAL). If p has been declared as VAR p: POINTER TO T; the correspondences are as follows:

```
NEW(p)      => ALLOCATE(p, TSIZE(T))
DISPOSE(p) => DEALLOCATE(p, TSIZE(T))
```

Note that it is possible to provide more than one version of the library modules which handle memory management, although most systems only come with one, Storage. If a module which uses NEW imports VirtualMemory.ALLOCATE instead of Storage.ALLOCATE, for instance, calls on NEW may be handled differently. Of course, Storage may be implemented quite differently on different systems, such as using only a heap in main memory on one and paging on another.

2

Reserved Words and Standard Identifiers

Reserved words may *not* be used as identifiers of programmer-defined objects; any declaration such as

CONST BEGIN = 1984;

which tries to give a reserved word a new programmer-defined meaning is illegal. SYSTEM and its exports (as defined in Wirth, 1983; there may be other exports on your system) are included in this appendix for convenience. Even though the names of SYSTEM exports are not reserved, it is not a bad idea to treat them as if they were to avoid misunderstandings.

Standard identifiers such as ABS and NIL are predeclared, i.e., they are always imported automatically into every module. Standard identifiers may be used to name programmer-defined objects in declarations which are local to a subprogram, but it is not a good idea to do this because it makes programs harder to understand. In other words, the standard identifiers, such as the names of SYSTEM exports, should be treated as though they are reserved words.

ABS	Standard function
ADDRESS	SYSTEM export
ADR	SYSTEM export
AND	Reserved word
ARRAY	Reserved word
BEGIN	Reserved word
BITSET	Standard type
BOOLEAN	Standard type
BY	Reserved word

CAP	Standard function
CARDINAL	Standard type
CASE	Reserved word
CHAR	Standard type
CHR	Standard function
CONST	Reserved word
DEC	Standard procedure
DEFINITION	Reserved word
DISPOSE	Standard procedure
DIV	Reserved word
DO	Reserved word
ELSE	Reserved word
ELSIF	Reserved word
END	Reserved word
EXCL	Standard procedure
EXIT	Reserved word
EXPORT	Reserved word
FALSE	Predefined value
FLOAT	Standard function
FOR	Reserved word
FROM	Reserved word
HALT	Standard procedure
HIGH	Standard function
IF	Reserved word
IMPLEMENTATION	Reserved word
IMPORT	Reserved word
IN	Reserved word
INC	Standard procedure
INCL	Standard procedure
INTEGER	Standard type
LOOP	Reserved word
MOD	Reserved word
MODULE	Reserved word
NEW	Standard procedure
NEWPROCESS	SYSTEM export
NIL	Predefined value
NOT	Reserved word
ODD	Standard function
OF	Reserved word
OR	Reserved word
ORD	Standard function
POINTER	Reserved word
PROC	Standard type
PROCEDURE	Reserved word
PROCESS	SYSTEM export

QUALIFIED	Reserved word
REAL	Standard type
RECORD	Reserved word
REPEAT	Reserved word
RETURN	Reserved word
SET	Reserved word
SIZE	SYSTEM export
SYSTEM	Exports potentially system-dependent objects
THEN	Reserved word
TO	Reserved word
TRANSFER	SYSTEM export
TRUE	Predefined value
TRUNC	Standard function
TSIZE	SYSTEM export
TYPE	Reserved word
UNTIL	Reserved word
VAL	Standard function
VAR	Reserved word
WHILE	Reserved word
WITH	Reserved word
WORD	SYSTEM export

3

Formal Syntax Diagrams

In the charts which follow, any characters which appear inside ovals or circles are terminal symbols, i.e., symbols which appear in actual Modula-2 source code. Nonterminal symbols appear inside rectangles and refer to syntactic entities which are defined, in terms of terminals and/or nonterminals, elsewhere in this appendix. Readers who are not familiar with syntactic descriptions of programming languages are invited to consult the glossary and to study the examples given later in this introduction.

These charts are not simply a graphical version of the EBNF (Extended Backus-Naur Form) description of Modula-2 given in Wirth (1983). The extra nonterminal Char has been introduced to accommodate CHAR values such as 33C instead of incorporating them under the category of integers. Most nonterminals have been given names which are more descriptive than those in the EBNF description. The syntax for comments has been included. IntegerConstantTerms have been distinguished from other constant terms since it makes no sense to allow BITSETs, for instance, to specify absolute addresses or module priorities. In general, I have tried to incorporate a bit more semantic information into the syntax diagrams. The root symbol, i.e., the main nonterminal at which one must start when trying to trace a path through these charts to determine whether or not a given module is syntactically correct, is CompilationUnit. The nonterminal letter refers to any of the alphabetic characters, i.e., a, b, . . . , z, A . . . Z.

Readers who are not familiar with syntax diagrams may find the following examples useful. Suppose your compiler gives you an error message along the lines of "identifier expected" and indicates that the problem is somewhere in the declaration VAR 1984GNP: REAL;. By using the index to the syntax diagrams, you can find the page on which a nonterminal called Identifier is defined. If you try to trace that syntax chart using the characters in 1984GNP, you will see that 1984GNP is not a valid identifier in Modula-2; every identifier must begin with a letter. GNP1984 and US1984GNP are both valid identifiers since they consist of a letter followed by zero or more letters or digits, as the syntax diagram indicates an Identifier should.

Notice that the syntactic aspects of a language, although important, are by no means the only part of a given system one must deal with on a regular basis. For instance, the syntax diagram would accept an identifier 10,000 characters long. The length of an identifier is an example of a restriction which is implementation-dependent. One cannot expect to find such restrictions by looking in the syntax diagrams.

The syntax charts also contain very little semantic information, i.e., they say little or nothing about what a piece of Modula-2 code means. For instance, if you look up the syntax diagram for Char, you will see that a Char can be either a character (e.g., #, Y, k, !, ", or " ") or a sequence of OctalDigits followed by a capital C. The syntax charts do not tell one that 120C means character number 120 (in base 8; the same as 80 in base 10) in the ASCII character set, i.e., the syntax charts do not say "120C means P." As far as the syntax diagrams are concerned 54321C is a valid Char, but I know of no systems which recognize it as such.

Index to Syntax Diagrams

In the following index, the boldface number in each entry is the number of the syntax diagram which contains the definition of the entry. Successive numbers indicate uses of the entry in other diagrams. As indicated, a character is any ASCII character, and a letter is any alphabetic character (a . . . z, A . . . Z).

Note also that Wirth and a number of other implementors of Modula-2 have agreed upon some changes and extensions to the language (see Appendix 5). The syntax charts in this book are for the original version of Modula-2. The changes effect the syntax of CaseList, ConstantFactor, DefinitionModule, ExportList, Set, Subrange, Tag, and Variant.

ActualParameters   **59**, 58, 62
AdditionOperator   **17**, 15, 56
AnythingBut *) or (*   **95**, 93
ArrayReference   **53**, 52
ArrayType   **34**, 29
AssignmentStatement   **61**, 60

BasicType	**30,** 29, 34, 44
Block	**78,** 75, 83, 91
CaseLabel	**43,** 42
CaseLabelList	**42,** 41, 68
CaseList	**68,** 67
CaseStatement	**67,** 60
Char	**8,** 2
character	(Any ASCII Character) 8, 10, 95
character*	**10**
character#	**10**
Comment	**93,** 94
CompilationUnit	**92**
ConstantDeclaration	**12,** 79, 90
ConstantExpression	**13,** 12, 23, 27, 33, 43, 72
ConstantFactor	**23,** 19, 23
ConstantTerm	**19,** 15
Declaration	**79,** 78
Definition	**90,** 89
DefinitionModule	**89,** 92
Designator	**52,** 58, 61, 62, 74
Digit	**7,** 1, 3, 4, 5, 6, 8
Element	**27,** 26
ElementList	**26,** 25
ELSEPart	**66,** 64, 67
ELSIFPart	**65,** 64
Enumeration	**31,** 30
ExportList	**85,** 83, 89
Expression	**55,** 54, 58, 60, 61, 64, 65, 67, 69, 70, 71
ExpressionList	**54,** 53, 59
Factor	**58,** 57
Field	**37,** 36
FieldList	**36,** 35, 38, 41
FormalParameters	**80,** 76
FormalParameterSection	**81,** 80
FormalType	**82,** 48, 81
FormalTypeList	**48,** 46
ForStatement	**71,** 60
HexDigit	**6,** 3
Identifier	**1,** 11, 12, 28, 32, 39, 50, 52, 71, 77, 88, 90
IdentifierList	**32,** 31, 37, 81, 85, 86, 87
IFStatement	**64,** 60
ImportList	**86,** 83, 89, 91
Integer	**3,** 2
IntegerAdditionOperator	**18,** 16, 17
IntegerConstantFactor	**24,** 20
IntegerConstantTerm	**20,** 16

IntegerMultiplicationOperator	**22,** 20, 21
IntegerSimpleConstantExpression	**16,** 24, 51, 84
letter	(a . . . z, A . . . Z), 1
LoopStatement	**73,** 60
ModuleDeclaration	**83,** 79
ModuleIdentifier	**88,** 83, 86, 89, 91
ModuleIdentifierList	**87,** 86
MultiplicationOperator	**21,** 19, 57
Number	**2,** 23, 58
OctalDigit	**9,** 3, 7, 8
OptionalAddress	**51,** 50
OptionalBY	**72,** 71
OptionalComment	**94,** 93
OptionalVAR	**49,** 48, 81
PointerType	**45,** 29
Priority	**84,** 83, 91
ProcedureCall	**62,** 60
ProcedureDeclaration	**75,** 79
ProcedureHeading	**76,** 75, 90
ProcedureIdentifier	**77,** 75, 76
ProcedureType	**46,** 29
ProgramModule	**91,** 92
QualifiedIdentifier	**11,** 23, 25, 30, 39, 47, 52, 82
Real	**4,** 2
RecordType	**35,** 29
RelationalOperator	**14,** 13, 55
RepeatStatement	**70,** 60
ScaleFactor	**5,** 4
Set	**25,** 23, 58
SetType	**44,** 29
SimpleConstantExpression	**15,** 13
SimpleExpression	**56,** 55
Statement	**60,** 63
Statement Sequence	**63,** 64, 65, 66, 68, 69, 70, 71, 73, 74, 78
String	**10,** 23, 58
Subrange	**33,** 30
Tag	**39,** 38
Term	**57,** 56
Type	**29,** 28, 34, 37, 45, 50, 90
TypeDeclaration	**28,** 79
TypeReturned	**47,** 46, 80
VariableDeclaration	**50,** 79, 90
Variant	**41,** 40
VariantField	**38,** 37
VariantList	**40,** 38
WhileStatement	**69,** 60
WithStatement	**74,** 60

1. Identifier

2. Number

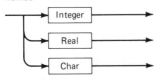

3. Integer

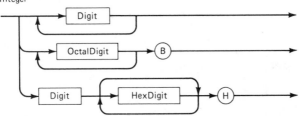

4. Real

5. ScaleFactor

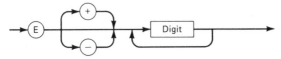

6. HexDigit

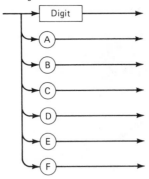

7. Digit

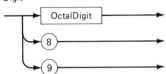

8. Char

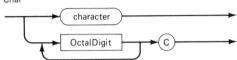

Some systems may allow Digit in place of OctalDigit

9. OctalDigit

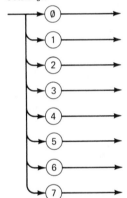

10. String

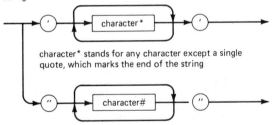

character* stands for any character except a single
quote, which marks the end of the string

character# stands for any character except a double
quote, which marks the end of the string

11. QualifiedIdentifier

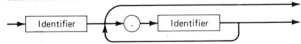

12. ConstantDeclaration

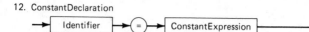

13. ConstantExpression

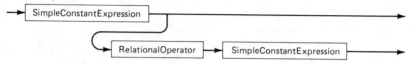

14. RelationalOperator

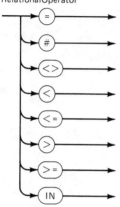

15. SimpleConstantExpression

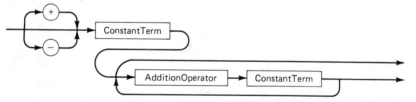

16. IntegerSimpleConstantExpression

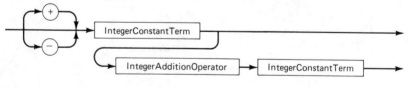

17. AdditionOperator

18. IntegerAdditionOperator

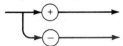

19. ConstantTerm

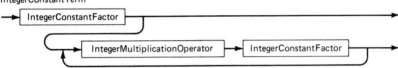

20. IntegerConstantTerm

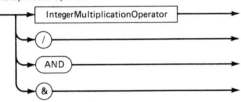

21. MultiplicationOperator

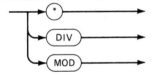

22. IntegerMultiplicationOperator

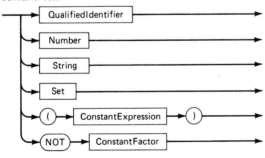

23. ConstantFactor

24. IntegerConstantFactor

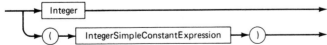

25. Set

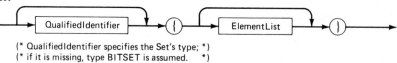

(* QualifiedIdentifier specifies the Set's type; *)
(* if it is missing, type BITSET is assumed. *)

26. ElementList

27. Element

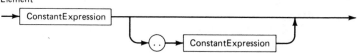

28. TypeDeclaration

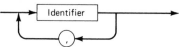

29. Type

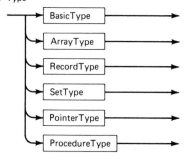

30. BasicType

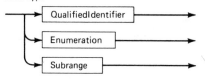

31. Enumeration

32. IdentifierList

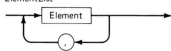

33. Subrange

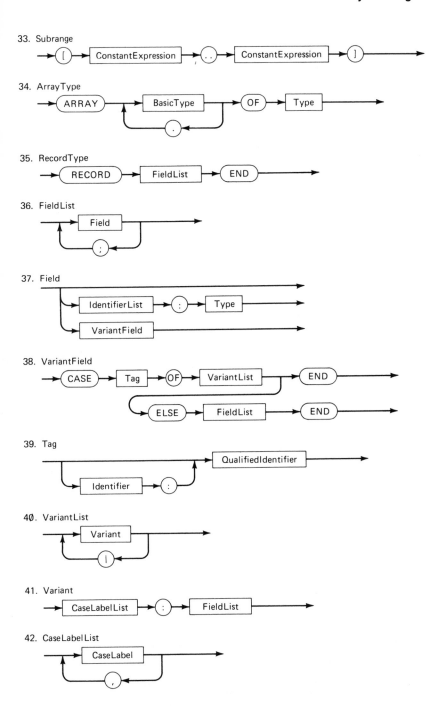

34. ArrayType

35. RecordType

36. FieldList

37. Field

38. VariantField

39. Tag

40. VariantList

41. Variant

42. CaseLabelList

43. CaseLabel

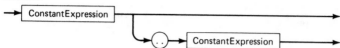

44. SetType

45. PointerType

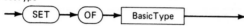

46. ProcedureType

47. TypeReturned

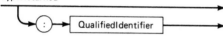

48. FormalTypeList

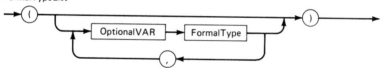

49. OptionalVAR

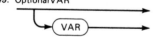

50. VariableDeclaration

51. OptionalAddress

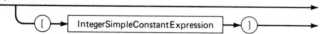

Some systems may only allow the first possibility, i.e.,
one might not be allowed to override the compiler's allocation scheme.

52. Designator

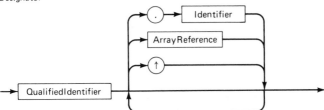

53. ArrayReference

54. ExpressionList

55. Expression

56. SimpleExpression

57. Term

58. Factor

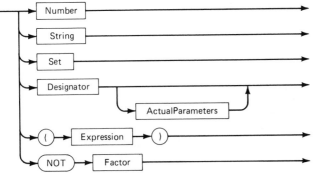

59. ActualParameters

60. Statement

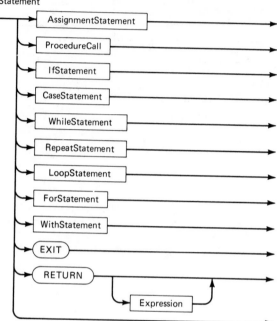

61. AssignmentStatement

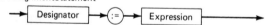

62. ProcedureCall

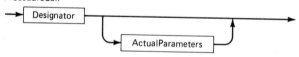

63. StatementSequence

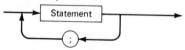

64. IfStatement

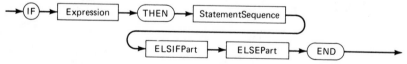

65. ELSIFPart

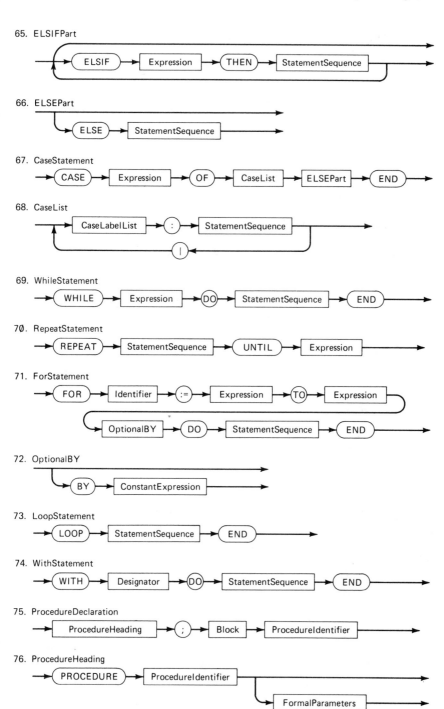

66. ELSEPart

67. CaseStatement

68. CaseList

69. WhileStatement

70. RepeatStatement

71. ForStatement

72. OptionalBY

73. LoopStatement

74. WithStatement

75. ProcedureDeclaration

76. ProcedureHeading

77. ProcedureIdentifier

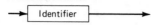

78. Block

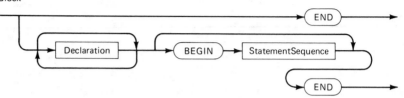

79. Declaration

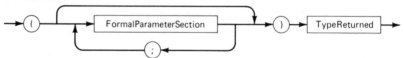

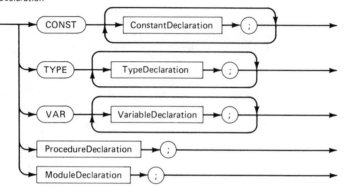

80. FormalParameters

81. FormalParameterSection

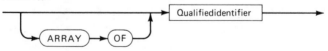

82. FormalType

83. ModuleDeclaration

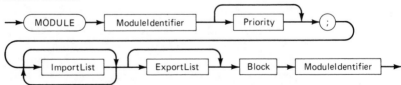

84. Priority

85. ExportList

86. ImportList

87. ModuleIdentifierList

88. ModuleIdentifier

89. DefinitionModule

90. Definition

91. ProgramModule

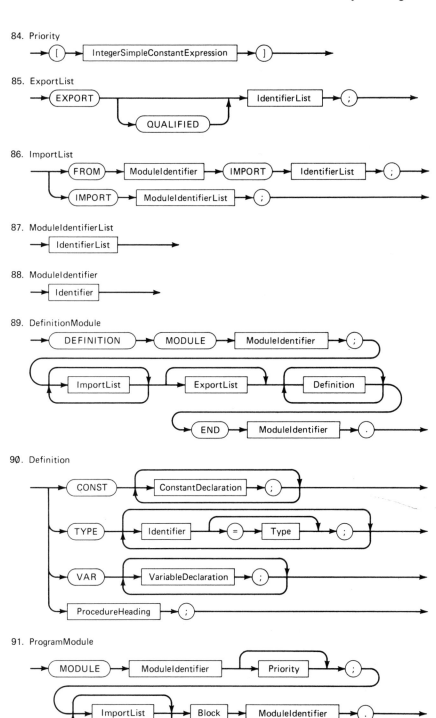

92. CompilationUnit

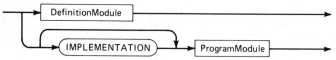

93. Comment

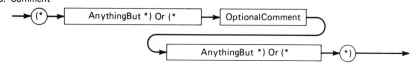

94. OptionalComment

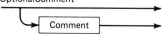

95. AnythingBut *) Or (*

This includes any stream of ASCII characters which does not
contain either of the two comment delimiters *) and (*.
Certain control characters might also need to be excluded from
commented text to satisfy a given implementation of Modula-2.

4

Other Sources of Information on Modula-2

For the most part, the sources listed in the bibliography have not been repeated in this appendix.

Magazines and Journals

ACM SIGPLAN Notices
11 W. 42nd St.
New York, NY 10036
(212) 869-7440

BYTE
P.O. Box 328
Hancock, NH 03449
In particular, see the August 1984 issue, the article by McCormack and Gleaves in the April 1983 issue (pp 385–395), and some of Jerry Pournelle's fairly recent columns.

Journal of Pascal, Ada and Modula-2
P.O. Box 384
Orem, Utah 84057
(801) 373-4094
This is a good source of free (once the magazine is paid for) Modula-2 software, as well as the best single on-going source of information on Modula-2.

Vendors

Fachbereich Für Informatik
Universität Hamburg
Schlüterstrasse 70
D-2000 Hamburg 13
Germany
(For VAX-VMS systems)

Interface Technologies Corp.
3336 Richmond, Suite 200
Houston, Texas 77098

JRT Systems, Inc.
45 Camino Alto
Mill Valley, CA 94941
(415) 388-0530

Logitech, Inc.
165 University Avenue
Palo Alto, CA 94301
(415) 326-3885

Modula Research Institute, Modula Corporation
950 N. University Avenue
Provo, Utah 84604
(801) 375-7402, 1-800-LILITH2
The institute is nonprofit; they sell compilers for some 8- and 16-bit machines for ridiculously low prices. The toll free number is for Modula Corp., which sells Lilith computers and Modula-2 systems for the Apple Macintosh.

Dr. Josef A. Muheim
BBC AG
Abt. ESL/Werk Turgi
CH-5401 Baden
Switzerland
(For RSX11 on PDP-11s)

Mr. P. Robinson
Computer Laboratory
University of Cambridge
Corn Exchange Street
Cambridge CB23QG
England
(For VAX-UNIX systems)

Tartan Laboratories, Inc.
477 Melwood Avenue
Pittsburgh, PA 15213
(412) 621-2210

Volition Systems
P.O. Box 1236
Del Mar, CA 92014
(619) 481-2286

Western Research Laboratory
Digital Equipment Corporation
4410 El Camino Real
Los Altos, CA 94022
At the time of writing, DEC WRL had just made a Modula-2 compiler which runs on VAX machines under 4.2 BSD UNIX available to universities. It may or may not be a generally available, supported product by the time you read this.

Miscellaneous Sources

"Answers to Various Questions About Modula-2," N. Wirth, September 11, 1983, available from MRI. This paper briefly answers questions concerning such things as higher-precision arithmetic, functions which return structured types, opaque types, type coercion, types exported by SYSTEM, string handling, exception handling, module priorities, and some proposed changes to the language definition. The bibliography attached to this paper consists mainly of technical papers on the Lilith's architecture, the implementation of separate compilation, database systems on the Lilith, the Lilith's operating system, a text editor which makes use of the Lilith's bit-mapped display, and a local area network for Liliths.

Institut für Informatik
ETH Zentrum
CH 8092
Zürich, Switzerland
This is where most of the work on Modula-2 and the Lilith machine took place before Modula-2 was released to the public in 1981. If you need to get in touch with Niklaus Wirth, this is the place to write.

Modula-2: A Seafaring Manual and Shipyard Guide, E. Joyce, Addison-Wesley, Reading, Mass., 1985. This is an easy-going introduction to some of the most commonly used portions of Modula-2.

5

Revisions and Amendments to Modula-2

This appendix is a slightly annotated version of a brief entitled "Revisions and Amendments to Modula-2," by Niklaus Wirth. The brief is dated March 3, 1984, and is available from Modula Research Institute (see Appendix 4). Wirth writes, "Future implementors are encouraged to comply with these revisions, and existing compilers should be adapted."

Restrictions and Clarifications

1. Formal VAR parameters and their matching actual parameters must be of identical types, not merely of compatible types. The only exceptions involve ADDRESS and WORD. Formal ADDRESS parameters will match any pointer type, and formal WORD parameters will match any type which is stored in one word of memory on a given system.

2. Suppose a FOR loop begins

   FOR ControlVariable := <ExpressionOne> TO <ExpressionTwo> DO

   Then the types of the expressions must be fully compatible with ControlVariable, not merely assignment compatible. Recall that two types are assignment compatible if they are fully compatible (see Summary 5-1) or if both are INTEGER or CARDINAL or subranges of INTEGER or CARDINAL.

3. A coroutine may not call subprograms which are declared in modules whose priorities are lower than the priority of the module containing the coroutine. However, calls to procedures and functions

which are declared in a module that has no priority are allowed.

4. Compilers are only required to support opaque types which are pointers; one will not necessarily be able to opaquely export subranges, enumerations, or any other nonpointer type. Assignment and tests for equality and inequality are always defined for variables of an opaque type.

5. All imported modules are initialized before the importing module is initialized. If two or more modules import from each other in a circular fashion, the order of initialization is implementation-dependent.

Changes

Extended Backus-Naur Formalism is used in what follows to describe the syntax of the second public version of Modula-2. Reserved words are capitalized, as usual. Special characters such as semicolons, periods, and vertical bars, which appear in Modula-2 source code, are shown inside double quotes. Unquoted vertical bars separate different choices, so we could represent the syntax for BasicType, for instance, with the following production:

BasicType = QualifiedIdentifier | Enumeration | Subrange

Any portion of a production which is surrounded by square brackets is optional; it may be used once or not at all. Portions enclosed by curly braces may be used zero or more times. Thus,

OptionalVAR = [VAR]

and

FieldList = Field {";" Field}

are representations of syntax diagrams 49 and 36, respectively (see Appendix 3).

1. All objects declared in a definition module are exported; explicit export lists are no longer used. Wirth writes, "The definition module may be regarded as the implementation module's separated and extended export list." The new syntax is

DefinitionModule = DEFINITION MODULE ModuleIdentifier ";"
        {ImportList} {Definition} END ModuleIdentifier "."

2. The syntax for Tag has been changed from

Tag = [Identifier ":"] QualifiedIdentifier

to

Tag = [Identifier] ":" QualifiedIdentifier

The reason for the new syntax is: "The fact that the colon is always present makes it evident which part was omitted, if any."

Extensions

1. The syntax of CASE statements and variant record declarations has been changed to allow the insertion of superfluous vertical bars in the same way that the legality of empty statements makes it possible to insert superfluous semicolons. The new syntax is obtained by replacing

CaseLabelList ":" StatementSequence

in the production for CaseList by

[CaseLabelList ":" StatementSequence]

Similarly,

Variant = CaseLabelList ":" FieldList

is replaced by

Variant = [CaseLabelList ":" FieldList]

2. Strings of length 1 are assignment compatible with type CHAR. In other words, CHAR variables and values can be matched to formal ARRAY OF CHAR parameters.

3. The syntax for Subrange types is changed from

Subrange = "[" ConstantExpression".." ConstantExpression "]"

to

Subrange = [Identifier] "[" ConstantExpression
                    ".." ConstantExpression "]"

The optional identifier allows one to specify the base type of the subrange, for instance,

TYPE OnePositiveDigit = INTEGER[1..9];

Without this, of course, subranges with nonnegative lower bounds are automatically of type CARDINAL, and all others are of type INTEGER.

4. Elements of sets no longer need to be constants. The new syntax looks like this:

ConstantFactor = . . . | ConstantSet | . . .
ConstantSet = [QualifiedIdentifier] "{" ConstantElementList "}"
ConstantElementList = ConstantElement { "," ConstantElement }
ConstantElement = ConstantExpression [".." ConstantExpression]

Factor = . . . | Set | . . .
Set = [QualifiedIdentifier] "{" ElementList "}"
ElementList = Element { "," Element }
Element = Expression [".." Expression]

5. The character ~ may be used as a synonym for NOT just as & is a synonym for AND in both versions of Modula-2.

6. The identifiers LONGCARD, LONGINT, and LONGREAL denote predefined types. These types will not necessarily be available on all implementations, and the number of bits involved is not specified.

7. The type ADDRESS is compatible with all pointer types and with types CARDINAL and LONGCARD. The interpretation of addresses as numbers is implementation-dependent.

8. Two new standard functions have been added: MIN and MAX. They return, respectively, the minimum and maximum value of any scalar type, including REAL. For instance,

MIN(CARDINAL) = 0

Glossary

Each entry in this glossary is in boldface, as is the first reference to an item which is described in some other glossary entry, e.g., "**array:** Array **variables** are **indexed** collections . . . ." Words which bear a strong tie to the actual entry have sometimes been printed in boldface when it would have been awkward to use the exact entry. Thus, "**port**" in ". . . easy to **port** to another machine . . ." refers to the entry on **portability.**

Modula-2 reserved words and identifiers, which are enumerated in Appendix 2, have been capitalized since that is what the language definition calls for. However, a few of the capitalized entries, such as CPU and ASCII, do not correspond to a reserved identifier. Note also that this glossary is not complete by any standard. It is meant as an additional aid to understanding Modula-2, not as an independent source of indisputable information. It is not to be expected that everyone will agree with all the definitions given, but I believe I am close to the prevailing consensus in most cases.

abstract data type Abstract data types consist of a **data structure** and some **operators** which are defined on instances of the data structure. Thus, the **tree** data structure and the operators CAR, CDR, LIST, APPEND, etc., defined in Listings 13-1 and 13-2 implement an abstract data type. The **predefined data type BITSET** and the operators defined for this type in Chapter 4 provide another example of an **implementation** of an abstract data type. Strictly speaking, an abstract data type exists separately from its various implementations, much as an **algorithm** is distinct from the **programs** which implement it. For instance, the fact that the two sets {}, {1} are not equal is true whether sets are implemented with **linked lists**, with **arrays**, or with something else.

activation record Each time a **procedure** or **function** is **called**, a new activation **record** for that call of the **subprogram** is placed on the **run-time stack.** This record typically contains storage space for the subprogram's **local variables** and **value parameters**, the **addresses** of any **variables** which were passed as **reference parameters**, links to data at global and intermediate levels, and the priority of the **module** containing the subprogram. The activation record always contains a return address, i.e., a pointer to the **instruction** which should be **executed** after the subprogram finishes execution.

actual parameters   These are the values which get matched to the **formal parameters** of a **subprogram** at the point at which the subprogram is **called**. See Chapter 7 and the glossary entries for **procedure, semantic checks, assignment statement,** and **calling environment.**

address   A computer's **memory** can be viewed as a row of cells which is numbered sequentially from zero (say) to some value such as 65,535 (giving 64K locations in this case). This use of a "linear address space" is a common approach, but other methods are also used, especially on multi-user **systems.** In any case, each cell is known as a **word.** Each word in this sequence of cells has its own address. The address of a word is constant and is distinct from the contents stored in the word, which may change during the **execution** of a **program.** The contents might be a representation of an INTEGER or BOOLEAN value, a code denoting some **low-level** operation such as LOAD or STORE, or an address which **points** to another memory cell.

    Variable names represent the addresses of one or more words which will be used to store the variable's successive values during program **execution.** The allocation of memory space for a given variable is usually done by the **compiler,** but if the variable is allocated **dynamically,** the **operating system** performs the allocation. In either case, the absolute addresses used for a particular variable will generally differ from one execution to the next unless the scheme described in Chapter 19 is used to override the compiler's normal memory assignments.

ADDRESS   This Modula-2 type is usually **exported** from module **SYSTEM.** Different **implementations** may assume that an **octal, hexadecimal,** or other representation is being used for ADDRESS values. ADDRESS is compatible with all **pointer data types.** See Chapter 19 for details concerning the use of this type. See also the glossary entry for **address.**

algorithm   An algorithm is a sequence of steps which, if followed, will produce a solution to a given problem. The description of an algorithm always assumes some knowledge on the part of the reader. For example, "Start at 0 and keep adding 1 and writing the result until the result just written is 100" is an algorithm for writing the first 100 positive integers. This algorithm assumes, among other things, that the user knows how to add, that the work is being done in **base 10** so that 100 represents one hundred (see **binary arithmetic**), that the user can see the result after it has been written and can check to see whether or not it equals 100, and that all additions except the first are being made to the result of the previous addition.

    Notice that an algorithm is distinct from its **implementation(s)** in some particular language(s). A **program** may or may not correctly implement an algorithm; much depends on whether or not the knowledge assumed by the person who wrote the algorithm is available to the person who wrote the program. See also the glossary entries for **pseudocode** and **structured programming.**

array Array **variables** are **indexed** collections of a finite number of variables which are all of the same **data type**. For example, the Modula-2 declaration VAR ArrayVar: ARRAY[23..25] OF CHAR; creates an array variable named ArrayVar which consists of three **CHAR** variables named ArrayVar[23], ArrayVar[24], and ArrayVar[25]. See Chapter 11 and the syntax diagrams in Appendix 3 for more details and examples.

ASCII See Table 4-3.

assembly and machine languages Machine language programs are the end product of the **compilation** of a Modula-2 program; see Chapter 8 and the glossary entry for **instruction**. Assembly language is similar to machine language, but it is not quite as dependent on the specific characteristics of a particular piece of computing **hardware**. Assembly language is extremely powerful and is commonly used for relatively small programs which need to perform as efficiently as possible, such as mathematical **library** routines.

Programming in a low-level language requires that one keep track of a number of details which can be ignored when one writes in a **high-level language** such as Modula-2. Also, it is generally difficult or impossible to **port** programs written in assembly or machine language from one machine to another which uses a different **CPU**. There is a large body of material available on **low-level** programming. It is possible to do some, but not all, of the things which were previously possible only in assembly or machine language in some of the currently available high-level languages such as C, Ada, and Modula-2. Certain Modula-2 **implementations** also allow one to include direct **calls** on low-level **subprograms** inside a program.

assignment statements These **statements** are used to assign values to **variables**. Syntactically, they are of the form

Designator ':=' Expression

Four actions are caused by the **execution** of an assignment statement. First, the Designator is evaluated to find the variable to which the assignment is being made. This is necessary because variables can be designated (in extreme cases) by things such as

OtherModule.RecordVariable.FieldName ↑ .ArrayVariable[3*x + 2]

The second step in executing an assignment statement is to evaluate the Expression to yield some value. This might involve arithmetic **operations, function calls,** comparisons to yield **BOOLEAN** values, or other computations.

The third step is to check for **type compatibility** between the Expression and the Designator. Finally, if no errors have been detected, the value obtained from the Expression is assigned to the designated variable. That is, some (**binary, hexadecimal, octal,** or other) representation of the value is written in the **word(s)** currently allocated to the variable. Note that calls on a **subprogram** which has a **value parameter** involve an implicit assignment statement since an **actual parameter** must be evaluated and that value must be assigned to the **formal** value parameter before execution of the subprogram's body can begin.

base 2, base 8, base 10, base 16 See the glossary entries on **binary, octal, decimal,** and **hexadecimal** arithmetic, respectively.

binary arithmetic Binary arithmetic is arithmetic done in **base 2**. The arithmetic most of us are used to is done in **base 10**; numbers are represented using powers of 10. Any of the **decimal** digits 0, 1, 2, 3, 4, 5, 6, 7, 8, 9 may appear. For instance, 235 base 10 = 2 * (10 * 10) + 3 * (10) + 5 * (1). In binary arithmetic, numbers are represented using powers of 2, and the only digits allowed are 0 and 1. Thus, 5 is written as 101 in base 2, since 5 = 1 * (2 * 2) + 0 * (2) + 1 * (1). Similarly, 14 in base 10 is written as 1110 in base 2 since 14 = 1 * (2 * 2 * 2) + 1 * (2 * 2) + 1 * (2) + 0 * (1). Since the switches used in a computer are generally viewed as being either on or off, binary arithmetic is very useful. Given four switches, for instance, one can represent the decimal number 14 by turning the switches to the configuration on on on off, i.e., 1110. See also the glossary entries on **octal** and **hexadecimal** arithmetic.

bit Bit stands for binary digit; see **binary arithmetic**. A computer's **memory** consists of a sequence of **words**, as discussed in the glossary entry for **address**. Each word in turn contains a number of bits. The number of bits per word is generally fixed for a particular machine; 16 and 32 are common values for a machine's **word size**. A bit can hold either of the values 0, 1. Bit operations allow one to manipulate the individual bits in a memory cell. For example, a left shift might replace 00101101 by 01011010 in an 8-bit word. Modula-2 does not provide any **predefined** bit operations, although they are available in some **implementations**. BITSETs are often implemented by using individual bits to denote the presence or absence of each potential member of the set. For instance, Bitset := {0..7}; might be **executed** by placing 11111111 in the appropriate word in memory.

BITSET This is a **predeclared** Modula-2 **data type** which takes as its values sets of **CARDINAL**s less than some number N (N is usually the **word size**). See Chapter 4 and the glossary entry for **bit**.

block A block is a group of **constant, type, variable, procedure,** or **local module** declarations followed by a sequence of **statements** which (it is hoped) make use of the items declared to perform some computation. Blocks are found in **subprograms, program modules, implementation modules,** and **local modules.** Either the declarations in a block and/or the sequence of statements may be omitted. In the simplest case, a Modula-2 block consists of nothing more than the **reserved word** END; see Appendix 3. After the **thread of control** has left a block, the **visibility rules** ensure that the block's declarations are no longer **visible**. This allows the **memory** space required by the items which were declared in the block to be reused and also limits the amount of **source code** one must examine during **debugging**. The term block is also used at times to refer to a group of adjacent **words** in **memory**.

BOOLEAN This is a **predeclared** Modula-2 **data type** which takes either of the predefined values TRUE, FALSE; see Chapter 4.

bug See the glossary entry for **debug**.

CPU This stands for central processing unit, the heart of every computer. The CPU is what **executes** the bulk of the **machine language instructions** which are produced from a Modula-2 **program** by a **compiler**.

call   When one wishes to begin **execution** of a **subprogram**, one makes a call to the subprogram by giving its name and providing **actual parameters** which will match the subprogram's **formal parameters** if it has any. See Chapter 7 and the glossary entry for **calling environment**.

calling environment   This is the environment which surrounds a **call** on a **subprogram**. It includes some indication of the point in the **code** at which the call was made and the current values of all **variables** which were **visible** just before the call was made. See Chapter 7 for examples.

CARDINAL   This is a **predeclared data type** which takes integers from 0 to **MaxCard** as its value. See Chapter 4 and the glossary entry for **overflow**.

case sensitivity   Modula-2 is case sensitive. That is, a distinction is made between upper- and lowercase letters in every piece of **source code**. Thus, VariableName, VARIABLEName, and variablename all denote different **variables**; each identifier would be associated with a different **address**. **Reserved words** and certain other identifiers are always completely capitalized; see Appendix 2.

CHAR   This is a **predeclared data type** which takes **ASCII** characters as its value; see Chapter 4.

code   See the glossary entries for **source code** and **object code**.

compilation unit   This is the smallest section of Modula-2 **source code** which can be **compiled** separately. The only compilation units in Modula-2 are **definition modules**, **implementation modules**, and **program modules**. Therefore, one cannot, for instance, submit an isolated **procedure** or **function** for compilation.

compiler   Every **program** written in Modula-2 must be translated into **machine language** before it can be **executed**. Decisions must be made as to where **variable** values and machine language **instructions** will be stored, and checks must be made to ensure that the program submitted contains no detectable **syntactic** or **semantic errors**. Compilers do these and other things; see Chapter 8 for some of the details involved, as well as examples of **compile-time errors**. The input to a compiler is known as **source code**, and the output produced is **object code**.

compile-time error   This is an error which can be detected while a **program** is being **compiled**. This is in contrast to a **run-time error**, which only appears during the **execution** of a program. See Chapters 8 and 20 for some examples.

concurrency   True concurrency involves the simultaneous **execution** of several **programs** on several different **CPUs**. Each of the programs, together with information on its state (namely, the values of all **variables** and some indication of the **instruction** executed most recently), constitutes a **process**. Modula-2 does not support true concurrency. The type **PROCESS** should really be called COROUTINE, since Modula-2 assumes that only one CPU is available. This assumption greatly simplifies Modula-2 **compilers** (ask an Ada compiler writer). Processes which take turns executing on a **system** which has only one CPU are known as **coroutines**. See Chapter 18 for more details.

constants Modula-2 allows one to give symbolic names to all those string, **CHAR,** numeric, or **BITSET** values which do not change during the **execution** of a given **program.** Constants may be viewed as read-only **variables.** Using constant declarations cuts down on the **bugs** caused by changing the value of the constant between executions and helps clarify the constant's purpose. See Chapters 5 and 21.

control character Many of the **ASCII** characters are not printable. Instead, they are used for various types of control. On the **Lilith** machine running MEDOS V4, for instance, writing 15C causes a carriage return, 12C causes a line feed, and 10C causes the screen cursor to backspace. The meaning of a given control character is **implementation-dependent,** especially for characters which are used infrequently. Chapter 4 contains more details on type **CHAR,** but the meanings of the control characters on your system must be obtained from your system documentation or by trial and error.

conversion This term is used in contrast to **type transfer.** Type conversions are provided by **standard functions** such as FLOAT and TRUNC; see Appendix 1. Programs which use such conversions are reasonably portable. Type transfers or coercions, on the other hand, are **implementation-dependent** if only because they assume that both types involved use the same number of **bits** to represent values. Conversions and transfers are useful because Modula-2 is **strongly typed;** see Chapters 5 and 19 for more details.

coroutines See Chapter 18 and the glossary entries for **concurrency** and **process.**

crash A **program** is said to have crashed when its **execution** is terminated sooner than planned, without completing its assigned task. This usually happens as the result of a **run-time error,** although clumsy people with soft drinks can also be fatal. After a crash which was the result of an error in the **software,** the **thread of control** is usually returned to the **operating system.**

data structure A data structure is a collection of **variables,** possibly of several different **data types,** connected in various ways. Thus, **arrays** and **records** are both data structures. Pointers are often used to build **dynamically** changing data structures such as **linked lists** and **trees.**

data types Every Modula-2 **variable** must be declared to be of a certain data type. This **declaration** serves to restrict the range of values which the variable may take on so that errors can be detected. The declaration also helps clarify the variable's purpose and allows the **compiler** to allocate the correct amount of space in **memory** to hold the variable's successive values during **program** **execution.** Modula-2's **predeclared** data types are INTEGER, CARDINAL, REAL, BITSET, BOOLEAN, CHAR, and PROC. Programmers may also declare their own types, which may involve **arrays, records, pointers,** sets, enumerations, subranges, and **procedures.** The details of **type compatibility** are discussed in Chapter 5; see also the glossary entry for **strong typing.**

debug Errors in **programs** are known as bugs for the simple reason that the cause of an error in one of the early computers turned out to be a moth which was trapped when a switch tried to close. Debugging is the process of finding and removing the causes of errors in programs. Chapter 20 contains some suggestions on debugging Modula-2 programs. See also the glossary entries for **run-time errors** and **compile-time errors**.

decimal   This term refers to counting and arithmetic which is done in **base 10**, i.e., using powers of 10. The decimal digits are familiar: 0, 1, 2, 3, 4, 5, 6, 7, 8, 9. Arithmetic is often done in other bases in computer science, namely, **base 2 (binary arithmetic), base 8 (octal)**, and **base 16 (hexadecimal)**.

declaration   The standard types BITSET, BOOLEAN, CARDINAL, CHAR, INTEGER, PROC, and REAL are all **predeclared**. These types can be used freely without being declared, as can the **standard subprograms** described in Appendix 1 and the **predefined** values TRUE, FALSE, and NIL. Every other **constant, variable, type, procedure, function**, or **local module** used in a Modula-2 **program** must be declared; see Appendix 3 for the **syntax** guidelines. Declarations involve information about **data types, parameter modes, imports, exports**, and other characteristics of the item being declared, as appropriate. Chapter 5 discusses the declarations of constants, types, and variables. Procedures and functions are discussed in Chapter 7. Local modules are discussed in Chapter 9.

definition module   Library modules always come in pairs consisting of one definition module and one **implementation module**. The definition module defines the degrees of **visibility** of the items which are **implemented** in the implementation module. Definition modules also contain all the information on **data types** and **parameter modes** which is necessary for the **compiler** to perform **semantic checks** and tests for **type compatibility** on the **exports** when they are used in other **modules**. See Chapters 8 and 9 for the details.

down   Down, as in "the **system** is down," means that the **operating system** or some other vital component of the mix of **hardware** and **software** which is necessary to write, compile, execute, and debug **programs** is not working.

dynamic allocation   The standard procedures NEW and DISPOSE can be used while a **program** is **executing** to create and destroy **variables** which are pointed to by some **pointer** variable. Any **program module** which uses NEW and DISPOSE must generally **import** the **procedures** ALLOCATE and DE-ALLOCATE from a **library module** such as Storage; these procedures make calls on the **operating system** to reserve and release **blocks** of **memory**. Anything which is dynamic is taking place as the program runs, as opposed to taking place during **compilation**. See Chapter 12 for more details and examples.

execution   After a **program** has been written and **compiled**, it can be executed. When the **operating system** is given a command to execute some program, it will load part or all of the **machine language instructions** which comprise the **object code** version of the program into **memory** so that the **CPU** can start reading these instructions and carrying them out. The **thread of control** for the CPU is said to be "inside" the program while the program is executing. After the CPU runs out of instructions or reaches one that it cannot execute (see the glossary entry for **run-time errors**), the program stops running and returns control to the operating system. One also speaks of the execution of parts of programs, such as **subprogram** bodies or the bodies of **implementation modules** which perform **initializations** on **exported** items.

exports   Library modules make **constants, variables, data types, functions,** and **procedures** available to other library modules and to **program modules** by exporting them. If an object is not exported, it will not be **visible** outside the module containing its **declaration.** The only exception is that everything declared in a **definition module** is visible throughout the corresponding **implementation module.** Those modules which need to make use of an export must **import** it; see Chapters 8, 9, and 14 and Appendix 5 for details. Also, see the glossary entry for **qualified export.**

file   From the point of view of most Modula-2 programmers, a file is a sequence of **ASCII** characters. Files are generally stored on a magnetic disk or tape, but they reside partially or completely in main **memory** while they are being used by a **program.** One of the main tasks of an **operating system** is to make file manipulation relatively simple. A file may contain **source code, object code,** text combined with **control characters** which help format the text when it is printed, data, or other useful information. See your own **system's** documentation for more details and examples.

formal parameter   Formal parameters are **variables** which are **visible** only within a given **subprogram.** They are distinct from the **actual parameters** which are provided at each of the various **calls** to a subprogram and which are visible in the **calling environment.** Modula-2 allows the formal parameters which are used to pass values between a **subprogram** and its **calling environment** to be of two kinds. **Value parameters** act like **local variables** which are **initialized** by the values passed at the time the call is made. **Variable parameters** are identified with the **variables** matched to them when the subprogram is called. See Chapter 7 for more details.

function   Modula-2 functions are **parameterized** groups of **statements** which return values as a result of their **execution. Syntactically,** function **calls** are an instance of a Factor which contributes to an Expression, whereas **procedure** calls (the other kind of **subprogram** call) are statements; see Appendix 3. Thus,

Link := NextElement(List);

and

GetNextElement(List, Link);

are two statements involving subprogram calls in which NextElement is a function and GetNextElement is a procedure. The ability to return **structured types** from a function is **implementation-dependent;** in general, only **unstructured types** can be returned; see Chapter 7.

garbage value   In Modula-2, a **declaration** never **initializes a variable.** A declaration makes checks for **type compatibility** possible and allocates space in **memory** for the variable, but it never **assigns** the variable any value. Following declaration, the variable's value is whatever happens to be stored in the **memory words** it was just allocated. These old values are nothing but garbage from the point of view of the new variable. One must always be certain that an appropriate value has been assigned to a variable before one tries to use the variable's value in a computation.

goto statement   Modula-2 does not allow arbitrary unconditional jumps in the **thread of control**. Some other languages allow programmers to use goto statements of the form goto LabelName in which LabelName is a label associated with some other **statement**. Languages which allow goto statements require programmers to adhere to numerous special rules, e.g., do not jump into the middle of loops or **subprograms** from outside these constructs. General goto statements also make "spaghetti logic" possible, i.e., it is easy to write programs in which the thread of control resembles a big knot more than anything else. However, Modula-2 does provide for certain specialized jumps. For instance, a RETURN statement in a **procedure** may be viewed as a command to "goto the end of the procedure." An EXIT statement is an order to "goto the first statement outside this LOOP loop," and a **call** to TRANSFER is an order to "goto the statement in the named **coroutine** just after the point at which that coroutine was most recently suspended."

hardware   This is an all-encompassing term which denotes the physical equipment used in computations. Screens, keyboards, **CPUs**, disk drives, printers, and all the other devices now for sale in a myriad of locations are examples of computer hardware. This term is used in contrast to the term **software**. Generally speaking, each piece of hardware used will have specific characteristics which one must be aware of if one is to make the best use of the equipment. The term hardware-dependent refers to software which makes use of such specific characteristics.

hexadecimal   This term refers to arithmetic which is done in **base 16**. Modula-2 uses $0, 1, 2, 3, 4, 5, 6, 7, 8, 9, A, B, C, D, E, F$ as the hexadecimal digits. The number 25 is written, for instance, as 19 in hexadecimal since (in **base 10**) $25 = 1 * (16) + 9 * (1)$. Also, 26 is written as 1A, 27 as 1B, and 100 as 64 since 100 (base 10) $= 6 * (16) + 4 * (1)$. In Modula-2, hexadecimal values are followed by a capital H, e.g., 26 and 27 are written as 1AH and 1BH. See also the glossary entry for **binary arithmetic**.

high-level language   Originally, the main difference between **low-level assembly** and **machine languages** and high-level languages was **portability**. Since the high-level languages depended on **compilers** (or interpreters) to supply the appropriate **hardware**-dependent information when it was needed, it was relatively easy to port **programs** written in high-level languages from one machine to another. Programs written in low-level languages were difficult to port. All this is still true. However, since the advent of Pascal, another important distinction has emerged: high-level languages make **structured programming** easier. In principle, one cannot write programs using WHILE loops, for instance, that could not also be written using only lower-level machine language constructs. After all, a WHILE loop must be translated into machine language before it can be **executed**. In practice, however, it is much easier to write and **debug** programs if they are written in a high-level language such as Modula-2.

I/O   This stands for input/output.

implementation   This term is used in two slightly different ways. One may refer to the **operating system, compiler,** and **library modules** which support

Modula-2 on a particular machine as an implementation of the language. This is the intended meaning when one says that the value of **MaxInt**, for instance, is **implementation-dependent**. On the other hand, one might have a particular Modula-2 **program** or a particular set of library modules in mind when one speaks of an implementation. This is the intended meaning when one says that a **program module** implements the Fast Fourier Transform **algorithm** or that the **definition** and **implementation** modules in Listings 12-1 and 12-2 implement a **linked list abstract data type**. See Chapters 8 and 9 for details concerning the use of definition and implementation modules. See also the glossary entries for **system** and **implementation-dependent**.

implementation-dependent   This term is used to refer to any part of a **program** or language which makes some assumptions that might not be valid on another **system**; it is generally used synonymously with the term system-dependent. Some dependencies are caused mainly by **hardware**. The most common such dependence is the number of **bits** which are used to represent values of a particular **data type**. Other dependencies arise because some of the restrictions imposed by Modula-2 **compilers** vary from one compiler to another, including limits on the maximum size step allowed in a FOR loop, the length and complexity of expressions, the maximum number of **formal parameters** a **subprogram** may have, the maximum length of a subprogram or **module** body, and the maximum number of modules in an import tree.

Of course, the set of available **library modules** is also implementation-dependent since much of the library is often written by the programmers who use the system. In general, any **code** which involves **addresses** (except by way of **pointer variables**), **type transfers**, the order in which **actual parameters** are evaluated or **initializations** are performed, **exports** from module **SYSTEM**, nonpointer **opaque types**, and **MaxInt**, **MinInt**, or **MaxCard** should be re-evaluated whenever the code is **ported** to another system or whenever a new compiler release is used; see Chapter 19. The reaction to certain fairly obscure forms of bad code may also differ from one implementation to another; see Chapter 20. In spite of all this, it is usually reasonably easy to port a well-written Modula-2 program.

implementation modules   These contain the **implementations** of any **exported subprograms** or opaque types. Implementation modules may also contain code which is not actually exported but which supports the exports. See Chapters 8 and 9 and the glossary entries for **separate compilation, definition module, information hiding, nesting, thread of control, initialize**, and **implementation**.

imports   A **library module** or **program module** which wishes to make use of an item which is **exported** from some library module must use one of the two kinds of import lists described in Chapter 9 to import the item before it can be used. Modula-2 **compilers** perform the same **semantic checks** on imports as on those items declared within a given module. When an item appears in an import list in some **module**, it does not need to be **declared** in that module. The compiler will use the definition given in the exporting **definition module** instead (there is actually some difference between a definition and a declaration, but the two terms may be used synonymously as long as one knows whether the code in question is in a definition or an **implementation module**).

index   This term is used in two ways. FOR loops have an index associated with them which keeps track of the progress of the **thread of control** through the iterations of the body of the loop. Each time the body is **executed**, the index is incremented or decremented; see Chapter 6. **Arrays** also have indexes, which are used to distinguish their individual elements. See Chapter 11 for more details and examples.

information hiding   By controlling the **visibility** of items in **library modules,** it is possible to hide information inside **implementation modules.** One can hide the specific representations used to **implement opaque data types,** for instance. Other examples of items which may be hidden include the bodies of **exported subprograms,** subprograms which are used to support exports, **data types, constants** or **variables** which are used by exports but which are not exported themselves, and the **code** which **initializes** exports. See Chapters 8, 9, and 14.

initialize   One must initialize each Modula-2 **variable,** i.e., one must explicitly assign it an initial value before trying to use its value in a computation. Otherwise, some **garbage value** will be used. **Declarations** do not initialize variables. Note that this is the case even with **pointer** variables. One also sometimes refers to the **execution** of the body of an **implementation module** as an initialization since this **code** will always be executed before any **statements** in any **module** which **imports** an item from the implementation module.

instruction   This term refers to a **machine language** instruction. Any given Modula-2 **source code statement** is usually translated by a **compiler** into several simpler **low-level** instructions. These instructions incorporate details such as what **address** the current value of a **variable** is stored at or where the intermediate results of the evaluation of an expression are being kept. Another group of instructions includes the jump instructions that tell one where the **thread of control** is to go after a RETURN from a **subprogram,** an EXIT from a loop, or the completion of one of the cases in a CASE statement, for example.

INTEGER   This is a **predeclared data type** which takes integers in the range MinInt . . . MaxInt as its values; see Chapter 4.

K   In computer science, K after a number is an abbreviation for * 1024 (in decimal). For instance, a **memory** which contains 64K **words** can hold 64 * 1024 = 65,536 **CHAR** values if one value is stored in each word.

level of abstraction   The different **statements** in a **program** fall more or less naturally into separate groups according to how close they are to the user's view of the program or to the **operating system.** The **code** which controls the heads in a disk drive is at a much lower level of abstraction, for instance, than that which informs the user of the purpose of a given program and requests the first input. The separations between the various levels should be marked by grouping statements into **subprograms** and **modules.** See Chapters 7, 8, 9, 15, and 16 for more details and examples.

library modules   Every Modula-2 **implementation** comes with a number of library modules. These generally include **SYSTEM, I/O module(s),** a **file** system, some math **subprograms,** and other items. Programmers are free to add their own modules, which make other **constants, types, variables,** and **subprograms** available to **program modules** and other library modules. Library modules always come in pairs consisting of one **definition module** and one **implementation module.** One sometimes speaks of library module Exporter, for instance, when one actually has definition module Exporter, implementation module Exporter, or both in mind. See Chapters 8 and 9 for more details.

Lilith   This is the name of the **system** designed at ETH in Zurich by the creator of Modula-2, Prof. Niklaus Wirth (yes, he also created Pascal!) and his colleagues. The Lilith includes a **bit**-mapped display (594 × 768 pixels), a three-button mouse, and a terminal to communicate with the **128K** of 16-bit **words** in main **memory.** The secondary store consists of an arbitrary number of 10MB (10000K) magnetic hard disk cartridges. This book was written on a Lilith which uses a Canon LBP 10 laser printer to produce very nice hard copy. The **software** used was made available through the Modula Research Institute; see Appendix 4.

linked list   A linked list is an **implementation** of the list **data structure** which makes use of **pointers** and **records.** A special pointer points to the record which contains the list's first element in one of its fields; this pointer has the **predefined** value NIL if the list is empty. The initial record and all the others (if any) in the list contain at least two fields. One field contains an element of the list, and one contains a pointer (or link) to the next record. The pointer in the last record is set to NIL. See Listings 12-1 and 12-2 for an example.

local modules   These **modules** may be used to provide more control over **visibility** than one can readily achieve using **subprograms.** Local modules are not **compilation units** and may not be used as **library modules,** although they can appear within **program** or **implementation modules.** See Chapter 9 for more details, and see the glossary entry for **qualified export.** Local modules are the only kind of module which is not a **compilation unit.**

local variables   **Variables** which are declared within a particular **block** are said to be local to that block. They are not **visible** in the surrounding blocks unless the block containing the **declaration** is a **local module** and the variables have been **exported.** The variables may or may not be visible in blocks surrounded by the one containing their declarations; this depends on the way **subprograms** and local modules are used within the block containing the declaration. When one speaks of local variables, one is usually referring to variables which are declared locally in a subprogram. See Chapters 7, 8, and 9 for more details.

low-level facilities   These are facilities which are generally **implementation**- or **hardware**-dependent. They are useful for writing things such as **operating systems,** I/O device drivers, and **compilers.** See Chapter 19 for a list of the low-level facilities provided by Modula-2; your particular implementation may provide some others as well.

low-level language   This is term used collectively for **assembly** and **machine languages;** see also the glossary entry for **high-level language.**

machine language   Machine language **instructions** are those which are directly **executable** by a CPU. Machine language **programs** refer to **hardware**-dependent items such as the **addresses** on a particular machine, the parts of **memory** which are reserved for low-level **I/O** control, or some particular memory registers. Machine language programs are very difficult to **port** between machines which use different CPUs. A large body of literature on low-level programming is available to the interested reader.

MaxCard   This is the maximum value allowed for any **CARDINAL variable**; the minimal value, of course, is always zero. The value of MaxCard generally differs from one **implementation** of Modula-2 to another; see Chapter 4.

MaxInt   This is the maximum value allowed for any **INTEGER variable**; the minimal value allowed is **MinInt**. The values of both these constants may differ from one **implementation** of Modula-2 to another; see Chapter 4.

memory   All the user **programs, library modules**, utilities (**compiler, debugger, and file** manipulation programs), documents, data files, the **operating system**, and the other information and **instructions** used in computations must be stored someplace. One generally stores these things in files on a magnetic disk or tape while they are not being used. Information or instructions needed in a computation must be brought into so-called main memory in order to be used. When one says that a computer has, for instance, **64K** of memory, one is generally referring to the number of **words** in this main memory. CPUs generally have access to a small number of memory registers which can be read or written very quickly. Generally speaking, disk space is cheaper than main memory and cheaper by far than registers. Registers, on the other hand, can be accessed very quickly in comparison to main memory, which is nonetheless much faster than disk storage. See also the glossary entry for **address**.

MinInt   See the glossary entry for **MaxInt**.

mode of a parameter   See the glossary entry for **parameter modes**.

modifiability   **Programs** which are easy to **understand** and which do not require the **recompilation** of a large (relative to the amount of code one has modified) amount of **source code** are said to be easily modifiable. See Chapter 15 for some suggestions on ways to make your programs more easily modifiable.

modularity   This term is used interchangeably with **separate compilability** in some contexts. Both terms indicate that **programs** can be composed of pieces which were **compiled** at different times. This implies that a change in one of the **compilation units** that makes up a large program might only require the **recompilation** of that unit, rather than forcing one to recompile the entire program. One can make a distinction, however, between modularity and separate compilability, in that many languages force one to pay a price for modularity. In some languages (but not in Modula-2), certain **bugs** that would have been spotted as **compile-time errors** if the program was not broken into **modules** are missed by the compiler and show up instead only when the program **crashes**.

In Modula-2, however, the same **semantic checks** are made on items which are **imported** to a module as are made on those items **declared** within the module. One could therefore think of separate compilability in Modula-2 as the ability to get the same results from a compilation whether a program is broken into modules or not. In the case of a **strongly typed** language such as Modula-2, this implies that checks involving **parameter modes, type compatibility,** and so forth are performed across module boundaries just as if the boundaries did not exist.

module This term is used generally in computer science to denote a **compilation unit** or in an even wider sense to denote some section of a large **program.** In the context of Modula-2 programming, a module may be a **definition module,** an **implementation module,** a **program module,** or a **local module** (all of which except local modules are compilation units). Modules may be used to limit the amount of **source code** which must be **recompiled** to reflect a small change in a program. Modules also help organize programs and help prevent one from repeating similar code in many places by contributing to a **library** of **constants, variables, types,** and **subprograms** which are available to every program as **imports.** Module boundaries also mark limits of **visibility.** See Chapters 8 and 9 and the glossary entries for **information hiding** and **opaque types** for more details.

mutual recursion Suppose that SubprogramOne makes a **call** to SubprogramTwo and SubprogramTwo contains a call to SubprogramOne; the two **subprograms** are said to be mutually recursive. See Listing 5-2 for an example. Similarly, if the **declaration** of ItemOne refers to the declaration of ItemTwo and the declaration of ItemTwo refers to the declaration of ItemOne, the two declarations are said to be mutually recursive. Modula-2 allows arbitrary recursion among subprograms, but the only recursive declarations allowed are mutually recursive and involve pointers. For instance,

```
TYPE ListPointer  = POINTER TO ListElement;
TYPE ListElement = RECORD
                   Value : INTEGER;
                   NEXT: ListPointer;
                   END; (* RECORD *)
```

is legal, but the following declaration is not legal:

```
TYPE MixedUp = POINTER TO MixedUp;
```

The declaration of MixedUp is not an example of mutual recursion since this declaration refers to itself, not to a second declaration which then makes use of the first declaration. Declarations such as this which define things in terms of themselves are not allowed.

The two declarations below are mutually recursive, but neither of the types defined is a pointer to the other one, so the declarations are not legal:

```
TYPE ArrayOne = ARRAY[1..5] OF ArrayTwo;
TYPE ArrayTwo = ARRAY[1..5] OF ArrayOne;
```

The recursion leads in this case to an infinite nesting. Legal recursive declarations do make infinite lists, trees, or graphs possible, but NIL provides an escape hatch in these cases.

nesting   When the **thread of control** is given to a **statement** and then given to some other statement before the first statement has finished **execution**, the second statement is said to be nested inside the first. Statements which lend themselves to the nesting of other statements inside them are sometimes called compound statements. Examples in Modula-2 include the following kinds of statements: IF, CASE, WHILE, REPEAT..UNTIL, FOR, LOOP, and WITH. For instance, the following example shows two **assignment statements** and a WHILE loop which are nested inside a WITH statement. A LOOP loop and a **procedure call** are nested in the WHILE loop, and an IF statement and another procedure call are nested in the LOOP loop:

```
WITH SomeRecord DO
  NeedHelp := FALSE;
  NotDone := TRUE;
  WHILE NotDone DO
    LOOP
      DoSomething(NeedHelp);
      IF NeedHelp THEN
        EXIT;
      END; (* IF *)
    END; (* LOOP *)
    CheckStatus(NotDone);
  END; (* WHILE *)
END; (* WITH *)
```

See Chapters 6 and 12 for more examples of nested statements. **Structured programs** generally involve a fair amount of nesting. One can also speak of nested procedures; see Chapters 7 and 9. Finally, it should be noted here that **local modules** may be nested inside each other; as indicated in Chapter 9, they are always nested in a surrounding **program module** or implementation **module.**

object code   This is another name for the **machine language** code produced by a **compiler.** See also the glossary entry for **source code.**

octal numbers   The octal digits are 0, 1, 2, 3, 4, 5, 6, and 7. Octal arithmetic is done using powers of 8. Therefore 29 is denoted by 35 in octal form since (in **base 10**) $29 = 3 * (8) + 5 * (1)$. In Modula-2, octal values are followed by a capital B, e.g., 35B, to distinguish them from decimal or hexadecimal values since B resembles an 8. See also the glossary entry for **binary arithmetic.**

opaque types   These are generally **pointers** which are **exported** from a **definition module.** All the details of what they point to are hidden in the corresponding **implementation module** and are unavailable to users who **import** the opaque type. This form of **information hiding** is useful for **implementing abstract data types.** See Chapter 14 for more details and some examples.

open array formal parameters   An open array is a **formal parameter** of the form ARRAY OF <SomeType>; this kind of formal parameter will match any **actual parameter** which is a one-dimensional **array** of <SomeType> **variables.** The **standard function HIGH** returns the high **index** of the actual parameter passed; the low index is always zero. See Chapter 11 for more details.

operating system   This is the **program** which is responsible for controlling the use of most or all of the resources on a **system**. These resources may include a number of disk drives, one or more **CPUs**, some special **I/O** processors, and the main **memory**. To many programmers, the operating system is identical to its command interpreter portion, which recognizes and **executes** commands along the lines of "**Compile** SomeProgram," "Execute AnotherProgram," "Rename SomeFile to NewName," and "Edit MyProgram." However, the operating system also handles **dynamic memory allocation** and **file** management.

operator   Modula-2 provides various **predefined** operators. They include numeric operators (e.g., $+$, $-$, $*$, $/$, DIV, MOD), set operators (e.g., $+$, $-$, $:=$, $*$), relational operators (e.g., $=$, $<=$, $>$, #), boolean operators (AND, &, OR, NOT), and **standard procedures** and **functions** such as INC, EXCL, and HIGH. Programmer-defined **subprograms** can also be viewed as operators. The **precedence** of each of the predefined operators is given in Summary 4-1, but **programs** should normally use parentheses to make the order of evaluation in an expression clear, rather than relying on the precedence rules.

overflow: No matter which arithmetic is being used (**binary, octal, hexadecimal**, or some other), computer **memories** contain a finite number of **words,** and each word has a finite number of **bits**. Therefore one cannot, for instance, represent all possible cardinal values. As discussed in Chapter 4, there is a difference between cardinal values and **CARDINAL** values. Any attempt to assign a **CARDINAL** **variable** a value greater than **MaxCard** results in an overflow. Similarly, one can cause **INTEGER** or **REAL** overflows by trying to assign values which are outside the group of integers or reals which can be represented on a given system. **Address** overflows are caused when one tries to access an address beyond the range available on one's system; see the list of causes of **run-time errors** in Chapter 20. Overflows generally cause the **thread of control** to be returned to the **operating system.**

parameter   A parameter is a **variable** which is used to pass values between a **subprogram** and its **calling environment**. See Chapter 7 and the glossary entries for **value parameter, variable parameter, formal parameter, actual parameter, parameter modes,** and **procedure.**

parameter modes   Modula-2 parameters come in two modes, **value** and **variable**. See Chapter 7 and the glossary entries for **formal parameter** and **semantic checks.**

pointer   Programmers generally think of the pointers as pointing to a **record** or some other variable. The actual values stored in pointer variables are **addresses**. Since the **memory** assignments made by a **compiler** or an **operating system** generally differ from one **execution** of a **program** to the next, the addresses themselves are of no use after a program has finished execution. One would need to know where all the machine **instructions** and variable values concerned were stored in memory in order to make use of these absolute addresses. In a **linked list** or **tree data structure** which is **implemented** with pointer **variables,** one traverses the structure by chasing pointers; see Listings 12-1, 12-2, 13-1, 13-2, 16-6, 16-7, 16-8, and 16-9 for examples. See Chapter 19 and the glossary entry for type **ADDRESS.**

It is important to note that **declarations** of pointer variables do not **initialize** those variables. Pointer variables are not automatically set to NIL. For instance, if the space allocated for PointerVariable was last used by an INTEGER variable whose final value was 54321 and one tries to execute

X := PointerVariable ↑ ;

chances are quite good that the program will try to find address number 54321 so that it can assign the contents of that **word** to variable X. One must also be very careful when pointers are passed as **value parameters**; see Chapter 12.

portability   **Programs** written to **execute** on a particular **system** are called portable when it is relatively easy to get them to execute properly on another system. In many cases, the second system will be based on another kind of **CPU** or other different **hardware**. Porting a program which is written in a **low-level language** is generally quite difficult. Porting a program which is written in a **high-level language** may involve nothing more than **recompiling** the program's **source code** version on the new system. More often, however, a program will use some **implementation-dependent** items, so one must abstract out the **algorithms** used in the program and **implement** them all over again in another program which is written with the particular characteristics of the second system in mind. Modula-2's **modules** can be used to isolate implementation-dependent sections of a program; see the glossary entry for **SYSTEM**. Chapters 15 and 21 suggest several ways to make programs easier to port.

precedence (of operators)   In expressions such as $2 + 3 * 5$, one must have some sort of convention to decide the order in which the operations (addition and multiplication in this case) are to be performed. These conventions give certain **operators** precedence over other operators. The rules for Modula-2 are given in Summary 4-1. If the expression is at all complicated, one should normally use parentheses to make the order of evaluation clear, rather than relying on the precedence rules.

predeclared   See the glossary entry for **predefined**.

predefined   This term is used in contrast to programmer-defined. For our purposes, predeclared and predefined are synonymous. See the glossary entries for **declarations** and **standard**.

PROC   This **standard** Modula-2 **data type** takes **parameterless procedures** as its values; see Chapters 17 and 18. It may be considered to have the declaration

TYPE PROC = PROCEDURE;

procedure   A procedure is a group of **statements** which can be **called**, i.e., given the **thread of control**, from any place in a **program** in which the procedure is **visible**. **Parameters** may be used to pass values in and out of a procedure, allowing procedures to be used more easily to **implement** fairly general **algorithms** instead of being tied to a specific set of values. A search procedure, for instance, might take in a (**pointer** to a) **linked list** and set a **formal variable parameter** to (point to) the element of the list which contains the value passed into the procedure by way of a **value parameter**. Such a procedure might have a **declaration** which begins like this:

PROCEDURE SearchList(VAR Element: PointerToListElement; ToFind: Value);

The ability to pass values via parameters allows one to use the same group of statements, i.e., the same procedure body, to search for different elements in different lists. Chapter 7 contains many of the details one needs to be aware of to use procedures in Modula-2 programs. Procedures and **functions** are known collectively as **subprograms** and may be **nested** inside each other. Generally, most of the exports from the **library modules** on a **system** are programmer-defined procedures, functions, and **data types**. However, certain **standard** procedures are **predefined**; see Appendix 1. One can declare **variables** or parameters which take procedures as their values in Modula-2; see Chapter 17. See also the glossary entries for **block** and **local variable**.

process   A process consists of four parts: the **code** which defines the behavior of a **program**, the current values of all **variables** now **visible** to the program, some indication of the last **instruction executed**, and finally, an indication of which (if any) of a **system's CPUs** the program is executing on. If there are more processes on a system than there are CPUs, at any given time some of the processes must be suspended, i.e., they do not control any CPU. The marker which keeps track of the last instruction in the program which was executed and the values of all the visible variables are known collectively as the **state information** of the process.

The state information allows a suspended process to resume execution when it is given control of a CPU just as if it had been executing continuously except that the process will clearly require more real world time to finish execution than it would have needed had it not been suspended. The term **coroutine** is often used to describe a process on a single-CPU system. Since Modula-2 assumes a single-processor system, the type **PROCESS** should really have been called COROUTINE. See also the glossary entry for **concurrency** and Chapter 18.

PROCESS   This Modula-2 type is usually exported from module **SYSTEM**. See Chapter 18 and the glossary entries for **coroutine, process**, and **concurrency**.

program   A program is a sequence of **statements** which (it is hoped) perform some desired computation when they are **executed**. Computer programs often make use of some **constant, type, variable**, or **subprogram declarations** which are associated with the statements and which describe items manipulated by the program during the computation. Programs may also make use of some input which is provided during the program's execution by a human user or by another program. Programs are said to be executing or running while they have control of a **CPU**, i.e., while the CPU's actions are being directed by the **object code** version of the program. In Modula-2, a program always comes in the form of a **program module**, which may **import** various items from **library modules**. See also the glossary entries for **algorithm, compiler, debug, procedure, thread of control, implementation**, and, in fact, just about anything else listed.

program modules Modula-2 provides three kinds of **compilation units.** The **definition** and **implementation modules** on a given **system** form a **library**, and program modules **implement algorithms.** Program modules are the only compilation units which are directly **executable,** i.e., which can take the **thread of control** from the **operating system** and perform some computation. However, the **initializations** of **imported** implementation modules must be executed before any code in the importer is run. See the glossary entry for **program** and Chapters 8 and 9 for more details.

proper subset A proper subset of a set S is a set which contains only elements of S and which does not contain all of the elements of S. No set is a proper subset of itself, but every set is an improper subset of itself.

pseudocode This is a mixture of English or some other natural language and some programming language such as Modula-2. A pseudocode version of a **program** may serve as a useful bridge between an **algorithm** and one of its **implementations.** As an example, consider the following partial translation of the example given in the glossary entry for algorithm:

```
NowAt := 0;
WHILE (NowAt <> 100) DO
    Add one;
    Write result;
END; (* WHILE *)
```

The bits of English in a piece of pseudocode often represent portions of the algorithm which are relatively difficult to implement because they involve the assumptions made by whomever wrote the algorithm. For instance, one must decide that "add one" means "add one to the result of the previous addition or to 0 if this is the first addition" and that the results should be written to a particular place, e.g., the screen, before one can complete the translation from algorithm to source code:

```
NowAt := 0
WHILE (NowAt <> 100) DO
    INC(NowAt);
    WRITECardinal(NowAt,6);
END; (* WHILE *)
```

qualified export In the original version of Modula-2, all the **exports** from a **definition module** must be listed in that **module** as qualified exports; see any of the definition modules in the text for an example. The second version of Modula-2 handles exports differently; see Appendix 5. As shown in Listing 9-5, **exports** from **local modules** may be qualified but do not need to be. Each use of an **imported identifier** which was listed as a qualified export must be preceded in the importing **module** by the name of the module which exported the identifier. As explained in Chapter 9, this may be done in either of two ways. If an import list states

```
FROM SomeModule IMPORT SomeIdentifier;
```

the **compiler** will recognize that SomeIdentifier was exported from SomeModule. If, on the other hand, one writes

```
IMPORT SomeModule;
```

all uses of SomeIdentifier must be prefaced by SomeModule, using the dot notation: SomeModule.SomeIdentifier. Of course, if a module imports two items called SomeIdentifier (from different **library modules**), the dot notation must be used to distinguish them no matter what kind of import lists were used.

range error This is generally a **run-time error** which occurs when some **variable** exceeds the bounds placed on it by its **declaration**. The variable in question is generally of a subrange or enumeration **data type**, but CARDINAL or other **overflows** are also sometimes called range errors. Range errors are often associated with **arrays** since subrange types are commonly used to **index** arrays.

REAL This is a **predefined** Modula-2 type; see Chapter 4 and the glossary entry for **overflow**.

recompilation Whenever the **source code** version of a Modula-2 **program** is **modified**, such as during **debugging**, it is necessary to run the new version through a **compiler** to produce a corresponding **object code** version which can be **executed** directly by a **CPU**. See Chapter 15 for suggestions on ways to keep down the amount of recompilation made necessary by a change to a program.

record Record **variables** are collections of a finite number of other variables known as fields. Unlike **arrays**, the variables which make up a record may be of different **data types**; see Appendix 3 for the formal **syntax** involved. For examples of records in Modula-2, see Chapter 12. Chapter 13 discusses so-called variant records in which the group of fields defined for a given record variable may change **dynamically.**

recursion A **subprogram** which **calls** itself is said to be making a recursive call. See Chapter 7 and the glossary entry for **mutual recursion.**

reference parameter See the glossary entry for **variable parameter.**

relational operator Examples include =, <=, >, and <>. See Chapter 4 and the syntax charts in Appendix 3.

reserved words These are words such as BEGIN, CHAR, and **PROC** which have **predefined** meanings in Modula-2. They are always completely capitalized, and their meanings are fixed. For instance, one cannot name a **variable** MODULE because MODULE is a reserved word. Appendix 2 contains a complete list of Modula-2's reserved words and **standard** identifiers.

run-time errors These are errors which appear while a **program** is **executing,** after it has been **compiled** and its **compile-time errors** have been fixed. A run-time error generally causes a program to **crash** and to return the **thread of control** to the **operating system.** See Chapter 20 for some examples.

run-time stack This is an area of **memory** which is used by the **operating system** to store **subprogram activation records.** An attempt to perform an infinite **recursion** generally causes a stack **overflow** because the operating system runs out of space for activation records on the run-time stack.

semantic checks   These are checks made by the **compiler** to ensure that the rules of **type compatibility** are observed and to ensure that **subprograms** are passed the correct number and mode (see **parameter modes**) of **actual parameters**. Checks are made on **imported** items just as if they had been **declared** in the **module** being compiled. For instance, the compiler will not accept **constants** or expressions which are matched to **variable parameters** no matter what module the subprogram concerned was declared in. See Chapters 5, 8, and 20 for more details and examples of **semantic** errors.

semantics   The difference between **syntax** and semantics is fairly subjective. One classification holds that syntactic errors are the same as **compile-time errors** and **run-time errors** are semantic errors. This book takes another approach which says that syntax deals with the form of a **program** and semantics deals with the **code's** meaning. See Chapters 5, 8, and 20 for some examples of the various syntactic and semantic errors that are possible, as well as an overview of the **semantic checks** performed by Modula-2 **compilers**.

Listings 3-1 through 3-6 are roughly equivalent from a semantic point of view if one assumes that the meaning of a program is the relationship which the program defines between inputs and outputs. However, the syntactic differences between the various **high-level languages** used in these six listings are fairly obvious. See also the glossary entries for **strong typing** and **type compatibility** since errors involving these concepts are often viewed as semantic errors.

separate compilability   See the glossary entry for **modularity**.

short-circuit   This denotes a certain way of evaluating logical expressions, i.e., expressions which yield **BOOLEAN** values. If the value of (E1 AND E2) or of (E1 OR E2) can be determined by finding the value of E1, E2 is not evaluated. This can be handy if the evaluation of E2 may at times cause a **run-time error** or is particularly complex. See Chapter 4 and Summary 15-5 for more details and examples.

software   This is a general term covering all the **source code** and **object code** which is used or available on a given **system**. User **programs, library modules, operating systems, compilers, debuggers,** and text editors are examples of common software. See also the glossary entry for **hardware**.

software engineering   From one point of view, this is a general term for the application of a collection of techniques which can be used to make programming less an art and more a science. I would prefer to think of software engineering techniques as ways to make it easier to write, **understand, debug, port,** and generalize **programs**. In my view, software engineering helps make programming into a more powerful and refined mix of art and science, not into less of an art. For examples of some software engineering techniques which are particularly useful to Modula-2 programmers, see Chapter 15. Also, see the glossary entries for **modularity, modifiability, understandability, portability, information hiding,** and **SYSTEM**.

source code   This term refers to any sequence of **statements** which is written in a **high-level language** such as Modula-2. **Compilers** expect source code as input. The underlying assumption is that source code is different from the **machine** or **object code** which is **executed** by a **CPU** and that source code is easier for people to **understand**.

standard   Modula-2 provides a number of standard **data types** (BITSET, BOOLEAN, CARDINAL, CHAR, INTEGER, PROC, and REAL), standard **subprograms** (see Appendix 1), and three **predefined** values (NIL, TRUE, and FALSE). These standard items do not need to be **declared** by the programmer before use. See Appendixes 1 and 2 and Chapter 4 for more details. Note that the **I/O procedures** are not **predeclared**; they must be **imported** from some **library module** such as InOut.

starting address   The starting address for a **coroutine's workspace** is the lowest (or highest; it depends on the **system**) of the **addresses** of the **memory** locations used to store the coroutine's state information. It is generally assumed that the workspace consists of some number of adjacent memory locations; it is "all in one piece." One should use ALLOCATE or a similar **procedure** to obtain a safe starting address when creating a new **PROCESS**; see Chapters 18 and 19.

statement   These are the building blocks which, together with **declarations, import** and **export** lists, comments, and a few other constructs, make up the **source code** version of a Modula-2 **program**. Statements represent actions the **CPU** is to take as the program **executes**. Modula-2 supports the following kinds of statements: **assignment, procedure call,** IF, CASE, WHILE, REPEAT.. UNTIL, FOR, LOOP, WITH, EXIT, and RETURN. See Chapters 6, 7, and 12 and Appendix 3 for more details and examples. See also the glossary entry for **instruction**.

string   A string is a sequence of characters. In the most general sense, this might include **control characters,** but generally one is most interested in strings made up of alphabetic characters, blanks, a few punctuation marks, and some sort of null character which can be used to mark the end of the string. Modula-2 taken "as is" does not handle strings very well. One can remedy this to some extent by adding programmer-defined **types** and **subprograms** to the **library**; Chapters 11 and 19 contain some examples.

strong typing   Modula-2 is a strongly typed language. This means that it is illegal in general to mix operands of different **data types** in a single expression. Chapter 5 contains the details and some examples, but it is worth repeating here that Modula-2 performs virtually no transfer of values from one type to another unless the programmer explicitly requests such a **type transfer.** The only exception is that transfers are made, if possible, between **INTEGERs** and **CARDINALs** and their subranges if the **statement** concerned is of the form x := y;. For this reason, INTEGER, CARDINAL, and their subranges are said to be assignment compatible.

structured programming   Programs written in certain **high-level languages** such as Modula-2 are called structured when the interrelationships of the program's components express the structure of the **algorithms** the programs were derived from. In Modula-2, the program components might be **state-**

ments, declarations, subprograms, coroutines, or modules. The possible relationships among the components could involve the **threads of control** which might be followed during program **execution, nesting, importation, recursion,** iteration (i.e., repetition such as that exemplified by a loop), and **visibility.**

As a simple example, consider the final Modula-2 version of the example presented in the glossary entry for algorithms and continued in the entry for **pseudocode.** The algorithm was "Start at zero and keep adding one and writing the result until the result just written is 100." A structured Modula-2 **implementation** of this algorithm is

```
MODULE ToOneHundred;
    FROM InOut IMPORT WRITECardinal;
    VAR NowAt: CARDINAL;
BEGIN (* main body of ToOneHundred *)
    NowAt := 0;
    WHILE (NowAt <> 100) DO
        INC(NowAt);
        WRITECardinal(NowAt,6);
    END; (* WHILE *)
END ToOneHundred.
```

This **program module** is an example of structured programming because anyone who knows Modula-2 could easily use it to produce an algorithm which is equivalent to the original algorithm taken together with the assumptions made during the translation from pseudocode to Modula-2 (see the entry for pseudocode for some of the assumptions). In other words, the program expresses the algorithm clearly to anyone who knows Modula-2. Structured programming makes programs easier to **understand, debug, modify,** and **port.**

structured types   Record **data types, array types,** and programmer-defined set types, all of whose values may have several components, are called structured types in Modula-2. BITSET, enumeration types, **pointer** types, **procedure** types, the basic types discussed in Chapter 4, and all other types are known as unstructured types. The distinction is important because **functions** are only required to be able to return unstructured types and because the rules of **type compatibility** are somewhat different for unstructured and structured types. See Chapter 5 for more details and examples.

subprogram   **Procedures** and **functions** are known collectively as subprograms.

syntax   See the glossary entry for **semantics.**

system   This term is often used interchangeably with the term **implementation.** I would prefer to make the distinction, however, that an implementation consists only of **software.** A system, on the other hand, is composed not only of software (which includes implementations of the various languages it supports) but of **hardware** as well. See also the glossary entries for **operating system, compiler, SYSTEM,** and **implementation-dependent.**

SYSTEM   This pseudomodule is provided with every **implementation** of Modula-2. SYSTEM is called a pseudomodule since it is actually more or less part of the **compiler** and is not really a separate pair of **library modules.**

SYSTEM exports various **implementation-dependent** items; see Chapter 19. By placing these items in SYSTEM, one improves **portability** and makes it easier to spot **system**-dependent **programs.**

thread of control This term refers to an imaginary path which is (or may be) traced through a **program** during its **execution.** The thread of control generally starts at the top of a program and simply goes from one **statement** to the next, but it may also be made to repeat statements as a result of WHILE, REPEAT..UNTIL, LOOP, or FOR loops. Calls on **subprograms** cause the thread to move into the statements defining the body of the **procedure** or **function.** When the end of the subprogram is reached or when a RETURN statement is executed, the thread of control moves back to the statement following the **call.**

The thread of control can be made to jump between **coroutines** by calling the **SYSTEM** procedure TRANSFER. Control runs through all the bodies of the **implementation modules** imported by a given module, executing the **exporting** modules' **initializations** in an **implementation-dependent** order before passing to the first statement in the body of the module which did the importing. One generally views each **CPU** in a **system** as having its own distinct thread of control and thinks of the thread as being passed from the **operating system** to a **compiler,** text editor, or user program, for instance, and then back to the operating system.

tree A tree is an **abstract data type** which is often **implemented** with **pointers** and **records.** A special pointer points to a record which is known as the root of the tree; this pointer has the **predefined** value NIL if the tree is empty. The root record and all the other records (if any) in the tree each contain at least two fields. One field contains the value of the node; this might be a **CARDINAL** value or a **string,** for instance. One or more of the other fields contain pointers (or links) to the record's "child" nodes. If every node has at most one child, the tree is actually a **linked list.** If every node has at most two children, the tree is called binary. Pointer fields which do not point to another node are set to NIL. Nodes which have no children are called "leaf" nodes. See Listings 13-1 and 13-2, and Figure 13-1 for an example.

truncate Two methods which are commonly used to change real values to integer values are rounding and truncation. If one rounds up, 2.7 becomes 3, and if one truncates, 2.7 becomes 2. All **implementations** of Modula-2 provide a **predefined type conversion function** TRUNC which produces **INTEGER** or **CARDINAL** values from **REAL** values by lopping off the decimal point and everything to the right of it.

type compatibility See the glossary entry for **strong typing.**

type transfer function Modula-2 allows one to use the name of any type <SomeType> as the name of a **function** which accepts values of any **data type** that is sufficiently similar to <SomeType> and returns "corresponding" <SomeType> values. This facility makes programs less **portable** because transfers can only be made between types whose values are represented internally with the same number of **bits.** See Chapter 19 and the glossary entry for **conversion.** Type transfers are also known as type coercions.

understandability   This is a very desirable quality in a **program**. See Chapter 15 for some suggestions on ways to make your programs easier to understand and thereby easier to **debug, port**, and **modify**.

unstructured types   These include INTEGER, CARDINAL, REAL, BITSET, BOOLEAN, CHAR, PROC, enumeration types, **pointer** types, **procedure** types, and subranges of these types. See the glossary entry for **structured types**.

value parameter   Also known as a call-by-value parameter in some contexts, this is a **formal parameter** which can be used to get values into a **subprogram** but cannot be used to get values back out to the **calling environment**. See Chapters 7 and 12 and the glossary entry for **variable parameter**.

variable parameter   Also known as a call-by-reference or reference parameter in some contexts, this is a **formal parameter** which can be used to get values into a **subprogram**, to pass them back out to the **calling environment**, or to do both. Any **variable** from the calling environment which is matched to a formal variable parameter in a subprogram **call** must be of the same **data type** as the formal parameter; this is one of the **semantic checks** Modula-2 **compilers** perform. Some systems may only require parameters to be of compatible types.

variables   A variable may be viewed as a symbolic name for one or more **words** in **memory** which are used to store successive values (all of a given **data type**) while a **program** is **executing**. The actual **addresses** of the locations used to store the variable's values may differ from one program execution to the next. See Chapters 5 and 19 for more details and some examples.

variant records   The set of fields of a variant **record variable** may change during **program execution**; see Chapter 13 for examples.

visibility   Variables, constants, types, modules, and **subprograms** can only be legally referenced at those points in a **program** at which they are visible. Chapters 7 and 9 illustrate the ways one can use the **visibility rules** and **import** or **export** lists in connection with subprograms and (**local**) **modules** to control visibility. One mainly wishes to limit the visibility of an item for two reasons. First, it allows the **system** to re-allocate the **memory** space dedicated to any item once that item is no longer visible. Second, computations never involve items which are not visible, so the amount of **code** one must **understand** during the **debugging** or modification of a piece of code is limited. Also, one need not be constantly thinking up new names for things. See also the glossary entries for **block** and **local variable**.

visibility rules   These are the rules which determine the parts of a **program** in which a given **constant, variable, type, subprogram**, or **local module** is **visible**. The main methods Modula-2 provides for controlling visibility involve **import** and **export** lists, local modules, **opaque exports**, and **local variables** in subprograms. These methods are described in Chapters 7, 9, and 14.

word   A unit of **memory** which is used to hold **variable** values, **instructions, addresses** or other information that is needed during computations. See the glossary entries for **address, memory, bit**, and **word size**.

word size   Memory is broken into a (fairly large) number of words, each with its own **address**. The word size on a given **system** is the number of **bits** in each word in memory. The word size and the number of words used for a **data type** determine the number of different values which can be assigned to a **variable** of that type on a given system. If one uses 16-bit words and represents **CARDI-NAL**s using **binary arithmetic** in a single word, for instance, **MaxCard** = $(2 \uparrow 16) - 1 = 65535$.

workspace   This is a region of **memory** used to maintain the state information of a **PROCESS**. See Chapter 18 and the glossary entries on **starting address, process,** and **coroutines**.

Answers to the Exercises

Chapter 4

1. INTEGERs and REALs are mixed; div should be DIV since reserved words are capitalized. Large values are written without commas: 13002, not 13,002.

2. BITSETs are written with braces, not parentheses, e.g., {1, 2}, not (1, 2). Also, the elements of a BITSET must be CARDINALs. This excludes negative numbers.

3. FALSE.

4. (a) CARDINAL. Do not use INTEGER because the number of children is never negative. (b) Probably REAL, although you could use INTEGER if you shift the decimal and MaxInt is large enough, e.g., represent $123.45 by 12345. If you shift the decimal and your balance is never negative, you could use CARDINAL. However, MaxInt and MaxCard are almost certainly not large enough for these last two types; see the glossary entries. (c) BOOLEAN since the statement is either TRUE or FALSE.

5. Without parentheses: H / K * H / K * H / K. With parentheses: (H * H * H) / (K * K * K). Because of the left-to-right evaluation of operators such as * and / which have the same precedence, H * H * H / K * K * K evaluates as H cubed times K squared divided by K, or H * H * H * K; the first and second Ks cancel.

Chapter 5

1. (a) Legal, but hard to read; RealEstate is better. (b) Illegal; no blanks allowed. (c) Legal. (d) Illegal; must start with a letter. (e) Illegal; nothing but letters and digits allowed. (f) Legal. (g) Illegal; cannot use a reserved word as a variable name. (h) Illegal; nothing but letters and digits allowed.

2. (*a*) Illegal. (*b*) Illegal. (*c*) Legal. (*d*) Legal. (*e*) Illegal. (*f*) Legal; try r = s = 2.5. (*g*) Legal; functions can call other functions as long as the types are correct at each stage. If you have these on your system, you might do some experiments. For instance, is card = CARDINAL(TRUNC(FLOAT(card))) for all values of card? What about real = FLOAT(CARDINAL(TRUNC(real)))?

Chapter 6

1. Note that the formulation as an IF statement is preferable if EmployeeNumber, ForemanNumber, BossNumber, and PresidentNumber are not close to each other in value.

```
CASE IDNumber OF
  EmployeeNumber: WriteString("Hello, employee.");|
  ForemanNumber : WriteString("Hello, foreman"); |
  BossNumber    : WriteString("Hello, boss");     |
  PresidentNumber: WriteString("Hello, Mr. President.");
ELSE
  WriteString("Sorry, I can't let you in.");
END; (* CASE IDNumber *)
```

The second IF, THEN, ELSIF, ELSE statement does not translate easily enough into a CASE statement to make it worth the trouble. The reason is that different variables, PatientCondition and StomachCondition, are used in the conditions; a CASE statement makes a choice based on the value of a single variable or expression.

2. Any value of AmountOwed except 5, 50, 500, or 5000 leaves the computer with no idea what to do. A program containing a CASE statement such as the one shown may get past the compiler, but it usually will not be reliable. Compare the behavior of the CASE statement given when AmountOwed = 7, for instance, with that of the IF statement below. The second problem with the given CASE statement is that the labels are not close in value. Because of the gap between 5 and 5000, this statement will probably execute considerably more slowly than a logically equivalent IF statement such as the one below would.

```
IF AmountOwed = 5 THEN
  WriteString("Have you sent your payment?");
ELSIF AmountOwed = 50 THEN
  WriteString("Hurry up; You owe us money.");
ELSIF AmountOwed = 500 THEN
  WriteString("We've impounded your car.");
ELSIF AmountOwed = 5000 THEN
  WriteString("We're taking possession of your house.");
END; (* IF AmountOwed = 5 *)
```

3. The rewritten code is as follows:

```
CubeLowerLimit, CubeUpperLimit:INTEGER;
  (* Limits on summation of cubes. *)
```

```
TotalCube, CubeSumIndex        :INTEGER;
.
.
TotalCube := 0;
FOR CubeSumIndex := CubeLowerLimit TO CubeUpperLimit DO
  TotalCube := TotalCube + CubeSumIndex*CubeSumIndex*CubeSumIndex;
END; (* FOR *)
```

4. The initial value of Index, 3, is not changed by the WHILE loop. The condition Index <= 35 is always TRUE, so the loop is never exited. The code is equivalent to this infinite sequence of statements:

```
Total := 0;
Index := 3;
Total := Total + Index;
Total := Total + Index;
Total := Total + Index;
Total := Total + Index;
.
.
.
```

Total will be infinite after this. In practice, you will receive some error message such as "INTEGER overflow" as soon as Total + Index is greater than MaxInt.

5. (a) The loop is never exited; both Total and Index head toward infinity. Index takes the successive values 1, 3, 5, 7, etc., skipping 6. (b) This is another infinite loop. Index takes the successive values 1, 3, 0, 2, 0, 2, 0, 2, ... Index is never greater than 5.

6. The loops are:

```
SumOfOdds := 0;
FOR Index  := LowerLimit TO UpperLimit BY 2 DO
  SumOfOdds := SumOfOdds + Index;
END; (* FOR Index := LowerLimit TO UpperLimit BY 2 *)
(* SumOfOdds = LowerLimit if LowerLimit = UpperLimit *)
(* SumOfOdds = 0 if LowerLimit > UpperLimit *)

SumOfOdds := 0;
Index := LowerLimit;
WHILE Index <= UpperLimit DO
  SumOfOdds := SumOfOdds + Index;
  Index := Index + 2;
END; (* WHILE Index <= UpperLimit *)
(* SumOfOdds = LowerLimit if LowerLimit = UpperLimit *)
(* SumOfOdds = 0 if LowerLimit > UpperLimit *)

SumOfOdds := 0;
Index := LowerLimit;
REPEAT
  SumOfOdds := SumOfOdds + Index;
  Index := Index + 2;
```

UNTIL Index > UpperLimit;
(∗ SumOfOdds = LowerLimit if LowerLimit = UpperLimit ∗)
(∗ SumOfOdds = LowerLimit if LowerLimit > UpperLimit ∗)
SumOfOdds := 0;
Index := LowerLimit;
LOOP (∗ sums odd numbers ∗)
  IF Index > UpperLimit THEN EXIT; END;
  SumOfOdds := SumOfOdds + Index;
  Index := Index + 2;
END; (∗ LOOP to sum odd numbers ∗)
(∗ SumOfOdds = LowerLimit if LowerLimit = UpperLimit ∗)
(∗ SumOfOdds = 0 if LowerLimit > UpperLimit ∗)

7. George is assigned the value FALSE 10 times, once for each value of Index from 2 to 11, inclusive. By using some new variables, we can pull out of the loop all computations which do not depend on the current value of the loop counter Index:

George := FALSE;
FOR Index := 2 TO 11 DO
  Total := Total + Index;
END; (∗ FOR Index := 2 TO 11 ∗)
LoopUpperLimit := 3∗UpperLimit − 2;
NewLimit := OldLimit − UpperLimit;
Factors1And2 := Factor1∗(1-Factor2);
WHILE Index < LoopUpperLimit DO
  Total := Factors1And2 + Factor3∗Index;
END; (∗ WHILE Index < LoopUpperLimit ∗)

Chapter 7

1. (a) Example(x, y, z);. Inside Example, i is initialized with x's value at the time of the call, which is 4. The y local to Example is initialized with the global y's value, 0, and the variable j is associated with the variable z. The value of j coming into the body of Example is 3, the value of z. The first assignment i := 5; changes the value of i from 4 to 5; the value of x is unchanged since i is a value parameter.

The second assignment j := i + y; changes the value of j to 5 plus the value of the local y, 0, i.e., j now has the value 5 instead of the value 3. Since j is a variable parameter, this new value is also assigned to its formal parameter, z. Finally, the third assignment y := y + 1; changes the local y to 1 but leaves the global y untouched since the local y is a value parameter. Therefore after the call, the values are as follows: x = 4; (global) y = 0; z = 5; i = 5; (local) y = 1; j = 5.

The rest of the calls on procedure Example will be traced by giving the values of all variables just before the first assignment i := 5; and then after each of the three assignment statements. For instance, the trace of this first call looks like

Last statement executed	Values of variables					
	x	(global) y	z	i	(local) y	j
BEGIN	4	0	3	4	0	3
i := 5;	4	0	3	5	0	3
j := i + y;	4	0	5	5	0	5
y := y + 1;	4	0	5	5	1	5

(b) Example(b, y, z);

Last statement executed	Values of variables					
	x	(global) y	z	i	(local) y	j
BEGIN	4	0	3	2	0	3
i := 5;	4	0	3	5	0	3
j := i + y;	4	0	5	5	0	5
y := y + 1;	4	0	5	5	1	5

(c) Example(x, y, b);. This call will not be accepted by the compiler because we have tried to match the variable parameter j to a constant b.

(d) Example(z, y, z);

Last statement executed	Values of variables					
	x	(global) y	z	i	(local) y	j
BEGIN	4	0	3	3	0	3
i := 5;	4	0	3	5	0	3
j := i + y;	4	0	5	5	0	5
y := y + 1;	4	0	5	5	1	5

(e) Example(y, y, b);. This call will not be accepted by the compiler because we have tried to match the variable parameter j to a constant b.

(f) Example(x, y, x+z);. This call will not be accepted by the compiler because we have tried to match the variable parameter j to an expression, x + z.

(g) Example(x+y, y, z);.

Last statement executed	Values of variables					
	x	(global) y	z	i	(local) y	j
BEGIN	4	0	3	4	0	3
i := 5;	4	0	3	5	0	3
j := i + y;	4	0	5	5	0	5
y := y + 1;	4	0	5	5	1	5

(h) Example(x, y, w);. This call will not be accepted by the compiler because we have tried to match REAL w to CARDINAL j.

Chapter 10

1. Notice how much easier it is to use INCL when working with a variable:

```
IF ThisToss = Edge THEN
  ResultsUpToNow := ResultsUpToNow + CoinTosses{Edge};
ELSIF ThisToss = Tail THEN
  ResultsUpToNow := ResultsUpToNow + CoinTosses{Tail};
ELSE
  ResultsUpToNow := ResultsUpToNow + CoinTosses{Head};
END; (* IF ThisToss = Edge *)

CASE ThisToss OF
  Edge : ResultsUpToNow := ResultsUpToNow + CoinTosses{Edge};|
  Tail : ResultsUpToNow := ResultsUpToNow + CoinTosses{Tail};|
  Head : ResultsUpToNow := ResultsUpToNow + CoinTosses{Head};
END; (* CASE ThisToss *)

INCL(ResultsUpToNow,ThisToss);
```

2. The definition should read TYPE Verbs =, not TYPE Verbs is. Modula-2 uses parentheses (,) for enumeration types; do not use square brackets. DO is a reserved word, although Do is not. HALT is also a reserved word, although we have not seen it much. The values listed for an enumeration type must be identifiers; exclamation marks are not allowed. Type definitions must be followed by a semicolon. An acceptable version would be

```
TYPE Verbs = (Run, Jump, Do, See, Halt);
ORD(See) = 3.
```

3. One can make 2^n different sets, including the empty set, from a collection of n values. If SomeType contains 3 values, SET OF SomeType contains 2^3 or 8 different values.

4. If the type CARDINAL was defined as a subrange [0..MaxInt] of INTEGER, only half as many CARDINAL values would be available as could be used otherwise. Recall that INTEGER values range from MinInt to MaxInt, a total of MaxInt − MinInt + 1 values. For instance, on a machine with word size 4, one can represent 2^4, or 16 values, so one might take MaxInt = 7, MinInt = −8. But for the type CARDINAL, only positive values are needed, so one should take the 16 CARDINAL values to be 0 through MaxCard = 15, instead of using 0 through MaxInt = 7.

Chapter 11

1. The functions are

```
PROCEDURE STRINGLessThan( One, Two: ARRAY OF CHAR ): BOOLEAN;
VAR Index    : CARDINAL;
BEGIN
  IF STRINGSAreEqual(One,Two) THEN
    RETURN FALSE;
  ELSE (* Look for first point at which the strings differ. *)
    Index := 0;
    WHILE ((Index <= HIGH(One)) AND (Index <= HIGH(Two))
          AND (One[Index] = Two[Index])) DO
      INC(Index);
    END; (* WHILE *)
    IF (Index > HIGH(One)) THEN
      (* Meaningful portion of One fills array One, and all *)
      (* the characters in One match the corresponding      *)
      (* character in Two.                                  *)
      IF (Index <= HIGH(Two)) THEN
        RETURN (Two[Index] <> NULLChar);
      ELSE
        RETURN FALSE;
      END; (* IF *)
    ELSIF (Index > HIGH(Two)) THEN
      RETURN FALSE;
    ELSE
      RETURN (One[Index] < Two[Index]);
    END; (* IF *)
  END; (* IF *)
END STRINGLessThan;

PROCEDURE STRINGLength( String: ARRAY OF CHAR ): CARDINAL;
VAR Index: CARDINAL;
BEGIN
  Index := 0;
  WHILE ((Index <= HIGH(String))
        AND (String[Index] <> NULLChar)) DO
    INC(Index);
  END; (* WHILE *)
  RETURN Index;
END STRINGLength;
```

2. Assume the visibility of the declaration

```
CONST NULLChar = 0C;

PROCEDURE ASCIIToCardinal(String: ARRAY OF CHAR): CARDINAL;
VAR Value, Index, ArrayUpperBound: CARDINAL;
BEGIN
  ArrayUpperBound := HIGH(String);
  Value := 0;
  Index := 0;
  LOOP
    IF ((Index > ArrayUpperBound)
        OR (String[Index] = NULLChar)) THEN
```

```
   EXIT;
   END; (* IF *)
   IF ((String[Index] < "0") OR (String[Index] > "g")) THEN
      WRITEString("ASCIIToCardinal passed non-digit character");
      EXIT;
   END; (* IF *)
   Value := 10*Value + (CARDINAL(String[Index]) - CARDINAL("0"));
   INC(Index);
   END; (* LOOP *)
   RETURN Value;
END ASCIIToCardinal;
PROCEDURE InitializedCardinalArray(
         VAR CardinalArray: ARRAY OF CARDINAL;
             InitialValues:  ARRAY OF CHAR      ): BOOLEAN;
CONST MaxDigitsInCardinal = 5;
VAR    NextValue: ARRAY[0..MaxDigitsInCardinal-1]OF CHAR;
       LastComma, CardinalIndex, ValuesIndex: CARDINAL;
BEGIN
   CardinalIndex := 0;
   LastComma := 0;
   WHILE ((CardinalIndex <= HIGH(CardinalArray))
         AND (LastComma <= HIGH(InitialValues))) DO
   (* Separate next initial value from the rest of the string. *)
   ValuesIndex := 0;
   WHILE ((LastComma <= HIGH(InitialValues))
          AND (ValuesIndex <= MaxDigitsInCardinal-1)
          AND (InitialValues[LastComma] <> ",")) DO
      NextValue[ValuesIndex] := InitialValues[LastComma];
      INC(ValuesIndex);
      INC(LastComma);
   END; (* WHILE *)
   INC(LastComma);
   IF  (ValuesIndex <= MaxDigitsInCardinal-1) THEN
      NextValue[ValuesIndex] := NULLChar;
   END; (* IF *)
   (* If string just obtained represents an initial value which *)
   (* is in the machine's range, insert the value in the array. *)
   IF (ValuesIndex <= MaxDigitsInCardinal-1) THEN
      CardinalArray[CardinalIndex] := ASCIIToCardinal(NextValue);
   ELSE
      WRITEString("InitializedCardinalArray");
      WRITEString("passed too many initial values");
   END; (* IF *)
   INC(CardinalIndex);
   END; (* WHILE *)
   IF (CardinalIndex > HIGH(CardinalArray)) THEN
   (* Ran out of room in array; are there more initial values? *)
   RETURN (LastComma > HIGH(InitialValues));
   ELSE
   (* Array large enough to hold all the initial values given. *)
   RETURN TRUE;
   END; (* IF *)
END InitializedCardinalArray;
```

Chapter 12

1. PrintList requires an added import clause such as

FROM InOut IMPORT WRITEString;

```
PROCEDURE DELETEName( NameToDelete: ARRAY OF CHAR;
                     VAR NameFound: BOOLEAN;
                     VAR FirstInList: NAMEListElement );
(* Deletes the specified name if a name which matches it for *)
(* the first K characters is found in the list. K is the     *)
(* minimum of NAMELength and the number of meaningful *)
(* characters in NameToDelete.                         *)
   VAR CurrentButOne, CurrentElement: NAMEListElement;
BEGIN
   IF (FirstInList = NIL) THEN
      (* List is empty. *)
      NameFound := FALSE;
   ELSIF (FirstInList ↑ .Next = NIL) THEN
      (* List has one element *)
      IF (STRINGSAreEqual(FirstInList ↑ .Name, NameToDelete)) THEN
         (* Delete first element of list. *)
         CurrentElement := FirstInList ↑ .Next;
         DISPOSE(FirstInList);
         FirstInList := CurrentElement;
         NameFound := TRUE;
      ELSE
         NameFound := FALSE;
      END; (* IF NameToDelete is in first element *)
   ELSE
      (* Search list for NameToDelete *)
      CurrentButOne := FirstInList;
      CurrentElement := FirstInList ↑ .Next;
      WHILE ((NOT STRINGSAreEqual(CurrentElement ↑ .Name, NameToDelete))
             AND (CurrentElement ↑ .Next <> NIL)) DO
         CurrentElement := CurrentElement ↑ .Next;
         CurrentButOne := CurrentButOne ↑ .Next;
      END; (* WHILE *)
      IF (STRINGSAreEqual(CurrentElement ↑ .Name, NameToDelete)) THEN
         NameFound := TRUE;
         IF (CurrentElement ↑ .Next = NIL) THEN
            (* NameToDelete is in last element of the list. *)
            CurrentButOne ↑ .Next := NIL;
         ELSE
            (* NameToDelete is in an interior element of the list. *)
            CurrentButOne ↑ .Next := CurrentElement ↑ .Next;
         END; (* IF *)
         DISPOSE(CurrentElement);
      ELSE
         (* Entire list was searched without finding NameToDelete *)
         NameFound := FALSE;
      END; (* IF current name is name to delete *)
   END; (* IF list is empty *)
END DELETEName;
PROCEDURE PRINTList( NextToPrint: NAMEListElement );
```

```
(* Prints the indicated list of names. *)
BEGIN
  IF (NextToPrint = NIL) THEN
    WRITEString("No names in list");
  ELSE (* List has more than one element. *)
    WRITEString(NextToPrint ↑ .Name);
    WHILE (NextToPrint ↑ .Next <> NIL) DO
      NextToPrint := NextToPrint ↑ .Next;
      WRITEString(NextToPrint ↑ .Name);
    END; (* WHILE *)
  END; (* IF NextToPrint = NIL *)
END PRINTList;
```

Chapter 13

1. The declaration is
```
TYPE OKSubTypes = (SubTypeOne, SubTypeTwo);
(* Assumes these identifiers are not needed to name the invariant *)
(* record types, which are not used since SuperType is visible.   *)
TYPE SuperType = RECORD
                   NewOneATwoB: INTEGER;
                   CASE SubType: OKSubTypes OF
                     SubTypeOne: NewOneB: CHAR;
                                 NewOneC: BOOLEAN; |
                     SubTypeTwo: NewTwoA: BITSET;
                                 NewTwoC: REAL;
                   END; (* Variant Fields *)
                 END; (* RECORD *)
```

Chapter 18

1. TryWorkspaceSizeGuess will ask the user for a guess for the size of workspace needed by One. If the user's guess is too small, execution will either hang as though the processor was in an infinite loop or else execution will be terminated and there will be a message from the operating system along the lines of "stack overflow" or "insufficient memory allocated." If the user's guess is large enough, Inside One will be printed. In either case, Inside Two will never be printed. The reason for this is that control is never explicitly passed back from the first PROCESS, which received control via the TRANSFER made as a result of the call

TryWorkspaceSizeGuess(One);

If a coroutine reaches the end of its body and then terminates without TRANSFERring control, the entire program containing the coroutine terminates. An analogy may be useful to understand this. Every procedure may be thought of as containing an implicit "goto the statement after the one which made this call" as its final statement. Every PROCESS may be viewed as if it ended in the statement "goto the operating system."

Bibliography

Alfred V. Aho and Margaret J. Corasick, "Efficient String Matching: An Aid to Bibliographic Search," *Communications of the ACM*, vol. 18, no. 6, 1975, pp. 333-340.

Stowe Boyd, "Modular C," *ACM SIGPLAN Notices*, vol. 18, no. 4, April 1983.

William F. Clocksin and Christopher S. Mellish, *Programming in Prolog*, Springer-Verlag, New York, 1981.

Richard Gleaves, *Modula-2 for Pascal Programmers*, Springer-Verlag, New York, 1984.

Adele Goldberg and David Robson, *Smalltalk-Eighty: The Language and Its Implementation*, Addison-Wesley, Reading, Mass., 1983.

C. A. R. Hoare, "Hints on Programming Language Design," reprinted in *Programming Languages: A Grand Tour*, E. Horowitz (ed.), Computer Science Press, Rockville, Md., 1983.

Hausi, A. Muller, "Differences between Modula-2 and Pascal," *ACM SIGPLAN Notices*, vol. 19, no. 10, October 1984.

John W. L. Ogilvie, "On the Translation of Modula-2 into Ada," Master's Thesis, University of Utah, June 1984.

Michael L. Powell, "Modula-2: Good News and Bad News," *CompCon '84 Proceedings*, IEEE, 1984.

Michael L. Powell, "Using Modula-2 for System Programming with UNIX," USENIX Association 1984 Summer Conference Proceedings, 1984.

David Spector, "Ambiguities and Insecurities in Modula-2," *ACM SIGPLAN Notices*, vol. 17, no. 8, August 1982.

Richard S. Wiener, "Dynamic Multidimensional Arrays," *Journal of Pascal and Ada*, vol. 2, no. 6, November/December 1983.

Richard Wiener and Richard Sincovec, *Software Engineering with Modula-2 and Ada*, John Wiley, New York, 1984.

Niklaus Wirth, "On the Design of Programming Languages," reprinted in *Programming Languages: A Grand Tour*, E. Horowitz (ed.), Computer Science Press, Rockville, Md. 1983.

Niklaus Wirth, *Programming in Modula-2*, 2d ed., Springer-Verlag, New York, 1983.

Niklaus Wirth, "Data Structures and Algorithms," *Scientific American*, September 1984.

Readers should note that Appendix 4 contains other sources of information on Modula-2 which were not explicitly referenced in the text.

Index

NOTE: Readers who do not find the information they desire in this index are encouraged to consult the glossary, which begins on page 262, and the index to syntax diagrams, which begins on page 239.

ABS (standard function), 21, 232
Abstract data types, 138, 262
Abstraction, level of, 55, 137–140, 143–144, 272
Actual parameter, 59–63, 78–79, 263
Ada, Modula-2 versus, 1, 12, 15–16, 266
ADDRESS (SYSTEM data type), 201–202, 263
  arithmetic, 202
  pointers versus, 121, 261
Address, 263
  absolute, 36, 203–204, 218
  starting, 202, 283
ADR (SYSTEM function), 201–202
ALLOCATE (procedure):
  parameters of, 190
  pointers and, 120, 233–234
  use of, with DEALLOCATE, 215, 218
Arrays, 264
  constant, 113
  declaring, 105–107
  dynamic, 214–215
  errors involving, 217, 218
  FOR loops and, 107
  initializing, 113–114, 295
  operators on, 107, 227
  records versus, 115–116
  type transfers of, 210–212
  (See also HIGH; Open arrays; Strings)
ASCII character set, 27
Assignment compatible types, 40, 258
Assignment statements, 21, 61, 264
Associativity of operators, 28, 30, 31, 288
Availability of program components, 149–150

Base type of a subrange type, 101, 260
BASIC, Modula-2 versus, 1, 13–14, 18
Basic data types (see BITSET; BOOLEAN; CARDINAL; CHAR; INTEGER; REAL)
BITSET (standard data type), 27–29, 265
  exercise involving, 30, 31
BOOLEAN (standard data type), 24–26, 100, 265
  de Morgan's law for, 25–26
  exercise involving, 30, 31
  IF statements and, 44
  "short-circuit" evaluation of, 25, 148, 282
BYTE (data type), 204

C, Modula-2 versus, 1, 13, 16–18
CAP (standard function), 212, 228, 232
CARDINAL (standard data type), 22–23, 266
  BITSET and, 28
  conversion to, 114, 212, 294–295
  example of, 5–7, 31
  initializing arrays of, 295
  INTEGER versus, 104, 293
  LONGCARD, 22, 228, 261
  operators on, 22
  overflow, 22, 218
Case, significance of, 8, 217, 230–231, 266
CASE statements, 44–46
  comments and, 45, 222
  errors involving, 218
  examples of, 289, 293
  IF statements versus, 53, 289

CASE statements (*Cont.*):
  revised syntax of, 260
  variant records and, 126
CHAR (standard data type), 26–27, 266
  ARRAY OF CHAR versus, 107, 227–228, 260
  ASCII character set, 27
  CharSetHandler modules, 174–178
  identifiers versus, 99–100
CHR (standard function), 212, 232
Comments:
  errors involving, 217
  syntax of, 32–33, 230–231
  use of, 143–144, 221–223
Compatibility (*see* Assignment compatible types; Types)
Compilation:
  checks made during, 3, 78–79, 216, 282
  dependency trees, 92–94
  options for, 33
Compilation unit, 266
Compilers for Modula-2, 2, 256–257, 266
Constant array, 113
Constant declarations, 33–34
Constant records, 116
Constants, 267
Control characters, 27
Coroutines, 267
  creation of, 190–195
  errors involving, 194–195, 217
  examples of, 195–199
  module priorities and, 258
  PROCESSes and, 188
  subprograms versus, 189–192
  workspace for, 190–194, 217, 297
Correctness of programs, 145

Data types (*see specific type names*)
DEALLOCATE (procedure):
  pointers and, 120, 233–234
  use of, with ALLOCATE, 215, 218
Debugging, 216–220, 267–268
  HALT and, 233
  techniques for, 219–220
  use of comments in, 33
  (*See also* Errors)
DEC (standard procedure), 21–22, 98, 228, 233
Declarations, 268
  comments and, 222

Declarations (*Cont.*):
  order of, 36
  reserved words in, 235
  (*See also* Visibility; Visibility rules)
Definition modules:
  description of, 3, 73–77, 268
  desirable qualities of, 138, 141–150, 222
  examples of: CharSetHandler, 175
    EasyOutput, 205
    Exporter, 93
    GraphHandler, 166
    LispInModula2, 129–130
    NameListHandler, 121
    PlaneGeometry, 75
    PMFunctions, 160
    STRINGHandler, 213
    StringSetHandler, 169–170
    StringStuff, 109–110
    SYSTEM, 201–202
  recompilation of, 79–80
  (*See also* Exports; Implementation modules; Library modules)
de Morgan's law, 25–26
Dereferencing operator, 121
Discriminator in a variant record, 126–128
DISPOSE (standard procedure), 119–121, 217, 233–234
Documentation of programs, 145, 221–225
Durability of programs, 148–149
Dynamic memory allocation, 118–120, 212–215, 268

Efficiency, 17–18, 147–148
Enumeration types, 98–100
  errors involving, 218, 293
  exercises involving, 103, 104, 293
  identifiers and, 99–100
Environment, 90, 92–93, 266
Errors:
  causes of, 217–219
  compile-time, 216, 266
  kinds of, 216
  reporting, 225
  run-time, 281
  (*See also* Debugging)
EXCL (standard procedure), 29, 98, 102–103, 233
EXIT statements, 51, 227
  (*See also* LOOP loops)

Exports, 76, 269
  list of, 76, 259
  local modules and, 94–97
  opaque, 137–140, 259, 276
  qualified, 96–97, 280–281
  read-only, 227
  visibility of, 89–92, 139–140

FALSE (predefined BOOLEAN value), 24
FLOAT (standard function):
  description of, 232
  reason for name of, 230–231
  type conversion using, 6–7, 42, 212
FOR loops, 48–50, 258
  array assignment using, 107
  comments and, 222
  errors involving, 217
  exercises involving, 54, 290–291
Formal parameter, 59–63, 107, 269
FORTRAN, Modula-2 versus, 1, 14, 18–19, 228
Functions, 63–64, 269
  errors involving, 217, 218
  examples of: CubeOf, 63
    Fibonacci, 70–71
    MayLogin, 43–44
  headings of, 59, 77, 224
  naming, 64
  parameters of (see Parameters of subprograms)
  procedures versus, 59
  reasons to use, 55–56
  type transfer, 209–212, 223, 285
  variable parameters in, 64, 143, 217
  visibility in, 65–69

Goto statement, lack of, 4, 270
Graph, representation of, 156, 166–169

HALT (standard procedure), 218, 229, 233
Hexadecimal values, 22, 270
HIGH (standard function):
  description of, 232
  drawbacks of, 229
  example of, 108, 148, 213, 217

Identifiers:
  CHAR values versus, 99–100
  enumeration types and, 99–100
  standard, 235–237
  syntax of, 36, 42, 227
  use of cryptic, 35, 142, 223

IF statements, 43–44
  CASE statement versus, 53, 289
  comments and, 45, 222
  examples of, 43–44, 289, 293
Implementation-dependent items (see System-dependent items)
Implementation modules:
  description of, 3, 73, 271
  desirable qualities of, 141–150
  examples of: CharSetHandler, 176–178
    CoroutineHandler, 193–194
    EasyOutput, 205–208
    Exporter, 93
    GraphHandler, 167–169, 178–179
    LispInModula2, 130–134
    NameListHandler, 122–123
    PlaneGeometry, 76
    PMFunctions, 160–166, 178–179
    STRINGHandler, 214–215
    StringSetHandler, 170–174
    StringStuff, 110–112
  opaque types and, 138–139
  recompilation of, 79–80
Import trees, 92–94
Imports, 271
  capitalization of, 8–9
  list of, 89, 229–230
IN (set operator), 29
INC (standard procedure), 8, 21, 98, 228, 233
INCL (standard procedure), 29, 98, 102–103, 233, 293
Initialization:
  of array, 113–114, 295
  of module, 77, 218, 259, 272
  of variable, 35, 217, 272
Input/output (I/O):
  EasyOutput modules for, 205–209
  errors involving, 218
  InOut modules for, 5–9
  lack of standard procedures for, 228, 283
INTEGER (standard data type), 20–22, 272
  CARDINAL versus, 104, 293
  hexadecimal, 22
  LONGINT, 20, 228, 261
  octal, 22
  operators on, 20–22

Library modules, 272–273
  benefits of using, 88–89

Library modules (*Cont.*):
  compilation of, 79–80
  description of, 3, 73–75
  desirable qualities of, 141–150
  lack of standard, 5, 8–9, 228
  (*See also* Definition modules;
    Implementation modules;
    Initialization, of module)
Linked lists, 118, 121–124, 273, 296
LISP, 129–136
Local modules, 94–97, 273
LOOP loops, 51–54
  arbitrarily long, 52–53
  comments and, 222
  errors involving, 217
  exercises involving, 54, 290–291
Loop statements (*see* FOR loops; LOOP
  loops; REPEAT..UNTIL loops;
  WHILE loops)
Loops, unnecessary computation in, 48,
  54, 291
Low-level facilities, 3, 201–215, 273
  (*See also* SYSTEM; System-dependent
  items)

Machine-dependent (*see* System-
  dependent items)
Memory, 218, 274
  (*See also* Storage)
Modifiability of programs, 146, 274
Modula, Modula-2 versus, 2
Modula-2:
  brief description of, 3–4
  comparison of, with other languages,
    10–19
  compilers for, 2, 256–257, 266
  extensions to, 239, 258–261
  origins of, 2
  shortcomings of, 226–231
  time required to learn, 1–2
Modules:
  dividing programs into, 155–178
  initialization of, 77, 218, 259, 272
  kinds of, 3, 73–77, 275
  priority of, 199–200, 258
  reasons for using, 3, 77–79
  (*See also* Definition modules;
    Implementation modules; Library
    modules; Local modules; Program
    modules)
Monitor module, 199–200

Nesting, 276
  modules, 94–97, 273
  procedures, 87–88
  statements, 227
NEW (standard procedure), 119–121,
  233–234
NEWPROCESS (SYSTEM procedure),
  190, 201–202
NIL (predefined pointer value), 120,
  217

Octal values, 22, 276
ODD (standard function), 21, 232
Opaque exports, 137–140, 259, 276
Open arrays, 276
  CHAR versus ARRAY OF CHAR, 107,
    227–228, 260
  declaring and using, 107–109, 229
  errors involving, 119
  storage requirements of, 203
  type WORD and, 204
Operators, 277
  array, 107, 227
  associativity of, 28, 30, 31, 288
  BOOLEAN, 24
  CARDINAL, 22
  INTEGER, 20–22
  precedence of, 28–31, 278
  REAL, 24
  record, 116, 227
  relational, 21
  set, 29
ORD (standard function), 26, 98–100,
  212, 232

Parameters of subprograms, 59–63, 277
  actual, 59–63, 78–79, 263
  evaluation of, 218, 291–293
  formal, 59–63, 107, 269
  modes of, 60–63, 71–72
  open array, 107–109
  value, 60–63, 124–125, 286
  variable, 60–64, 217, 258, 286
Pascal, 1, 2, 10–12, 14–15
Pattern matcher (example program), 151–
  179
Pointers, 277–278
  ADDRESS versus, 121, 261
  arithmetic with, 121
  dangling, 119, 217

Pointers (*Cont.*):
  declaring and using, 118–125, 143
  NIL, 120, 217
  opaquely exported, 138, 259
  operations on, 121
  type compatibility and, 118
  value parameters and, 124–125
Portability of programs, 149, 278
Predeclared (*see* Predefined)
Predefined, 235–237, 278, 283
  subprograms, 210, 261
  types, 20–29, 181–182
  values, 32
Priority of modules, 199–200, 258
PROC (standard type), 181, 278
Procedure types, 180–187, 203
Procedures, 55–59, 278–279
  errors involving, 218
  examples of: CountDown, 69
    LookForCharacter, 51–52
    MonitorVatTemperature, 52–53
  exercises involving, 71–72, 291–293
  functions versus, 59
  headings of, 59, 77, 224
  naming, 64
  nesting, 87–88
  parameters of (*see* Parameters of
    subprograms)
  reasons to use, 55–56
  visibility in, 65–69
PROCESS (SYSTEM data type), 188–199,
    201, 279
  (*See also* Coroutines)
Program modules:
  description of, 3, 73, 280
  desirable qualities of, 141–150
  examples of: AdaptiveDataRetrieval,
    183–184
    Editor, 83–87
    Example, 124
    FindMax, 11
    FirstExample, 5–9
    Geometer, 56–59
    ImportEnvironment, 93
    OuterMost, 95–96
    PatternMatcher, 157–159
    TestForRepetition, 74–75
    TextProcessor, 195–199
    VisibilityExample, 66

Qualified export, 96–97, 280–281

REAL (standard data type), 23–24, 281
  LONGREAL, 23, 228, 261
  operators, 24
  (*See also* FLOAT)
Records, 281
  arrays versus, 115–116
  constant, 116
  declaring, 115–117
  dot notation for, 116
  examples of, 122–123, 167–174, 214–
    215
  operators on, 116, 227
  variant (*see* Variant records)
Recursion, 38–39, 69–71, 217, 275, 281
REPEAT..UNTIL loops, 50–51, 54
  comments and, 222
  errors involving, 217
  exercises involving, 54, 290–291
  infinite, 51
Reserved words, 235–237, 281
RETURN statements, 63, 218

Scope (*see* Visibility; Visibility rules)
Semantics:
  compiler checks on, 3, 78–79, 216, 282
  syntax versus, 238–239, 282
Set types, 102–103
  number of values for, 293
  operations on, 29
  restrictions on, 102, 228, 260–261
"Short-circuit" BOOLEAN evaluation, 25,
    148, 282
Side effect, 217
SIZE (SYSTEM function), 201–203
Software engineering, 141–150, 282
Standard subprograms and identifiers
  (*see* Predefined)
Storage (library module), 120, 190, 215,
    234
  (*See also* ALLOCATE; DEALLOCATE;
    Dynamic memory allocation;
    Memory)
Strings, 283
  CHAR arrays as, 107
  constant, 34, 227
  empty, 229
  handling, 109–114, 169–174, 212–215,
    228, 294
  LISP, 135
Strong typing, 39–42
Structured types, 37, 63, 210–211, 284

Style, programming, 142–145, 221–225
Subprograms, 284
    coroutines versus, 189–192
    exported, 77
    environment of, 90, 92–93
    nested, 87–88, 181–182
    organization of, 81–89
    parameters of (*see* Parameters of
        subprograms)
    predefined, 210, 261
    reasons to use, 55
    (*See also* Functions; Procedures)
Subrange types, 100–102, 209, 260
Syntax diagrams:
    index to, 239–241
    of Modula-2, 238–254
    semantics versus, 238–239, 282
SYSTEM (standard module), 201–204,
    222, 235–237, 284–285
System-dependent items:
    absolute addresses, 36
    comments near, 149, 222–223
    functions as, 63
    opaque exports as, 138
    PROCESSes, 190
    and standard source, 227
    SYSTEM exports, 149
    type conversions, 39
    (*See also* Low-level facilities; SYSTEM)

TRANSFER (SYSTEM procedure), 188–
    189, 201–202, 217–218
Trees, 124, 135, 262, 285
TRUE (predefined BOOLEAN value), 24
TRUNC (standard function), 21, 42, 212,
    233, 285
TSIZE (SYSTEM function), 201–203
Type transfer functions, 209–212, 223,
    285
Types, 267
    anonymous, 211–212
    basic data, 20–28
    coercion of, 209–212, 223, 285
    compatibility of, 39–42, 107, 118, 204,
        209–212, 227–228
    conversion of, 6–7, 39, 120, 209, 212,
        232–233, 267

Types (*Cont.*):
    declaring, 36–38
    predefined, 20–29, 181–182
    reasons for using, 37
    structured versus unstructured, 37, 63,
        210–211, 284
    (*See also* Abstract data types; *and*
        specific type names)

Understandability of programs, 142–145,
    286
Unstructured types, 286

VAL (standard function), 98, 212, 233
Value parameter, 60–63, 124–125, 286
Variable parameter, 60–64, 217, 258, 286
Variables:
    declaring, 34–36, 217
    initialization of, 35, 217, 272
    specifying address of, 36
Variant records, 126–136, 143, 286
    discriminators of, 126–128
    dot notation for, 127
    errors involving, 127–128, 217
    storage requirements of, 203
Visibility, 286
    block diagrams of, 67, 82, 83, 96
    examples of, 65–68
    of exports, 89–92, 139–140
    global versus local, 65–69
Visibility rules, 286
    for exports, 89–92, 139–140
    for modules, 97
    for subprograms, 65

WHILE loops, 50–51, 54
    comments and, 222
    errors involving, 217
    exercises involving, 54, 290–291
    infinite, 47, 50
Wirth, Niklaus, 2
WITH statements, 117–118, 217, 222
WORD (SYSTEM data type), 201, 204–
    209, 286

ABOUT THE AUTHOR
John W. L. Ogilvie received his M.S. in computer science
in 1984 from the University of Utah after completing
a thesis "On the Translation of Modula-2 into Ada."
Several of his articles have been published in the
Journal of Pascal, Ada, and Modula-2. He now works
at Modula Corporation in Provo, Utah.